Extreme Programming
Applied

The XP Series

Kent Beck, Series Advisor

Extreme Programming, familiarly known as XP, is a discipline of business and software development that focuses both parties on common, reachable goals. XP teams produce quality software at a sustainable pace. The practices that make up "book" XP are chosen for their dependence on human creativity and acceptance of human frailty.

Although XP is often presented as a list of practices, XP is not a finish line. You don't get better and better grades at doing XP until you finally receive the coveted gold star. XP is a starting line. It asks the question, "How little can we do and still build great software?"

The beginning of the answer is that, if we want to leave software development uncluttered, we must be prepared to completely embrace the few practices we adopt. Half measures leave problems unsolved to be addressed by further half measures. Eventually you are surrounded by so many half measures that you can no longer see that the heart of the value programmers create comes from programming.

I say, "The beginning of the answer …" because there is no final answer. The authors in the XP Series have been that and done there, and returned to tell their story. The books in this series are the signposts they have planted along the way: "Here lie dragons," "Scenic drive next 15 km," "Slippery when wet."

Excuse me, I gotta go program.

Titles in the Series

Extreme Programming Applied: Playing to Win, Ken Auer and Roy Miller

Extreme Programming Examined, Giancarlo Succi and Michele Marchesi

Extreme Programming Explained: Embrace Change, Kent Beck

Extreme Programming Explored, William C. Wake

Extreme Programming in Practice, James Newkirk and Robert C. Martin

Extreme Programming Installed, Ron Jeffries, Ann Anderson, and Chet Hendrickson

Planning Extreme Programming, Kent Beck and Martin Fowler

Extreme Programming Applied
Playing to Win

Ken Auer
Roy Miller

ADDISON–WESLEY

Boston • San Francisco • New York • Toronto • Montreal
London • Munich • Paris • Madrid
Capetown • Sydney • Tokyo • Singapore • Mexico City

The publisher offers discounts on this book when ordered in quantity for special sales. For more information, please contact:

Pearson Education Corporate Sales Division
201 W. 103rd Street
Indianapolis, IN 46290
(800) 428-5331
corpsales@pearsoned.com

Visit us on the Web at www.aw.com/cseng/

Library of Congress Cataloging-in-Publication Data

Auer, Ken.
    Extreme programming applied : playing to win / Ken Auer, Roy Miller.
        p. cm.—(XP series)
    Includes bibliographical references and index.
    ISBN 0-201-61640-8
    1. Computer software—Development.   2. eXtreme programming.   I. Miller, Roy (Roy W.) II. Title. III. Series.

    QA76.76.D47 A84 2002
    005.1'1—dc21

                        2001046253

ISBN 0-201-61640-8
Text printed on recycled paper
1 2 3 4 5 6 7 8 9 10—MA—0504030201
First printing, October 2001

To the Lord Jesus Christ
—K.A.

To God and my family
—R.M.

Contents

List of Pioneer Stories

Pioneer stories appear throughout the book. If you read only these stories, rather than the surrounding text, you will gain some good insights. You may wish to use this list to find stories for future reference.

Foreword

Extreme Programming asks the simple question, what is the best way for a small group of ordinary developers to deliver the most value to a customer? This book answers that question. The answer comes from authors who like to deliver value, not get into methodological arguments. They've listened to the arguments, all right. They've dug into them, torn them apart, applied the pieces and even the whole. They know what works and why.

Ken Auer was early into object-oriented programming, the defining technology of the last decade, the technology that is simply assumed as we move into the next. Ken understood objects intuitively. Ken sought to share that intuition, first as a developer, then as a consultant to developers, and now as the founder of a development company. Sharing what is obvious to him hasn't been easy, especially as he has found himself addressing whole projects, then whole departments, and now whole enterprises. Through this progression Ken has maintained a customer focus and a keep-it-simple attitude, values at the core of Extreme Programming.

Roy Miller shares Ken's customer focus with a complementary career path. Roy's six years with a big five consultancy have presented him with all manner of enterprise needs. Roy has firsthand experience with methodological dogma applied and, too often, methodological dogma failed. Roy had to do all of the heavyweight process stuff and figure out how to get the work done too.

Together Ken and Roy tell us how they and a handful of similarly minded practical people have embraced Extreme Programming to the benefit of teams just trying to get a good job done. Consider this book an experience report. Ken and Roy have tracked the evolving conversation about object-oriented programming and related methods; they have tested the best ideas in the real work they do; and now they tell us what works and why. If you are a software developer, if you are the customer of software developers, or if you manage either of these, you will want to hear what Ken and Roy have to say.

Ken and Roy understand one more thing. They understand that once you embrace Extreme Programming, and have applied it to the work you do, you will want to help others do the same. First you may shake your head at the foolishness of others, but then you will want to help. The authors assume you want to help, not from a motivation of amassing control, power or wealth, but from a real desire to alleviate suffering. Much of the writing within addresses the needs of the corporate rebels known as change agents. Ken and Roy are exactly this—agents of change—and they can't help but share advice from this part of their experience too. Consultants, either those working from within a company or those providing to other companies, will find this information immediately applicable.

Ward Cunningham
Portland, Oregon

Preface

"You're a fool to think this will ever work."

People have said that to all of us about Extreme Programming (XP). We've said it to ourselves about XP.

People told Christopher Columbus he was nuts when he wanted to sail west. People told the Pilgrims this before they got on the *Mayflower*. People told many of the early settlers of the American frontier the same thing.

Yet they all headed west. Why? They believed there was something better out there, and somebody had to be the first one to find out if they were right.

The journey itself was treacherous for each of them. Once they got to their destination, there were more dangers. Some they suspected ahead of time. Some were total surprises. Of course, they were scared. But, as pioneers, they had no choice but to face their fears head-on. Sometimes they died. Sometimes they lived to face the next life-threatening challenge.

Stories from these brave fools made it back to the people they left behind, and then to people they didn't even know. Those who may not have been brave enough to take the first journey, or who didn't have the opportunity, were encouraged. They became the next wave of pioneers. They were better prepared than the first wave. Bravery and success (mixed with the excitement of knowing the risk they were taking) encouraged another wave. It didn't come easily, but eventually the West was settled.

We are the early pioneers. We don't have all the answers. We have cele-brated some victories. We've reflected on some failures. We certainly have learned a lot. These are our letters home. We hope they will encourage the next wave to head west.

Who Should Read This Book

We wrote this book for software developers and for technical managers who are interested in Extreme Programming (XP). Perhaps they don't know how to get started or don't know how to go further than they've already gone. Our goal was to create a practical volume that would provide advice based on real-world experience.

We assume that people reading this book have either read Kent Beck's *Extreme Programming Explained* or have otherwise gained a general under-standing of what Extreme Programming is. Kent's book is a manifesto that makes the case for XP. We accept the case as made, and we move on to helping those who want to act on it.

If you are a developer or a technical manager even mildly interested in XP, we assume you have at least one of these five burning questions:

1. Does XP work where it has been tried?
2. How does it work?
3. How can I make the case for it within my organization?
4. What's the best way to get started, given the resistance I'm likely to face?
5. Once I've made the case for it and gotten started, how do I make it work within my organization?

Although we may not be able to answer all of these questions definitively for you, we hope to give you enough guidance to act immediately.

How to Read This Book

You can read this book in three different ways:

1. As a collection of stories about how various people (including us) have started using XP in their organizations
2. As advice about how to start using XP in your organization
3. As a virtual coach to use as you begin introducing XP into your organi-zation in your own unique way

The list of pioneer stories provides a complete listing of all the stories in this book. Each story has a title that captures its primary thrust. You can read just these stories and get a feel for how to make the case for XP and how to start using it.

We embedded the stories within the chapters of the book, where we provide some context for them and some advice based on our own experiences. You can read the book from cover to cover, skipping the stories entirely (they are highlighted in the text) to get the advice in its nonillustrated form.

Perhaps the best way to read the book, though, is as a cohesive whole. The stories put the advice we're giving in the context of organizations and projects with human beings acted on by real forces. It is the next best thing to having tried XP yourself.

Ultimately, we hope you *do* try it yourself. Think of this book as an instruction manual for achieving the goal Kent outlined in *Extreme Programming Explained*.

XP on the Web

A good reference bookshelf is an invaluable tool. The Internet puts mounds of information at your fingertips, but it hides it under a lot of junk. Finding what you need can be a needle-in-a-haystack exercise.

If you want to find out more about XP and some of the things we've referred to in this book, check out our XP Portal at http://www.rolemodelsoft.com/xp. There you will find things like pointers to

- Laurie Williams and Alistair Cockburn's research on pair programming
- Integration procedures using VisualAge for Java Enterprise
- A JAccept™ overview

We will update this portal over time.

Acknowledgments

Writing a book is both a joy and a pain in the neck. We could have written one without help from any reviewers, but it would have stunk. So, thanks to all of the people who gave us detailed feedback and reviews: Ann Anderson, Paul Chisholm, Randy Coulman, Rick Evans, Martin Fowler, Chet Hendrickson, Jim Highsmith, Ron Jeffries, Joshua Kerievsky, Jeff McKenna, Bill Pyritz, Bill Wake, and Frank Westphal. A special thanks to Paul Chisholm who really put his all into reviewing the book to the finest detail.

Thanks also to the pioneers who contributed to the book. Without them, there would have been far less to write about. You can read more about them at the end of the Introduction. We acknowledge them by name directly in the text, but that doesn't begin to express our appreciation for their contributions.

We couldn't have done this without the RoleModel Software team. Their contributions over the last couple of years have been tremendous. Many of them didn't end up in the book by name, but their participation and support along the way has been incredible. We love you guys.

Ken

First and foremost, I'd like to thank my Lord, Jesus Christ for creating everything and dying for me and for being the one who makes all things possible. ". . . in Him we live and move and exist" (Acts 17:28a). He also gave me enough confidence to start the XP journey and to write this book, as well as enough humility to seek help along the way.

Thanks to my excellent wife, Carol, who has been an incredible encouragement and support and has demonstrated tremendous patience not only through the journey of writing this book, but throughout our life journey together. Carol has taught me so much about being aware of the thoughts and needs of people around me. I would have never appreciated XP without her, not to mention so many other things in life. Carol, your worth is far above rubies.

My children, Hope and Caleb, have also been a great encouragement to me. Having them around has taught me what it means to think of others first and "lay my ego at the door," as they reflect all of my character flaws and love me in spite of the ones they've learned not to reflect. You kids truly are a blessing from the Lord.

Although this book was started so long ago, it may have never made it to Addison-Wesley without Roy. His tireless contributions, his writing skill, and his insights are invaluable. Thanks for your patience and the many sacrifices you've made to be a part of RoleModel. You are a fine man, Ricky, Rasheed, or whatever your name is.

Ward Cunningham has been a great encouragement to me over the years in helping me focus on the essential. I'd like to thank him for believing in me, and encouraging me to write this stuff down and focus on what I'm passionate about. Thanks for your friendship and paying me the honor of writing the foreword for the book.

Kent Beck has been a tremendous catalyst for the software industry. Many don't realize that he was the driving force behind the use of software patterns in addition to contributing what has been called by Joshua Kerievsky "the most successful pattern language to date," Extreme Programming. Kent has always encouraged me to be confident in my own abilities and reach beyond my confidence level. As I look back over my career, I realize how he has instigated just about all of my risk-taking in some way. Kent, watching you finally jump out of that big redwood tree made me realize the value in not allowing my fears to hold me back. You're brilliant and I love you!

I need to thank Ron Jeffries for being the coach's coach. Ron has always been there when I didn't know what to do on that first big XP project. He even once pulled his car over in a cornfield in Iowa to patiently give me his sage advice. His tireless answering of a gazillion XP questions is much appreciated by me for so many reasons. No matter what anyone else says, Ron, I have seen firsthand your innate wit and charm.

Although Martin Fowler may be less extreme than the three "Extremos" mentioned above, it hasn't stopped him from being an extremely helpful counselor along the way. From the time I first saw you do your elephant routine, I knew we'd get along just fine. Thanks for being there whenever I called on you, and always taking the time to answer every question. And thanks for helping me learn how to draw bubbles and arrows when I need to.

I also need to thank Duff O'Melia, the world's most enthusiastic chronic learner. Thanks for making the drive from Virginia for three of the most exciting weeks of programming I've ever had. Thanks for starting the journey with me and helping me figure out how to put all of this stuff together. I couldn't have picked a better pair partner with whom to start applying XP. Thanks for sticking with me when other opportunities arose. I look forward to the rest of the journey.

I need to thank God for sending Nathaniel Talbott into my life. When I thought it was time to hire an apprentice and build the studio, I had no idea that He would provide the consummate XP apprentice. Thanks, Nathaniel, for listening as I talked about what I thought it would look like, acting on every one of my whims, and doing everything you were asked to do to get this thing off the ground. Thanks even more for sharing the wisdom beyond your years. It's sometimes hard to tell who is the master and who is the apprentice. Remember me when you have eclipsed everything I've accomplished in my life by the time you are twenty-five.

Thanks to Jeff Canna, who was crazy enough to think this XP Software Studio would work when all we had was a single project and an attic office. Your deep thought on XP and everything else is a great encouragement. You took the risk when most old guys with families would have written it all off and I've reaped a great reward. Thanks for sticking by me when the going got tough.

I also need to thank the other XPers who have worked with me at Role-Model over the past couple of years for asking a lot of tough questions, and challenging me always to move forward: Chris Carpenter, Chris Collins, Michael Hale, and Adam Williams. You are all my dear brothers.

I also need to thank all of the people on the Stagville project, especially my fellow XPers—David Blythe, John DeMichiel, Andy Fekete, Karen Read, Chris Stark, and Richelieu Tah—and the other members of the team: Roger Elkins, Velinda Moore, Lisa Morelli, Carl Nuckols, Cynthia Traynham, and David Trogdon. You've come up with a lot of hard problems and have helped us work through them. A special thanks to John DeMichiel for believing in me enough to let me indoctrinate his project with XP, even though you never said I wasn't a crackpot. I'd also like to thank Lisa Morelli for working hard to figure out what the customer is supposed to do.

My mom and dad were the first people who showed me unconditional love, or more accurately, contraconditional love. Thanks for making all the sacrifices you did over the years for me when I gave you every reason to give up on me. The older I grow, the deeper I understand how much you gave me. A special thanks for your example of honoring your commitments and working hard.

There are so many others who have offered me encouragement along the way: my church family at Fellowship Bible Church, Reed Phillips and so many of my colleagues at the old Knowledge Systems Corporation, The Hillside Group, my sisters, my wonderful in-laws, my clients (especially Graham Poor and Margaret Mahoney), my business associates, and my friends.

I personally want to thank our editor, Mike Hendrickson. Mike, your patience and encouragement when the book just wasn't moving forward is greatly appreciated. I hope you get a great return on your investment in me.

Last, but certainly not least, I need to thank Jon Vickers. Jon, neither RoleModel nor I would be standing if you hadn't come along to take care of all of the stuff that has nothing to do with programming. Outside of the Lord and my wife, there is no one I've leaned on more over the past couple of years. You've put up with all of the stuff I've dumped on you at the last minute and still smiled about it. There is no man I trust more. You are a true RoleModel and I'm blessed to have you in my life.

Roy

Thanks to God for giving me a good brain and then requiring that I use it. He deserves ultimate credit for anything good that I do. The mistakes are all mine.

Thanks to Ken for giving me the opportunity to write this book with him. It was an opportunity I wasn't expecting. I hope I made the most of it.

Thanks to my mother, who taught me how to value my family, to speak my mind, and to laugh at myself. And how to fold a fitted sheet—man, that really comes in handy. Thanks for loving me when other people didn't, Mom.

Thanks to my father, who showed me what it's like to be a man of character. Any courage I have, any grace under pressure, any optimism when the going gets tough, I learned from him. You're a real man, Dad.

Finally, thanks to my sister, the most amazing person I have ever known. I look forward to seeing where your life will take you, and I hope I can come along for the ride now and then. Know this, though. Even if you achieve nothing (impossible), even if you become nothing (you're already a miracle), I will always be as in awe of you as I was when I held you for the first time. I will love my little sister forever, no matter what. Without you, Rachel, I wouldn't be who I am.

The folks at Addison-Wesley have all been great from the first day the book was conceived. They are truly a first-class organization, and we can't imagine a better publisher to work with. There were a lot of people involved with creating this book, and we're grateful to all of them. We would specifically like to thank Mike Hendrickson, Heather Olszyk, Ross Venables, Tyrrell Albaugh, and Kim Arney Mulcahy. We couldn't have produced this book without their help, especially at the end when it got hairy.

Introduction: Playing to Win!

We shouldn't ever have to survive another software project.

Survival is a good thing. But when it is your focus, it's not that fun or rewarding. In the end, you are not much better off than when you started. In some ways, you are worse off. That's not where you want to be. And once you've realized you survived, it certainly feels better, but you don't want to start the journey over again.

There are all sorts of books about surviving software projects. Some say that the best you can hope for is survival. Many experienced in the industry say the same thing. If you were counseling a young person about his future career options, you would not say, "Think about a career in software—with a lot of hard work, and by learning a few key techniques, you can survive."

If you are a professional reading this book, whether you just live in a world with room for improvement or dwell in the depths of despair, you are probably looking for something better than the status quo. You are hoping that Extreme Programming (XP) is something better, and you want to find out whether the promise that others have seen in XP has actually panned out. You see a lot of obstacles between you and that wonderful place you'd like to be. You wonder whether "The Promised Land" is even attainable, and whether the journey is worth taking.

Like many promising things that have come before it, XP is no silver bullet. It does not offer a formula for wild success on your next (or current) software project. On the other hand, XP, when executed well, allows you to shake off many of the problems of mainstream approaches that can keep you from succeeding.

To illustrate some of the problems with mainstream approaches, we offer the following composites of real people we have met in the software world.

The Pitiful Programmer

Many very intelligent programmers we know seem to go from one failed project to another. Often the next project seems full of promise. There's new technology to learn and you look forward to learning it. Often, you start with enthusiasm, but it goes south in a hurry.

It becomes clear that your leadership has made unreasonable promises and set the bar too high. The inevitable technical and organizational obstacles spring up, but the deadline does not change. Scope creeps. Maybe, after Herculean efforts (often at the expense of family, social life, and physical or mental health), the project actually produces something. Not something to be truly proud of, mind you, but something. Equally likely, the project gets cancelled, to no one's surprise. The warning signs of impending failure were all over the place and screaming for attention.

This is the norm. Being part of a project that provides an enriching learning environment, produces something good, and doesn't kill you along the way is a fantasy, an unattainable dream. The pitiful programmer comes to believe that success is just luck, and the chances of success are too slim to count on. The best you can hope for is to survive without being maimed.

The Die-Hard Developer

Many very intelligent and talented programmers we know seem to have overcome some great obstacles to produce software that actually ships. Life is not so bad, most of the time. You were given part of the software to develop, figured it out, used some of the best design practices in the industry, and worked hard to hit your deadlines. Then came integration.

On the project plan, there is this little block of time where everything comes together. You and everybody on the team cross your fingers. Soon, each of you finds out a few assumptions others made about your software. Of course, the process of getting there is not pretty. Things are going wrong and you have to spend just as much time defending your work as you do trying to get all of the software to come together as planned. You work late into the night to pull it out, but you are bruised and battered. The pristine software you submitted to be integrated has been patched and hacked in so many ways, it's barely recognizable. Management may appreciate these heroics or lay blame for the problems that required the heroics.

This is the norm. Being part of a project that provides a way to avoid these intense storms is a fantasy, an unattainable dream. The die-hard developer believes there has to be a way to avoid this, but hasn't yet seen it. The best you can hope for is to survive the storms to get to the next relative calm.

The Sad Sponsor

Many business people we know doubt that they'll ever get quality software delivered on time and within budget. Who can blame them? They ran the numbers before the project started. They vetted the numbers with all the right people and got a unanimous "go," after a painfully slow process in which the company spent a bunch of indirect money deciding whether to spend the direct money. Everyone was excited about the possibilities. Then reality set in.

Several months into the project, the software team started requesting additional resources in order to hit the target date. They blame you for changing the requirements or for providing vague requirements in the first place. After reluctantly cutting into the hoped-for profit, you learn that the software team doubts it will ship anywhere close to the planned release date. And the "minor" functionality changes that some stakeholders requested produce a groundswell of resistance from the developers, who get the shakes when asked to deliver. They seem to have forgotten that the stakeholders are the ones paying their salaries.

The software must ship or the budget will have been blown with nothing to show for it. Even if it does ship, there's still a good chance you will get fired for incompetence because the incremental profit promised won't materialize. The next release doesn't look any better. Is there any chance you can survive in this organization with this reputation?

This is the norm. The best you can hope for is to survive without looking like an idiot.

The Smelly Software

Both the developer and the sponsor are battered and bloody at the end of the typical project. The project delivered either subpar software or decent software over budget. The end user identifies a handful of significant problems in the software. There are some nice features, but not the ones that really give the users the desired bang for the bucks they spent. Everyone is at least a little bit ashamed of what they shipped . . . in private.

This shouldn't be surprising. Scope got out of hand fast and changing requirements invalidated the original design. Pretty soon, nobody even remembered the original design anymore. Under the intense time pressure, developers took all sorts of shortcuts and did all sorts of dumb things. The sponsor spent a lot of time dealing with the concerns coming out of development and missed some significant needs of the end users. Remember, sponsors, developers, and programmers are all just trying to survive. Communication broke down, too. Who had time for meetings or coordination? Alternatively, who had time for anything but meetings and rationalization?

In the end, the software they created is not in the best shape. It's full of bugs, or is a patchwork of fixes commented with "Not sure why this works— DON'T TOUCH!" It's brittle. Changing it is so risky that developers perform unnatural acts to squeeze new features into spots not made to accept anything new, because that's the only way to avoid new bugs. Management and customers don't understand why it seems to be so hard to get the new features in for the next release. Now the pressure is on again.

Developers don't want to produce software like this. Customers don't want to buy and use it either.

How Things Got So Bad

We made our own mess.

Software development as a discipline hasn't been around very long. It came about almost by accident. In the beginning, it wasn't even considered a discipline, because there weren't enough people doing it. Then it exploded.

Practitioners cast about looking for some guiding principles to increase professionalism, to improve the quality of the software they were making, and to make life easier. Along the way, both practitioners and theorists with good intentions made some very bad assumptions. These assumptions led to faulty conclusions and bad practice. And that made the mess.

The Methodologists' Solution

For years, methodologists have told us that the way to clean up the software mess is to learn from other engineering disciplines, and many have gone along for the ride. Other engineering disciplines would never accept the sorry state of affairs that exists in software. If engineers—or even house builders—worked this way they'd be bankrupt in no time flat. Methodologists tell us that we should learn from them.

What do other engineers do? They spend a lot of time gathering requirements to make sure they understand what the customer wants. Next, they figure out what raw materials are needed and how to assemble them, culminating in a standard diagram. After reviewing this diagram carefully they approve it and get down to the business of creating something real. The product undergoes rigorous testing and inspections to make sure it's acceptable before any end customer gets hold of it. They can't afford to miss their estimate by very much, or so the theory goes.

The methodologists say we should build software the way civil engineers build bridges, to pick one example. After all, they've been doing what they do for far longer than "software" has even been a word. Using their approach will make us successful. We'd be arrogant and foolish to think it should be done any differently.

As the British say, this is utter tosh. It's bunk. Let that sink in.

Remembering the "Soft" in Software

Software is fundamentally different from physical stuff. It is expected to change. That's why it is called *soft*ware. The stuff that we understand, that we can set in cement, goes into the hardware. The stuff we don't understand gets left to the software developers. We know the hardware development process isn't easy or perfect, either. But that doesn't invalidate the point about the word "soft."

When we treat software development like a civil engineering project, we sign up for the baggage that comes along with that approach. We have to get all of the diagrams signed off. We have to keep them up to date. We have to go up several layers of management to get permission to put a new feature into a project that's in a code freeze. That's the equivalent of getting permission to put a jackhammer to hardened concrete. It's a lousy way to build software.

Engineers typically build models when designing complex physical things like bridges, buildings, planes, etc. because the models are cheap and flexible. They create paper, cardboard, or plastic models to get a feel for the end product. Often they build software models for the things that are hard to verify without actually building them. They may write down some thoughts and draw some sketches, but they don't rely on those thoughts or sketches to verify their design. Once they've verified their design, they produce the plans for sign off before actual construction.

Why do we build things that are impossible to verify (documents and diagrams) as models for things that are directly verifiable? We can create lots of documents using a conversational language and lots of diagrams using a modeling language. Neither one can verify that we will produce the desired behavior. (The process of writing this book has verified that!) The most verifiable model for software is a program written in a programming language. And when you are done verifying it, you're done. You don't have to get everything signed off so you can start to build the real thing.

Why do we want to apply a process for building stuff with "hard materials" to building something with "soft materials?" Let's stop acting as if there was any real merit in this approach and throw it out! It is not a way to win. It's not even a good way to survive.

We should plan and execute differently, in a way that respects the fundamental differences between soft things and hard things. The civil engineering approach doesn't work for software. It often produces brittle systems—late. That has profound implications for the economics of software development.

The Dreaded "Cost of Change" Curve

When you build a bridge, you end up with something big that's tough to change and probably will last for over a hundred years, until it decays and collapses. All of these are good characteristics for a structure you trust your life to. But what if the bridge needed to change significantly next month? What if it needed to change tomorrow?

The common assumption, and common reality, on most software projects is that the cost of changing software rises exponentially over time, just like it would for a bridge. Most software projects, whether or not they are aware of it when they start, are living with what has become the self-fulfilling reality of this "cost of change" curve. It looks like Figure I.1.

The original premise of the curve has gone away due to changes in the tools we use for most of today's software. The curve began as a reflection of the cost of change related to the waterfall model of development. Most no longer use that approach. Interestingly, for many, the fundamental shape of the curve hasn't changed significantly. It's still exponential. Teams might not be building software in phases quite as regimented as in the waterfall approach, but change still costs more over time. Why?

The biggest reason is that typical formal development approaches, although not strictly waterfall anymore, still delay the build phase by doing lots

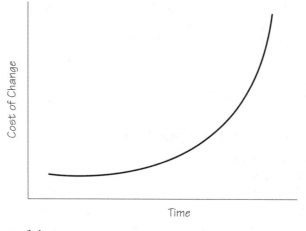

FIGURE I.1 Cost of change curve

of other things in big chunks up front. Typically, this means design. This leaves precious little time to steer as you learn. If you encounter a show-stopping design flaw, it's too late to "rearchitect" the system. You've got to press on the best you can. This leads to brittle code that's difficult to change.

Another big reason is that some software development approaches do little beyond the build phase. They ignore many of the best practices of the industry and they try to move forward continuously against increasingly significant self-made obstacles.

Let's face it. A software project begins with excitement. It's full of promise. At that point, given the curve, there are two traditional ways you can go. You can try to defy it, or you can respect it. The problem is, neither one works.

Defying the Curve

You can produce something quickly by ignoring the curve. Just get a few tools and people who can manipulate the tools well, and it's amazing what you can produce in a short amount of time. You begin to feel invincible.

Then, a few months into the project, you try to make the first significant change to the software. The super programmers get it to work, but it feels like you're moving slower than you were. Before you know it, you seem to be crawling, and the list of problems is growing faster than you can fix them. You're climbing the steep part of the curve, and it isn't much fun. The curve was intended to discourage this kind of behavior.

How did you get there? You ignored the waterfall model because everyone knows it doesn't work. There are a lot of reasons you may have ignored it, but here are a few common ones.

Incomplete Understanding of the Requirements

You probably began before you understood all of the requirements. You knew enough to get moving, and you knew the requirements would change over time anyway. You didn't bother with any significant design issues to plan for flexibility in the right places. You didn't do anything to ensure quality up front. People copied and pasted stuff that seemed to work in one place and now doesn't work, for slightly different reasons, all over the place. Now you are in "code and fix" mode, mostly "fix."

Reliance on Tools

There are a lot of good tools out there that claim you won't have to code much to develop software with them. Many of them have "visual" in the product name. Most do a great job on the mundane stuff that can be prone to error otherwise, but the bar on what's mundane gets higher all the time. This is both a blessing and a curse. The tool designer's understanding of the problem is often much greater than the user's understanding. So more naive people (who will work at a cheaper rate) can use the tool to produce things they really don't understand very deeply. When the tool falls short of solving the hard part of the problem, the naive users are lost. They are already well down a road that got them 80 percent of the way to their desired destination, but it's a dead end. The two choices seem to be back up and start over, or take out a machete and try to extend the road. You may end up with a complete road, but the last 20 percent will be a treacherous uphill climb.

Inexperienced People

You might have employed only craftsmen wannabes who know just enough about good development practices to be dangerous. They really didn't know how to handle the hard problems. They also didn't know enough to identify the riskiest parts of the project up front.

Skilled People Distracted by Other Things

You may have had one or two craftsmen who got things rolling competently and quickly, then got too busy attending meetings to help the less skilled developers turn their competently blazed trail into a useful road. When less skilled developers stray off the road, he may not even realize the difference in the ride. When he comes across an obstacle, he might just decide he can handle it himself. He takes out the machetes and climbs (or creates) the steep curve.

Poor Communication

The communication between the people defining the requirements and the development team might have been poor and the hard problems identified at the wrong time.

Time Pressure

When the pressure is on to get in "all of the functionality," you may have cut corners. Now you're spending more time servicing the resulting problems than tackling the business problems.

Turnover

When stuff isn't getting produced fast anymore, the positive strokes the "geniuses" got when they whipped together the first demo can turn to threats. It's not fun anymore—and the "geniuses" leave. Unfortunately, they were the only ones who understood any of the software you are now trying to make it work.

The bottom line is that there is a plethora of things that make the curve steep before you ever get to deployment. When you ignore all the things that can go wrong, most of them will.

Respecting the Curve

You probably don't want to end up in this predicament. So you embrace the curve and resolve to heed its wisdom. You spend lots of time understanding requirements, drawing pictures, documenting everything under the sun, and getting all the right sign-offs. You produce mostly paper in the beginning, but it proves you really thought about everything. Then the requirements change, or you find out you misunderstood something, and the house of cards collapses, but the ship date can't move. You spend more time trying to recover gracefully, but give up in frustration as time pressure grows intense. You decide you'll just get the thing to work and cram in as many "fixes" as you can. Before you know it, what is about to get shipped to the customer has only a vague resemblance to all of the diagrams you drew, and you don't have the energy or desire to go back and update them. Nobody reads them anyway.

Despite your best efforts up front to minimize costs late in the game, the curve poked you in the eye anyway. The wonderful design is gone and so are its creators. And so are your chances of getting it back to a system designed for flexibility.

When you use a process meant for building inflexible things like bridges to build flexible things like software, it shouldn't shock you that later change costs more. Whether you ignore the curve or embrace it, you'll end up climbing it because you're using hard methods to produce soft stuff. But when you use soft methods to produce soft stuff, the curve doesn't apply anymore. That is the beauty of XP.

XP Flattens the Curve

Change is the reality of software development. You can't anticipate everything, no matter how much you plan. Traditional approaches to software development force you to climb an exponential cost of change curve. The only way to produce good software, and to stay sane, is to use a curve that looks like Figure I.2.

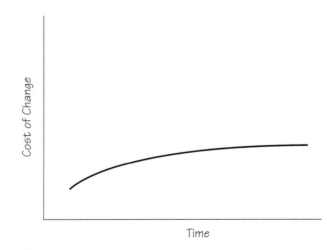

FIGURE I.2 The XP cost of change curve

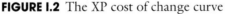

If you want to win, you've got to flatten the curve and keep it flat. XP focuses on living in the self-fulfilling reality of a flatter curve, and it gives you the tools to get there.

Developing software is a challenge, no matter how you go about it. But XP proposes that we apply four values consistently to give ourselves a better chance to succeed:

1. Simplicity
2. Communication
3. Feedback
4. Courage

The fundamental premise of XP is that applying these values through consistent practices will flatten the curve. Those values and practices accept the reality that requirements change, that scope creeps; that two people working together are simply more productive than the same two people working alone, that not every programmer is Einstein, and that some things are out of your control. Stuff happens: Accept it and get going.

XP is no silver bullet. There are still forces outside our control (competitors, human fallibility, etc.). But if the curve is flatter, you can walk or run instead of slowly clawing your way up the curve, wasting a significant amount of time and energy trying not to fall.

XP also isn't just a spin on undisciplined hacking. Applying the values and practices takes discipline. It takes discipline to write tests first, to integrate often, to get all the tests to run before moving on, to pair program. In fact, the one lesson we should draw from "hard" engineering is that discipline is important.

The difference between the discipline needed for XP and the discipline needed for civil software engineering is in the results. XP increases your chances of producing reliable, flexible software on a routine basis. You can win with that, whether you have the diagrams or not.

When XP gets a fair shot, both programmers and business people enjoy it. And why wouldn't they? Fighting uphill battles is tiring. The flatter the terrain, the less fatiguing the battle. In fact, it often doesn't even feel like a battle, especially to those who are used to fighting on a slope.

Wagons Ho!

Prior to adopting XP, we saw lots of different ways to develop software, and we struggled with the curve. Often we felt defeated. We watched many others struggle and go down to defeat. Of course, it wasn't always that bad. Along the way, we had experiences that were enjoyable and less of a struggle. We got over some obstacles in ways that made us feel like winners.

We recognized, however, that just about all of the victories involved most or all of the four values of simplicity, courage, communication, and feedback. When we heard about XP, we hoped that following it would lead to a better place where victory was more easily attainable. We were looking for a place where good, hard work commonly resulted in the achievement of desired goals rather than mere survival.

So we decided to begin the XP journey. Along the way, we met other pioneers on the same journey, looking for the same promise. Some had harder journeys, some easier. Some turned back for one reason or another. But many of us have kept going.

The road hasn't always been easy, but taking the first steps has been the hardest part. We've got some arrows in our backs from those who suspected us to be enemies, to be sure. We also took a few wrong turns. The good news is that we not only survived but also achieved much of what we set out to do. We've also found that the journey is never really over. In many ways, XP is just the beginning of a journey to a better place where the four values abound. The terrain of the flatter curve makes the journey less treacherous and victory more attainable.

The better news for you, the reader, is that we made a map and there are now some established settlements. There is certainly uncharted territory. But we hope this map can make the journey less treacherous for those who follow. The odds are good you'll make it out alive. In fact, we believe this book will greatly reduce the stress of your journey and help you enjoy the blessing of the four values more readily.

XP is the best way we've seen to keep the curve flat. It can help average programmers become more effective. It can make excellent programmers phenomenal. Even more importantly, it creates collaborative winning teams. And everyone's life is more fun when you are winning.

Software development should be about more than surviving. It should be about progressing toward noble goals, while living life to the fullest and developing meaningful relationships. History has stacked the deck so that survival is the primary concern. XP is a way of thinking and behaving that can help you move beyond that.

Meet the Pioneers

This book is full of real-world experiences. Many of them come from us (your authors). Others come from friends we've met or become reacquainted with along the way. The following is an introduction to the pioneers mentioned in this book. We'll often refer to them on a first-name basis. Maybe you will too by the time you're done reading the book.

Ken Auer is President, Founder and Master Craftsman of RoleModel Software, Inc. He has been active in the development of object-oriented software since 1985. Through the years, he has collaborated on many occasions with Kent Beck and Ward Cunningham, and was fortunate enough to visit the famed Chrysler Comprehensive Compensation (C3) project in 1996. In late 1998, RoleModel Software began building the first eXtreme Programming Software Studio, based on his vision. This is a place where apprentices, skilled journeymen, and software masters work together in an environment of continuous learning with extremely effective modes of collaboration to produce unusually adaptable and robust software for its clients.

Roy Miller is a Software Developer at RoleModel Software, Inc. Prior to joining RoleModel, Roy spent six years with Andersen Consulting (now Accenture), most recently as a Project Manager. Roy came to RoleModel after reading *Extreme Programming Explained*. The contrast between XP and the way he was used to doing things was so exciting, he had to try it. RoleModel Software promised the opportunity, so he jumped at the chance, believing that a company using XP would provide the environment of success and camaraderie in which he wanted to work. His enthusiasm and insights into what made XP work quickly led Ken to invite him to coauthor this book.

The rest of the pioneers who have contributed to this book are listed in alphabetical order to avoid offending any of them that are particularly touchy.

Kent Beck is the "articulator" of Extreme Programming. His introduction of the process at Chrysler in 1995, and his seminal work, *Extreme Programming Explained*, have been the inspiration for many of the XP pioneers. He also coauthored *Planning Extreme Programming* with Martin Fowler. He didn't supply any stories directly and you probably know who he is by now anyway. We quote him now and again, and often refer to him merely as "Kent." So, when you see the name Kent, we do not mean to imply Ken, the coauthor of *this* book. Whenever something refers to both Ken and Kent we will use the short form of Ken(t). Don't worry, it doesn't happen very often.

Rob Billington has been a software developer and manager for many years. He was first introduced to XP in 1999 at StorageTek and embraced it wholeheartedly. As a manager of a software development group, he had to encourage his team to get over the initial hurdles.

Jack Bolles is a software consultant with ThoughtWorks and cofounder of the Bay Area (San Francisco) XP Users Group. He has delivered several large-scale financial systems using a variety of methodologies. He initially gravitated toward XP because it reflected how he likes to work. Jack finds agile development both harder to do right and much more rewarding than other processes he has worked with.

Jeff Canna is a Senior Software Developer at RoleModel Software, Inc. Jeff joined RoleModel Software in the summer of 1999 after spending about six months talking to Ken, reading about XP, and trying to figure out whether it was really a better way to develop software. Although he developed software for almost 17 years for Wang, Compugraphics, IBM, and MGV America prior to joining RoleModel, he claims he has learned more in the last two years in an XP environment than in all of his previous years combined.

Alistair Cockburn is founder of Humans & Technology and is recognized as a leader in the research of the human impact on software processes. He doesn't actually do XP, but he admires it from afar. He's got some great papers that back up a lot of our subjective experience, and we quote him often enough to give him more than a footnote.

Chris Collins is a Senior Software Developer at TYBRIN. After working in a collaborative environment and then going to a heavy "big design up front" project, he enjoyed the best one and a half years of his life doing XP as much as possible at RoleModel Software, Inc. before moving back to Florida to be close to family. He has taught computer science courses at North Carolina State and the University of West Florida.

Ward Cunningham is a principal at Cunningham & Cunningham and has been developing object-oriented software in various roles since the early 1980s. He is credited by Kent Beck as the inspiration for XP. In 1989, Ward formed a team that used all of the principles and many of the practices of XP at Wyatt Software. Since then he has introduced many of the practices and principles of XP into many organizations as a consultant.

Michael Feathers is a member of the team at ObjectMentor, Inc. His life changed when he attended a pair-programming BOF given by Ward and Kent at OOPSLA'97. He was stunned to find a community of people intent on making programming easier rather than harder, who loved programming but cared more about how we can all be more effective in a very human way. A few years after that, he joined ObjectMentor, where the same values are held. Michael is currently helping organizations transition to XP and satisfying his programming itch whenever he can. The interests that currently keep him awake at night are team culture, micro-incremental test-first design, and large-scale systems evolution.

Martin Fowler is Chief Scientist at ThoughtWorks and perhaps one of the best bald-headed object-oriented application software developers on the planet (but give Ken a few more years as the diminishing number of hairs on his head rapidly approaches zero). Martin has authored many best-selling books, including *Refactoring*, arguably the first XP-related book to be published. He coauthored *Planning Extreme Programming* with Kent Beck. Although Martin didn't contribute any stories directly to this book (too busy writing his own books, he says), he certainly has said a lot of good things that we find worth quoting.

Steve Freeman is a consultant in the United Kingdom who has been involved in object-oriented software development for 15 years. He has implemented XP on several projects, beginning at Lombard Risk Systems and then on various Web-based projects. He is a member of the Extreme Tuesday Club in London.

Uros Grajfoner and **Matevz Rostaher** both work at FJA OdaTeam in Slovenia. Working in an environment where many of the values of XP were already in place, they began to adopt the practices in 1999. The nature of their business led them to make some interesting adaptations that allowed them to work closely with a small number of customers at the customer site.

Travis Griggs is a Senior Software Engineer with Key Technology. He got excited about XP at OOPSLA'98 in Vancouver, where the C3 team was prancing around in their cool shirts. He spent the next couple of weeks after hours with a colleague writing tests and pair programming a VisualWorks Wiki implementation. That taste was enough; he and colleagues launched full-heartedly into implementing and practicing XP at Key Tech.

Steve Hayes is an insightful and experienced software developer and manager who helped extract the vision for the XP Software Studio from Ken's head at a 1998 OOPSLA workshop. He has been involved in object-oriented software for over 10 years, in a variety of positions. Most recently, he was Vice President of Technology at a prominent Wall Street bank, where he successfully formed an XP team. Steve is currently back in his native Australia introducing his new bride to his family and friends and advocating XP practices through his company, Khatovar Technology.

Jim Highsmith has 30 years' experience as a consultant, software developer, project manager, and writer. He has published dozens of articles in industry publications and is the author of *Adaptive Software Development: A Collaborative Approach to Managing Complex Systems*. Jim has worked with companies in the United States, Canada, Europe, New Zealand, Japan, and Australia to assist them in accelerating development in increasingly complex, extreme environments. He is a thought leader in agile methods and has offered some excellent ideas on how to think about and measure their effectiveness.

Ron Jeffries of ObjectMentor is known to many in the XP community as its most zealous promoter, and the pioneer with the most arrows in his back. Brought in as the Assistant Coach and then Head Coach on the C3 archetypal XP project, he may be one of the foremost authorities on "how to do XP right." He coauthored *XP Installed* to tell us what the promised land of XP looks like. We've asked him to share some insights on the struggles of keeping even the best XP projects on process.

Kay Johansen and **Ron Stauffer** are both software developers. Kay has a background in application development at WordPerfect, and Ron has experience in accounting and in developing information systems. They met at e-automate Corporation, where they tried many of the XP practices as a pair. They liked what they experienced and wanted to form an XP team. Rather than driving XP from the development team only, or from management only, Kay and Ron were able to coordinate their efforts to create a team environment that encouraged developers to use XP.

Kevin Johnson is a Principal Software Engineer at Medtronic, Inc. and has been doing pair programming since before Kent Beck came up with the name Extreme Programming. Kevin learned Smalltalk while in graduate school and at the same time followed the early development of XP in Kent's column in *The Smalltalk Report* magazine. Later, while still hanging out in the academic world trying to decide what he wanted to be when he grew up, Kevin used pair programming (among other XP ideas) to teach Smalltalk and object-oriented design. He is now working on introducing ideas from XP and other agile methods into the challenging environment of software development for medical instruments.

Susan Johnson (no relation to Kevin) is a Senior Principal Software Engineer at Medtronic, Inc. In 1998 and 1999 she worked on a joint project with Object Technology International that to the best of our knowledge was as close to Geographically Distributed XP as anyone has ever achieved.

Tom Kubit is a consultant in the Ann Arbor, Michigan area who has been involved in object-oriented development for over 13 years. In 1997, he was introduced to XP by Don Wells and, rumor has it, dragged into it kicking and screaming. Once brainwashed, he began evangelizing XP, and has introduced and been involved with XP development with a variety of teams and environments.

Kyle Larson has been in software development since 1983 and object-oriented development since 1993, and is currently Chief XP Coach and Best Practice Mentor for the consulting firm Advanced Technologies Integration. He attempted test first by intention and pair programming in 1998 with mixed success but with rejuvenated interest in both XP and in software development as a profession. Convinced that XP was a more effective and more humane approach to software development, he joined ATI in 1999 to build its XP practice and is currently working on his fourth XP project.

Jeff McKenna has been doing consulting on object-oriented projects for 15 years and has been involved with software for so long that he has threatened to introduce "GeezerFest" at a future OOPSLA. After spending years doing big design up front, he found that, although adopting XP practices is quite natural to him in many aspects, old habits are still hard to break. He is actively consulting on XP projects.

Rob Mee has been coaching XP projects since 1998. He is currently Director of Engineering (aka XP coach) at Evant, an e-commerce software provider in San Francisco and an XP shop from top to bottom.

Duff O'Melia is a Senior Software Developer at RoleModel Software, Inc. Ken introduced Duff to the concepts of XP in early 1998. Before the end of the year, Ken and Duff had convinced a common client to allow them to work together in XP style for a segment of a project. Duff was hooked and later joined RoleModel Software on its first full XP project. Although he started as a subcontractor, Duff eventually realized that RoleModel was the best place in the world to work and decided to shut down his own business and join the team full time.

Joseph Pelrine is an independent consultant living in Switzerland when he's not on the road. Having worked with Kent Beck during Kent's two-year stint in Europe, Joseph has been known to flinch occasionally when he sees a rolled-up newspaper. He's been involved in object-oriented software development, primarily in Smalltalk, for over 13 years and has developed some particularly well-formed practices in the area of testing and packaging in an XP environment.

Don Roberts, "Redneck Smalltalker," is a consultant with the Refactory, Inc. and has been doing object-oriented programming for several years. He had been studying refactoring for several years, primarily in the area of framework design and evolution, before he heard Kent utter the phrase "Extreme Programming." Don's principle contribution to this community has been the Refactoring Browser (for Smalltalk), the first commercial refactoring tool, which he developed along with John Brant during their decade at the University of Illinois.

Nathaniel Talbott is a Software Developer at RoleModel Software, Inc. Nathaniel started his first programming job at age 16, and joined RoleModel as an apprentice and Ken's first hire at the age of 18 in 1998. He was one of Ken's first XP guinea pigs and helped Ken figure out a lot of the infrastructure that would need to be put in place to develop the XP Software Studio. He was on RoleModel's first full XP project and has been a key contributor to its success. Don't let this young man's age fool you. He is already a key player in the XP community.

Frank Westphal is a software consultant based in Germany who has implemented XP on several projects. XP seemed familiar enough to make sense to him, yet he felt challenged to become a master of the craft, so he experimented with it on many occasions. He finally brought all the pieces together at Channel One, where his team has shipped several releases of a shrink-wrapped intranet application suite.

Laurie Williams is an Assistant Professor at North Carolina State University. In a past life, Laurie worked at IBM for nine years in Raleigh, North Carolina. While at University of Utah she began studying pair programming and conducting extensive research on its effectiveness. Since then, she has been studying other aspects of XP and adding to the growing body of empirical data about the process.

A Map of the Book

We've divided this book into five parts and suggest you read it in order (at least the first time).

Part 0—Before You Start

Part 0 contains a single chapter summarizing XP for those who have not read *Extreme Programming Explained* or who don't have a copy of it handy. If you can recite the four values and 12 practices, you can probably skip this section.

Part I—The Right Mindset

Part I covers the mental and emotional challenges we face in getting started with XP and offers you help in overcoming them. Some of these challenges come from within ourselves. Others come from outside forces, usually human.

Not all of these challenges apply to everyone, nor is our list comprehensive. We have found that most of the challenges of adopting XP are really mental and emotional ones, not mechanical. To many who have not yet adopted XP, this may be the most important section you'll read.

Part II—First Things First

One of the rules of XP is to do the things with the highest risk first. In Part II we suggest the practices that are most important to concentrate on early. We have found that once these practices are adopted, other things tend to fall into place. In addition, we provide advice based on our collective experience to help you develop a plan to adopt these practices in your own environment.

Part III—The Rest of the Story

If you just stop at the practices in Part II, you'll have overcome the greatest challenges, but you still won't be close to realizing the full value of XP. Part III advises you on how to bring the rest of the practices to bear. Again, we provide advice based on our collective experience to help you develop a plan to adopt these practices in your own environment.

Part IV—Uncharted Territory

Several questions commonly come up in discussions of XP in particular types of environments. Some of these won't apply at all to your environment; others might represent your biggest concern. Part IV describes the sketchy parts of the XP map that several have explored, but few, if any, have really conquered. We hope Part IV will set realistic expectations and warn you about the special challenges you will face in the journey ahead. Maybe the advice you will get here is just what you'll need to win!

Part 0

Before You Start

Extreme Programming Explained: Embrace Change is the XP manifesto. As we were starting to use XP, we often found ourselves wishing we had a brief outline to give other people to read or to use as a cheat sheet. That's what this section is.

If you can recite the four XP values and the 12 XP practices, you can probably skip this section. If you can't, we encourage you to read it before you dive into the rest of the book. Even if you can, this might be worth reading as a refresher.

Chapter 0

XP Distilled

XP combines industry best practices that have been around for years in a refreshingly different way to produce significantly better results than other approaches. Trying XP can be scary. Not trying it is even scarier.

Extreme Programming embraces the reality that people work with people to develop software. Successful software processes must maximize people's strengths and minimize their weaknesses. In our opinion, XP does the best job of addressing all the complementary forces that affect the people involved. XP represents the single biggest opportunity this decade has to bring radical innovation to the process of software development. It identifies clear roles based on the reality of people's area of expertise and encourages the people filling those roles to work as one team. Everybody contributes to the dialogue that must take place to develop software that meets business needs. Customers contribute stories, priorities, acceptance tests, and information on demand when programmers and managers need it. Programmers contribute estimates and running code with unit tests. Management mediates—balancing customer-defined value with development cost, resolving disputes, and determining the level of resources that can be dedicated to the project based on fluctuating business conditions.

This chapter is adapted from an article by Roy Miller and Chris Collins that was first published by IBM developerWorks at http://www.ibm.com/developer/.

XP prescribes a core set of values and practices that allow software developers do what they do best: develop software. XP eliminates the unnecessary artifacts of most heavyweight processes that distract from that goal by slowing down and draining the development staff. We recognize that something called "Extreme Programming" might be tough to sell to your management as a serious development process. But if your company needs software written, it behooves you to look past the name to the competitive advantage XP can provide.

Kent Beck outlined the core values of XP in his book *Extreme Programming Explained*. We summarize them here:

1. **Communication.** Problems with projects often can be traced back to somebody not talking to somebody else about something important at some point. XP makes it almost impossible not to communicate.
2. **Simplicity.** XP proposes that you always do the simplest thing that could possibly work with regard to process and writing code. The way Kent put it, "XP is making a bet. It is betting that it is better to do a simple thing today . . . than to do a more complicated thing today that may never be used anyway."
3. **Feedback.** Getting concrete feedback early and often from the customer, from the team, and from real end users gives you more opportunity to steer your efforts. This keeps you on the road and out of the ditch.
4. **Courage.** If you aren't moving at top speed, you'll fail. Courage lets you do that by giving you guts when it counts, such as when you need to throw code away or make a change late in the game.

The practices of XP translate these values into the things you should do every day as a developer. There isn't much new here. The XP practices have been recognized by the industry for years as "best practices." In fact, the word "extreme" in XP derives primarily from two things:

1. XP takes proven industry best practices and turns the knobs up to "ten."
2. XP combines those practices in a way that produces something greater than the sum of the parts.

What does this look like? Code reviews are good, so we do them all the time by writing code in pairs. Testing is good, so we do it all the time by writing tests before we write code. Documentation rarely stays in sync with the code, so we write only the minimum necessary and depend on clearly written code and tests for the rest. XP doesn't guarantee that people will do the right thing all the time, but it allows them to. It combines these "extreme" practices in a mutually supportive way that produces significant increases in speed and efficiency.

Let's take a closer look at the 12 practices to get a better understanding of what it means to do XP.

The Planning Game

Some people like to criticize XP as glorified hacking, just a bunch of cowboys cobbling together a system without any discipline. We disagree. XP is one of the few methodologies out there that recognizes that you can't know everything when you start. Because both the business team and the developers will learn things as the project progresses, only approaches that encourage and embrace such change will be effective. Status quo methodologies ignore change. XP listens. The way it listens is through the Planning Game.

The main idea behind the Planning Game is to make a rough plan quickly and refine it as things become clearer. The artifacts of the Planning Game are a stack of index cards containing customer stories (which will drive the project's iterations) and a rough plan for the next release or two. The critical factor that makes this style of planning work is letting the customer make business decisions and letting the development team make technical ones. Without that, the whole process falls apart.

The development team determines

- ✧ Estimates of how long it will take to develop a story
- ✧ The cost implications of using various technology options
- ✧ Team organization
- ✧ The risk of each story
- ✧ The order of story development within an iteration (doing risky items first can mitigate risk)

The customer determines

- ✧ Scope (the stories for a release and the stories for an iteration)
- ✧ Release dates
- ✧ Priorities (which features get developed first, based on business value)

Planning happens often. This provides frequent opportunities for either the customer or the developers to adjust the plan as they learn new things.

Testing

There are two kinds of testing in XP:

1. Unit testing
2. Acceptance testing

Developers write the unit tests as they write code. The customer writes acceptance tests after defining stories. Unit tests tell developers whether the system works at any point in time. Acceptance tests tell the entire team whether the system does what users want it to do.

Assuming the team is using an object-oriented language, developers write unit tests for every method that could possibly break, before they write the code for that method. Then they write just enough code to get the test to pass. People sometimes find this a little weird. The point is simple. Writing tests first gives you

- ✧ The most complete set of tests possible
- ✧ The simplest code that could possibly work
- ✧ A clear vision of the intent of the code

A developer cannot check code into the source code repository until all the unit tests pass. Unit tests give developers confidence that their code works. It leaves a trail for other developers to help them understand the original developers' intent (in fact, it's the best documentation we've ever seen). Unit tests also give developers the courage to undertake any refactoring, because a test failure will immediately tell the developer if something is broken. Unit tests should be automated and give a clear pass/fail result. xUnit frameworks do all this and more, so many XP teams use them.[1] Each framework lets developers create tests that have one or more assertions for specific test conditions. These tests can be executed automatically with the click of a button in a GUI. Results are displayed in some detail in a list at the bottom of the main window. The most prominent

---

1. xUnit is a family of free-testing frameworks built for unit testing. The "x" is typically replaced by letters indicating the target language, such as JUnit for Java code or VBUnit for VisualBasic. You can find out more at http://www.xprogramming.com.

visual feature of each framework is a color bar that grows as tests execute. The bar is green if all the tests pass and red if any test fails. (This is what we mean when we refer to the "green bar" and the "red bar" in various places in this book.)

Customers are responsible for making sure each story has acceptance tests to validate it. The customer can write the tests personally, can recruit other members of the organization (e.g., QA people, business analysts, etc.) to write them, or some combination of the two. These tests tell the customer whether the system has the features it is supposed to have and that those features work correctly. Ideally, customers will have acceptance tests for the stories in an iteration written before that iteration is finished. Acceptance tests should be automated and run frequently to ensure that developers are not breaking any existing features as they implement new ones. Typically customers will need some help from the development team to write acceptance tests. We developed an automated acceptance test framework that allows the customer to enter inputs and expected outputs in a simple editor. The framework converts the input to an XML file, runs the tests in the file, and spits out "pass" or "fail" for each. Customers love it.

Not all of the acceptance tests have to pass all the time. Acceptance tests simply help customers gauge how far along the project is. Acceptance tests also allow customers to make informed decisions about whether something is ready for release.

Pair Programming

In XP, pairs of developers write all production code. This is not as inefficient as it may sound. In fact, pair programming provides many benefits, economic and otherwise:

- ✧ All design decisions involve at least two brains.
- ✧ At least two people are familiar with every part of the system.
- ✧ Two people are less likely to neglect tests or other tasks.
- ✧ Changing pairs spreads knowledge throughout the team.
- ✧ Code is always being reviewed by at least one person.

Research also shows that programming in pairs is actually more efficient than programming alone.[2] You probably will (or will appear to) sacrifice a little bit of speed initially, but you will more than make up for that later on.

---

2. A. Cockburn, L. Williams. "The Costs and Benefits of Pair Programming." Reprinted in *Extreme Programming Examined,* by G. Succi and M. Marchesi. Addison-Wesley, 2001.

Refactoring

Refactoring is the technique of improving code without changing functionality. An XP team refactors mercilessly.

There are two key opportunities for refactoring: Before implementing a feature and after implementing it. Developers try to determine if changing existing code would make implementing the new feature easier. Developers look at the code they just wrote to see whether there is any way to simplify it. For example, if they see an opportunity for abstraction, they refactor to remove duplicate code from concrete implementations.

XP says you should write the simplest code that could possibly work, but it also says you'll learn along the way. Refactoring lets you incorporate that learning into your code without breaking the tests. It keeps your code clean. That means your code will survive longer, introduce fewer problems, and guide future developers in the right direction.

Simple Design

Detractors claim that XP neglects design. This isn't true. The problem is that most of the heavyweight approaches we've seen say you should take a static picture of the horizon, stay still, and chart a perfect course of how to get there. XP says design should not be done all at once, up front, under a delusion that things won't change. XP considers design so important that it should be a constant activity done in small chunks. We always try to use the simplest design that could possibly work at any point, changing it as we go to reflect emerging reality.

What is the simplest design that could possibly work? According to Kent it is the design that:

1. Runs all the tests
2. Contains no duplicate code
3. States the programmers' intent for all code clearly
4. Contains the fewest possible classes and methods

Requiring a design to be simple doesn't imply that the design must be small or trivial. The design just has to be as simple as possible and still work. Don't include extra features that aren't being used. We call such things YAGNI, which stands for "you aren't going to need it." Don't let YAGNI destroy your chances for success.

Collective Code Ownership

Every person on the team should have the authority to make changes to the code to improve it. Everybody owns all the code, meaning everybody is responsible for it. This allows people to make necessary changes to a piece of code without going through the individual code owner, who can sometimes be a bottleneck. The fact that everybody is responsible negates the chaos that ensues from no code ownership.

Saying that everybody owns all the code isn't the same as saying that nobody owns it. When nobody owns code, people can wreak havoc anywhere they want and bear no responsibility. In XP, "You break it, you fix it." Unit tests must run before and after each integration, and if you break something, it's your responsibility to fix it, no matter where it is in the code. This requires uncommon discipline.

Continuous Integration

Frequent code integration helps you avoid integration nightmares. XP teams integrate their code several times a day after they get all the unit tests for the system to run.

Frequent integration makes the cause of failure for any particular integration more obvious (the tests ran before, so the new stuff must have caused the problem). This keeps the team moving at maximum speed, rather than in the typical yo-yo fashion of traditional approaches. Those approaches tend to force developers to code a lot, do a big-bang integration, then spend a significant amount of time fixing the problems. This defers bug fixing. Continuous integration makes bug fixing part of the daily development flow. It keeps the code clean rather than letting bugs hide in the closet. Sooner or later, you'll have to clean that closet. Doing it along the way minimizes the pain.

On-Site Customer

To function optimally, an XP team needs to have a customer available on-site to clarify stories and to make critical business decisions that developers should not make alone. Having a customer available eliminates bottlenecks that can arise when developers have to wait for decisions or for clarification of desires and priorities.

XP does not pretend that a story card is all the direction a developer needs to deliver the necessary code. The story is a commitment to a later conversation between the customer and the developer to flesh out the details. The idea is that communicating face to face minimizes the chances of misunderstanding.

We have found that having the customer on-site is the best possible situation, but it's not the only scenario that will work. The bottom line is that the customer must be available whenever needed to answer questions and to provide direction for the team, based on business value. If that can happen without the customer being on-site with the team full time, great, but physical presence with the team makes this much easier. We strongly recommend it.

Small Releases

Releases should be as small as possible while still delivering enough business value to make them worthwhile.

Releasing the system as soon as it makes sense will provide value to the customer as early as possible (remember that money today is worth more than money tomorrow). It also will provide concrete feedback to developers on what meets customer needs and what doesn't. The team can include these lessons in its planning for the next release.

40-Hour Week

Kent says that he wants to be ". . . fresh and eager every morning, and tired and satisfied every night."[3] The 40-hour work week lets you do that. The principle is more important than the exact number of hours. Burning the oil for long periods kills performance. Tired developers make more mistakes, which will slow them down more in the long run than keeping a "normal" schedule will.

Even if developers could function well for longer periods, it doesn't mean they should. Eventually, they'll get tired of it and leave their jobs, or have problems outside work that will impact their performance. You mess with people's lives, you pay the price. Overtime isn't the answer to a project's problem. In fact, it's a symptom of a larger problem. If you need a death march, you screwed up.

Coding Standards

Having a coding standard does two things:

1. It keeps the team from being distracted by stupid arguments about things that don't matter as much as going at maximum speed.
2. It supports the other practices.

---

3. K. Beck. *Extreme Programming Explained: Embrace Change.* Addison-Wesley, 2000, p. 60.

Without coding standards, it is harder to refactor code, harder to switch pairs as often as you should, and harder to go fast. The goal should be that no one on the team can recognize who wrote which piece of code. Agree on a standard as a team, then stick to it. The goal isn't to have an exhaustive list of rules, but to provide guidelines that will make sure your code communicates clearly. Your coding standard should begin simply, then evolve over time based on team experience. You shouldn't make it a large, up-front exercise.

System Metaphor

What does an architecture do? It provides a picture of the various components of a system and how they interact. Developers can use this as a blueprint to see where new pieces will fit.

The system metaphor in XP is analogous to what most methodologies call architecture. The system metaphor gives the team a consistent picture it can use to describe the way the existing system works, where new parts fit, and what form they should take.

It is more important to have everyone understand how the system fits together than it is to have a beautiful metaphor. Sometimes, you just can't come up with a good one. It's great when you can.

The Practices Work Together

The whole is greater than the sum of the parts. You can implement single practices, or a small subset, and get great benefits over not using any. But you only get the maximum benefit if you implement all of them, because their power comes from their interaction.

Do XP by the book at first, then, once you understand how the practices interact, you can adapt them to your context. Remember that doing XP is not the goal, it is a means to an end. The goal is developing superior software quickly without messing up people's lives.

Part I

The Right Mindset

Education, experience, and peer pressure have conditioned software developers and their management to think about software development in certain ways. Sometimes these ways are wrong. They lead to inaccurate conclusions, which lead to misguided actions that do not produce the results the various parties want. Breaking this cycle requires a new way of thinking.

The existing XP literature talks a good bit about XP as a discipline and how to *do* things differently. More significant, though, is that XP requires software developers and their management to *think* differently about what they do. Without that different mindset, XP will not produce the best possible results. It might not even work.

XP questions things about software development that have been assumed for years. People with a vested interest in developing software the traditional way, and people who simply do so out of habit, probably will resist changing their minds. This is human. Questioning beliefs and habits can be a shock to the system.

In this section, we talk about the mindset required for XP, and why software developers and technical managers resist it.

Chapter 1

The Courage to Begin

Far better it is to dare mighty things, to win glorious triumphs, even though checkered by failure, than to take rank with those poor spirits who neither enjoy much nor suffer much, because they live in the gray twilight that knows neither victory nor defeat.

—Theodore Roosevelt

Trying XP can be scary, since it might very well entail some personal and professional risk. Not trying it is even scarier, since your organization probably can't survive as it is.

Organizations tend to be conservative. Proposing and trying new things within those organizations can be risky, both professionally and personally. This risk can range from mild ridicule from colleagues to losing your job.

The XP approach is a sharp departure from typical software development. Although the leadership of some organizations will adopt it enthusiastically as is, many will not like the idea initially. This means that proposing some or all of the XP practices can be risky. Implementing them can be even riskier.

The Organizational Imperative

Given that there might be some personal and professional risk involved with trying XP, why should you do it? You should take the risk because status quo software development in your organization probably isn't as firm a foundation as your leadership might think it is.

The formalism, documentation, and process of "heavyweight" software development approaches attempt to quell fear by reducing risk. Using a methodology created by people with more experience than they have—doing it "by the book"—gives company leaders confidence. Following predefined, reusable steps leads them to believe that they can connect the dots and succeed. Producing lots of reassuring artifacts makes them feel like they are making progress. If they haven't had much success in building software before, who could blame them for thinking this way?

This is a false sense of security. Following the steps and producing documents distracts people from building software and slows them down. When your team is confronting a deadline, do you want to focus on writing and testing code or on keeping documents up to date? Code wins every time. Focusing on all the other junk actually *increases* risk by building delusion into the process and impeding progress.

Traditional approaches to developing software threaten to destroy the companies that use them. These approaches force companies to move too slowly for the modern competitive environment, simply because these approaches incur significant overhead that distracts from creating the software that drives the business. This should be an uncomfortable position for the leadership of your company. If they choose to continue that way, mediocrity is the best they can hope for. Agile companies can lead. Slow ones get run over.

Your Role

If you are interested in seeing your organization survive, you should play an active role in keeping it healthy.

In 1965 John William Ward said, "Today the man who is the real risk taker is anonymous and nonheroic. He is the one trying to make institutions work."[1] That is exactly the role you may need to play within your company, if you currently use a traditional approach to software development. You can propose that your company do things differently, and you can make it work. How you do that is the topic of the next chapter.

---

1. J. W. Ward. *Time Magazine*, 17 November 1965.

Chapter 2

Introducing XP

*Even if you're on the right track you'll get
run over if you just sit there.*
—Will Rogers

When you are starting XP, do the simplest thing that could possibly work. Find a suitable project, use the simplest tools possible, and drive a spike to explore all of the practices.

One of the fascinating things about XP is that its values and principles aren't limited to creating software. They apply to all of human behavior. Nowhere is this more obvious than when you are starting to use XP.

One of the values of XP is to focus on doing the simplest thing that could possibly work. You should think and behave this way when you're trying XP for the first time. This is how you can do that:

- Find a trial project that is big enough to let you explore all the practices, but small enough to give you feedback soon.
- Make sure you have the materials you need to do the job.
- Drive a spike to learn.[1]

---

1. Defined in the XP Glossary (http://c2.com/cgi/wiki?XpGlossary) as "quick (typically minutes or hours) exploration by coding of an area the development team lacks confidence in." The spike is concluded when you learn what you needed to learn. So-called because a spike is "end to end, but very thin," like driving a spike all the way through a log. We've also used the expression to mean exploring an entire system as in the Exploration Phase described in Chapter 9.

Before you actually take the plunge, however, you can make it a little easier on yourself by bringing some company along.

Bring a Friend

Find a person to take the risk with you. This can be a fellow developer who's interested in XP and willing to try it, a team leader who wants to try something new, or a group of people who are tired of doing things the same old way.

You can do quite well by applying the principles and practices of XP by yourself. Your confidence and productivity will go up, and you'll be justifiably proud of what you produce. But XP is a group thing. You can't pair program alone.

You probably are not used to developing software the XP way. It is outrageously fun, but it takes discipline. You will feel stupid often. If you can be "in it together" with one or more other people, you can help each other solve the puzzles and get over the rough spots. If you bring a friend, a daunting risk can seem more like an adventure.

Find a Target

Once you find a person or small group willing to take risks and simulate an XP project, pick a project to start on.

An acquaintance of Ken's reacted this way to XP after Ken told him the basics and pointed him to *Extreme Programming Explained:*

> *I took you up on your advice about reading Kent Beck's* Extreme Programming Explained *book. It's amazing! . . . I'd really like to see this thing in practice day in and day out.*

This guy obviously "got" XP. But he had no clue about what his initial target should be. When Ken followed up to find out what the guy wanted to know, his first question was this:

> *If you were introducing XP into a company, especially a new company starting up, what practices would you introduce first? Obviously, XP is too big to dump into a company all at once.*

XP is not big or complicated. That is the beauty of it. It is unusual, which is the source of the fear of doing it all at once. If there is already a process in motion, identify a target where you can alleviate a source of pain. If the company is just starting up, avoid the pain from the beginning.

At a start-up company, yes, you would do it all at once! There is no better situation. Why would you use other approaches that will create a steeper curve? Just so you can flatten it? That's the wrong way to think about it. Get the entire organization focused on winning from day one. In fact, only hire people who want to work this way. Otherwise, you'll be fighting an uphill battle from the start.

Introducing XP the Wrong Way
by Ken Auer

The first client I tried to introduce to XP was the founder of a start-up company. He needed to refine a framework he was building. He had hired me because he knew I had the necessary experience, and he saw some wisdom in what I was saying when I talked about my craft. Once I understood what he was trying to do with the prototyped framework, I proposed building the production version with an XP approach. This intrigued him.

He and I had pair programmed together on portions of the prototype. He valued the collaboration, so he agreed to start with pairing to build the production version of the kernel. He wasn't convinced that this was the best way to build the framework, but he wanted to bring another developer (Duff) up to speed. He thought a few weeks of Duff working with me might facilitate that. Then Duff and I could split up and do our own tasks.

What we produced in three weeks boggled his mind. He, his partner, and his other employee were pleased at first. But when Duff and I suggested that we should continue using and pairing XP, the client wasn't so sure. Although he recognized my expertise, and respected Duff as a developer, he and his partner were confident that they knew how to build software and that XP wasn't it. They wanted applications built by other developers, so they wanted lots of documentation so others could understand the framework. Duff and I got our own assignments and were held to the fire to deliver. When we objected and suggested using XP, as we did often, we were accused of wasting time and working against them instead of just working on what we were told to work on. Several times, that was accurate.

Our client was scared. He was reverting to what made him feel comfortable. This is human. We didn't do a good job of convincing him and his partner that XP was a safer way. We hadn't taken the time to communicate clearly what we had learned in our first three weeks. We weren't that confident of it ourselves. We just felt that we were much more productive when we were doing

In an established company, the focus shouldn't be on the entire organization. You can introduce XP to a small group on a small project within an organization of any size. Start small and grow from there. That is the simplest thing that could possibly work.

Your first effort shouldn't be grandiose. As a matter of fact, biting off too much could make you choke. This is your "proof of concept" for XP in your organization, so start with something small. Ease into XP like a new exercise routine.

If you are starting a new project, you *can* introduce everything at once. You should probably pick something nontrivial, but not mission-critical. This will let you get used to XP in a relatively safe environment. You'll have a better chance of success if you pick something relatively small that you would like to implement and that you understand well enough to describe.

If you are in the middle of a sick project, you may have to ease into it an XP practice or two at a time. Identify where the pain in the project is, and use the practices as antidotes to the most nagging ailments. Repeat at the point of greatest pain. Before too long, you might have a healthy project.

Reversing the Tide
by Jack Bolles

Late in the year, a group of us were asked to join a project in trouble. Scheduled to go live in mid Q1, the project was missing and the team was running headlong into death march mode. So on top of whatever else had created this situation, we made the classic mistake of throwing bodies at the problem.

It worked.

The reinforcements consisted largely of developers who had delivered before. I think the key to this working was that we joined the team rather than taking it over. From the beginning, we resisted the "full speed ahead" urge common to this situation. Nor did anyone make high and mighty proclamations about "the right way." Change was introduced in the course of writing the application—kind of refactoring the process and methodology rather than making wholesale changes.

We all knew that the application's code base was not very extensible. To make the first deliverable, we stressed simplicity—do the simplest thing that will work rather than some high-minded principle. This was done mainly because we were afraid of what might happen each time we rebuilt the source. Of course, to deliver we still had functionality to add.

Being new to an existing project, we inevitably had questions. We handled communication very informally: "Hey Rob, could you tell me what's going on here so I can integrate my stuff?" Collectively, people introduced many best practices through individual emphasis and communication. Depending on whom you paired up with, one practice was stressed more than the other. We smoothed out the difference in styles later.

As for pair programming, another programmer and I did formally decide to try this, with mixed results. The work was good, but we were much more comfortable with parallel programming (two people working side by side constantly communicating). This was a theme that would continue, with true pair programming usually only happening when someone was coding to work out a design or as part of a learning process.

On the way to meeting our lofty goal, we had successfully begun to turn the project around. Of course, when you change directions, at some point it feels like the project is stopped. To outsiders, this can feel like moving backward. That exact moment came Wednesday before the customer was to make their "go/no go" decision. Nothing worked. A variety of unrelated things that were checked in together just prior to our nightly build added up so that the testers could no longer get through any of the test threads. Panic does not begin to describe the reaction from our analysts. But by the end of the next day, we had recovered and all the changes were synchronized, and miraculously, everything was back on track.

While elated that it was over, we managed to take some time to learn from our mistakes. As various best practices were introduced, someone stepped up and championed each one. And sometimes the champion was surprising; sometimes the champion was not the person who introduced it. This was an organic uprising, and not every practice was welcomed with open arms by each person. But strong support from the team made it easier to justify doing the right thing, and gave the people on the team the courage to take the extra steps necessary to improve the situation. A common belief that never again would we go through that, made each individual latch onto something(s) that had hindered them in the first place.

I've started calling this the "most necessary best practices" technique. Basically, everyone has a set of practices that they find essential to development. Say it was being able to integrate and build regularly and with ease. That developer would have a very difficult time doing anything else until they felt those basics were in place and working. A common set among the teams I've worked on includes

- Working and usable source control
- Build that works
- Readable codebase
- Tests

In my experience, many developers choose most necessary best practices for one of two reasons. Either it is essential to getting the app up and running or it's the developers' preferred way of getting familiar with the code and domain. Some preferred writing tests or creating a design/data model. I prefer to step through the code, refactoring anything I don't understand.

With something in production, coupled with some timely business decisions, we set up processes that would make our lives easier. We immediately began improving our build process. And though it wasn't an overnight success, we automated our build and promotion process so that

- Anyone could start or promote a build (between some environments the promotion decision is automated)
- The unit test suite would be integrated with the development build
- The build process used by developers locally would be the same as the one on the development box

Once that was in place, people started to attack testing. By that summer, the business wanted major focus change, and we felt confident refactoring, knowing that the tests were in place. By the end, I'd estimate the test suite had about 40% coverage spread across our code base. This could be better from a raw numbers point of view, but our most complicated code has very strong and in-depth tests. Others were driven to remove comments such as "Please! Please! Forgive me. It's 3 a.m. and I know this is a hack but it will work," as well as the resulting 150-line case statement.

By the time we finished, we went from being the project no one wanted to be on to the one that had the highest morale and arguably the highest standards in the company.

That's it. The great secret to introducing XP into your project is . . . don't. Rather, trust and empower the people you work with and for to do the things that make them most productive. When things work, embrace them. When things don't, drop them. Look up after a few months. We did, and saw that we were doing something very close to textbook XP. Maybe this is the best test of a methodology: Given no direction, would a team naturally gravitate in that direction?

Assemble the Right Tools

How many times have you gotten excited about a new hobby or interest, and gone out and bought lots of expensive gear to get started? You probably felt a little foolish once you realized you didn't really need all that stuff to do it right. You probably felt even more idiotic when you learned that the best practitioners often don't use the "best" equipment. Tiger Woods could probably drive a golf ball three hundred yards with an antique club he bought at a yard sale.

You don't need fancy stuff to get started with XP. In fact you need just a few things:

- ✧ Index cards for stories
- ✧ Someone to play the customer in the Planning Game
- ✧ A physical environment in which you can pair program
- ✧ One computer per pair of programmers
- ✧ Preferably, an object-oriented language to program in
- ✧ A unit testing framework for the language you chose

With this simple set of tools, you can explore most of the practices of XP.

Driving Spikes

The biggest barrier to getting started with XP is that you really don't know what you're doing. The idea may make perfect sense, you may be excited, but the silent challenge of the monitor gives you the shakes.

The simplest thing you can program that will convince you that you are on the right track is what we in XP call a "spike." "Driving a spike" means doing some useful work that lets you explore all areas of a problem quickly so that you can reduce your risk later on when you try to fill in the details. Try out all the practices of XP to get a feel for them. You might very well produce junk, but you'll learn and you'll get more comfortable with the process.

An important thing to recognize about driving spikes is that you gain a lot from doing it, but there is plenty left to be done afterward. There are many ways to drive spikes. We give a few examples on the next few pages. Most of them give the developer a feel for some of the practices they might be uncomfortable with, but fall short of providing the real feel for the all-important relationship between the customer and the developer. So beware—you'll get the feel of XP, but don't think you can really do XP without a team that includes all of the non-developers.

The Lone Wolf

If you can't find somebody to try XP with you, you can give it a go yourself. Run a miniature Planning Game. If you don't have a real customer handy, play the role of customer yourself. Write a couple of story cards and prioritize them. Then put on your developer hat and break the stories into small development tasks of a half day or less. Estimate the first few you think you should tackle. Then move on to development.

Exploring XP Alone
by Ken Auer

Before I hired my first employee, I was full of ideas of what he could do when he wasn't doing work directly for a client. In the past, I had worked on a drawing editor framework named Drawlets. It was a Java implementation based on the HotDraw concept originally developed in Smalltalk by Kent Beck and Ward Cunningham in the mid to late 1980s (and redeveloped by many others since then). I was familiar with many of the things that had been done with earlier HotDraws, and had a bunch of ideas of my own that had not been implemented.

I looked at my time commitments and realized that I only had the time to get a subset of the features done. So I started writing them down on cards. I wrote only enough to make it clear to myself as a developer what the "story" was. I played the role of the customer by asking which of the features would make the product most attractive. Once I had those sorted out, I played the role of developer by asking how long it would take to develop each feature. When the features were big, I laid them aside as a signal to ask the "customer" to break up the story further, if possible.

In less than an hour, I had created a stack of 40 or so stories and had sorted them into piles of high, medium, and low priority. It was clear that I wouldn't have enough time in the next few months to tackle all of the high priority items. I calculated the greatest amount of time I might have to spend on them and realized I would probably only have time to do two or three in the following two months. I learned an immense amount about the reality of what I could and could not do with Drawlets in the near future, and got a feel for the power of the Planning Game.

Next determine and write the tests that will demonstrate you've accomplished the first task. For each test, write the code and run the test until it passes. Once you've gotten a green bar, verify that the test is adequate and that the solution is as simple as possible. Refactor as necessary. Then wrap up development.

We strongly recommend doing this one test at a time. If it will take you three steps to accomplish the task, write the test for the first step and get the first step to work. Then write the second test. The moment you get xUnit to pass the first test, you will get your first taste of the exhilaration of knowing your code does what you wanted it to do. It only gets better.

Identify how long the task really took and record how accurate your estimate was. Do whatever sort of version control you need. You now have a baseline for future integration.

Move on to the next task and repeat the process: estimate; write tests; write code and get the tests to pass; refactor; record results and do version control. Feel the rhythm? Reflect on what you learned, share it with others, and determine how you could apply it to something mission-critical.

Congratulations. You've just done micro-XP. If no one is willing to join you, do things this way on your own. When you start producing results that others can only dream about, XP will catch on.

A Single Pair

The single pair approach looks almost like the Lone Wolf approach. The difference is that you write tests and code as a pair. Take turns being the "driver" of the pair (the one typing code) and the "navigator" (the one thinking ahead).

A Small Team

The small team approach expands on the single pair approach, giving you a fuller feel for what XP is really like. If at all possible, start this way.

When the team is running the Planning Game, have each person take ownership of and estimate a couple of tasks important to the group. Once the group has completed the Planning Game, discuss how you should describe the main objects in the system. This is the skeleton of a system metaphor. Don't worry about getting it exactly right, just agree on something.

Have a daily stand-up meeting to decide which tasks should be tackled first and how you should pair. Then pair up to write tests and code, switching pairs as often as you can. During development, integrate the versions of all tasks on a single machine, making sure you can run all tests each time you integrate. Resolve any conflicts with the existing integration base each time you integrate. Whenever a pair integrates, don't allow them to continue until they have integrated cleanly.

A Small Team with a Lead Developer

In a variant on the small team approach, add a lead developer who is confident in his abilities, perhaps someone with XP experience. This lead developer can bring a less confident team along. The lead developer follows the steps already outlined, demonstrating a simple version of each and then directing the team to try it in pairs. During the demonstration the leader is a developer working on a task with multiple development partners: the team.

Introducing XP with a Lead Developer
by Ken Auer

Our first XP client, and largest to date, was looking to bring in a strong Java development team to build its next-generation software product and to mentor its small team. The team was new to Java and to industry best practices in OO development. I convinced the client that XP would not only be the best process for the long run, but also the best way to work with their people to transfer the knowledge.

We taught them XP and Java at the same time. On the first day, we talked about XP and wrote our first JUnit test before their eyes. It was incredibly simple. I had my laptop attached to an LCD projector and asked them to tell me something they might need to do in their new system. They said they would need to collect "results" from their hardware device and associate them with an "Order." So I wrote a test that added two Results (objects that didn't exist) to an Order (another object that didn't exist) and tested that when the Order was asked how many Results it had, it would answer "2." I then wrote just enough class and method stubs to get the test to compile and ran the tests. Red bar. I implemented the "add" method and ran the test again. Red bar. I implemented the "getNumberOfResults" method and ran the test again. Green bar (applause from the other developers in the room). By the end of the day, we had seven tests running.

The next day, we discussed some simple things we might need to add to our baseline and told people to go off in pairs. Over the next couple of hours, each pair wrote tests and got them to pass, sometimes with my help. We went back to the conference room with the LCD several times, each time discussing another type of feature we wanted to add (UI, interfacing to a serial port, printing), sometimes adding a stub for some tests, and then going off in pairs.

At the end of the first week, we did a little Planning Game on a prototype of the new system. Then we were off.

It's All Right to Feel Awkward

When you first try XP, most of the practices will feel funny. This is normal You will write tests before you write any code. You will be coding with a pair all the time. You won't flesh out all the details before you start writing code. These things most likely will appear to be vastly different from the way you have been doing things for years. It may be a little scary. You will not understand everything completely when you start. This is a learning process. You won't know if you can do it until you try.

Chapter 3

Taming the Resistance

*Whatever course you decide upon, there is always some-
one to tell you you are wrong. There are always difficulties
arising which tempt you to believe that your critics are right.
To map out a course of action and follow it to the end,
requires some of the same courage which a soldier needs.*

—Ralph Waldo Emerson

*XP forces people out of their comfort zones. They will resist. This resistance
comes from fear and pride. Overcome this by focusing on using XP as a
strategy to increase their chances of winning.*

If you think your own fear and ignorance are the only obstacles you'll face when
starting XP, think again. That is just the beginning.

Other people will resist. They can't afford not to. They have a good bit of
time, effort, and ego invested in the way things have always been done. Change
might be risky, painful, or both. It also might cast doubt on their past judgment. You are pushing them out of their comfort zone, and they won't like it.

You'll get resistance from two primary sources: from managers and developers. If you are a manager, you might face resistance from the developers you
manage, from your management peers, or from a manager above you. If you're
a developer, you might face resistance from your manager or from the developers you work with. You probably won't be shot—beyond that, all bets are off.
We've seen everything from reasonable and open debate to screaming matches
and sabotage. It can get ugly.

The most likely form of resistance will be simple objections that XP is
wrong, stupid, or inferior for one reason or another. These objections are supposed to be based on principle, but most of the time they aren't.

Where Resistance Comes From

Managers and developers are people. We human beings are wired to fear the unknown and to think we are worth more than we are. If you don't believe this, you haven't been paying attention. Unfortunately, both of these natural behaviors can cause problems.

When we are afraid, we gravitate toward ways of thinking and acting that make us feel safe, even if they are unhealthy or unproductive. New ways of doing things can be scary, so people tend to slip back into old ways of doing things. This inertia is natural.

New approaches can be challenging in two ways. First, they force us to admit that there was at least one thing we didn't know (the new technique). Second, they force us to admit that our current approach might be wrong. Our pride makes it difficult to do either one.

Nobody likes to be ignorant or wrong, because that wounds our pride. Rather than risk that, we often resist new ways of doing things. That lets us stay comfortable. Unfortunately, admitting ignorance and mistakes is the only way to learn new approaches. It's rare to be an expert at a new technique when you start—mastery requires practice. It's also rare to find that there is no better way of doing things—there is *always* room for improvement.

Managers and developers alike often fall victim to pride. Both are frequently afraid of change and unwilling to admit that they have something to learn. This is at the core of a lot of the resistance you'll face from these groups. Not all the resistance you run into will be this simple, and it might not surface entirely in the beginning. You have to be ready to handle it at any time. Fortunately there is a simple strategy that seems to work most of the time: Focus on results.

The Result That Matters

In 1968, a lanky guy named Dick Fosbury revolutionized the sport of high jumping with a technique that became known as the "Fosbury flop." Instead of going face-first over the bar and scissor-kicking his legs like everybody else, he flopped over on his back and landed on his shoulders. It looked stupid, frankly. Lots of people said, "We've never done things this way" and "That'll never work." But at the 1968 Olympic games, Fosbury cleared every height up to 7'3¼" without a miss. He won the gold and set a new Olympic record. It is hard to knock the winner for using an unorthodox strategy.

XP is an unorthodox strategy for producing great software that delivers high business value on time, without forcing people to give up their lives. When you face resistance from managers and developers, remind them of this. Each group will have their own particular objections, which we'll talk about in the next couple of chapters, but they all want to "win" as they define it. If doing something new and different, like XP, will increase your chances of winning, then that's the smart thing to do. If you can't get people to agree that winning is the goal, it might be time to change jobs. Losing is a hard habit to break.

If you can get everyone to agree that winning is what's important, cast XP with each group as the best way to do that. Focus on the results XP produces that can help managers and developers win as they define it. This not only will focus attention on what's really important, but will also give you a standard to use when evaluating each practice against other options.

Approach every discussion by asking whether doing things the old way will make winning more likely. Make the strongest possible case for the old way. Talk about what it's missing. Then introduce the possibility that using the XP approach might be best, even if it goes against the gut reaction of most people. Finally, work hard to convince people that the best way to prove whether XP produces better results is to try it for a while.

If XP produces better results sooner and with less pain than the old way, it will be tough for managers and developers to say the team should go with the old way, just because it's familiar. If they do, you might want to consider leaving the organization.

What Not to Do

Managers and developers will object to particular practices. You will be tempted to defend them, or your support of them, on theoretical grounds. Don't. These things are irrelevant. Instead, discuss the objection in the context of winning. Remember that winning is the goal, not the individual practices *per se,* or being right. The practices are simply ways to help you win. They are not "good" or "bad"—they are only better or worse than the available alternatives.

The reality is that you will have to justify and defend XP practices eventually. If everyone involved agrees that getting results is the goal, you have a ready-made standard for evaluating XP practices against other options. If a practice increases your chances of getting results, do it. If it doesn't, scrap it or change it so that it does work in your environment.

Finally, don't focus on XP for the sake of XP. This will label you a zealot in a nonproductive religious war. Remember that getting results is the goal, not XP or you being right.

In Chapters 4 and 5 we discuss how to handle manager and developer resistance in more detail.

Chapter 4

Manager Resistance

Managers will resist XP because they make faulty assumptions about alternative approaches. Focus on flattening the software development cost curve to overcome their objections.

Most managers got where they are because they have at least some ability to think ahead. They are supposed to see issues before they become issues. Manager objections to XP relate to what they see as potential problems with the approach. Fortunately for you, the objections usually are based on faulty assumptions about alternatives.

If you are a developer, this chapter can help you overcome manager resistance you may face. If you are a manager yourself, this chapter can help you overcome resistance you may face from the managers above you or from the managers who work for you. This chapter also can show you how you are likely to resist XP and how to evaluate whether your resistance makes sense in the long run for you and your company.

The Manager Perspective on Winning

In our experience, there is nothing that overcomes manager resistance like undeniable progress toward the goals the manager will be measured by. Find out what these are and how you can use XP to help him make progress toward these goals. That is how a manager defines "winning."

Every organization is different. Every manager will be measured by different standards. But all managers in all organizations want to minimize risk.

Remember the exponential software development cost curve. Managers are consumed by minimizing the risks to their projects and to their careers implied by that curve. Their reaction to a new approach tends to be that it will cost too much and take too long, both of which increase project risk. When managers object to XP, often risk avoidance is behind it. If you want to be heard, you had better couch your responses in those terms. Focus on

- ⟡ The money costs of code development and modification
- ⟡ The time cost of code development and modification
- ⟡ Retention of highly skilled developers
- ⟡ Contribution of less skilled developers

These are all areas of risk that can make the curve exponential. If a given approach does a better job of flattening that curve, it wins.

Here are the most prevalent objections we've heard and how you can address each by focusing on flattening the curve. We hope this book will help reinforce the points made.

XP Is Too New to Trust

Almost nobody makes a habit of using Release 1.0 of a software product, because this increases project risk. To many, XP is at Release 1.0 right now. Maybe it is really at Release 1.x. So what?

When managers talk about new things like XP being risky, they are assuming that the status quo is safer. We have seen that it isn't. If you stay on the status quo curve, be ready to run out of oxygen. You cannot stay there and win. The only real way to find out if XP is too risky to use in your context is to try it. As we said in Chapter 2, you don't have to try it on a mission-critical project first. But you do have to try it so that you can get feedback on whether it produces the results you want in your environment.

If your manager doesn't micromanage, get a bunch of XP-friendly developers together and give it a try. Show your manager the results. If the results are great, you're on your way. If not, drop back and figure out why not. Then modify the process as necessary and try again.

If your manager has a more hands-on style, ask permission to try XP for two or three weeks. Then let the manager examine the results at the end of the trial period and draw his own conclusions. Ask whether extrapolating the results you saw on this first project would flatten the curve. If it would, you've got a powerful argument in favor of XP.

XP Is Simplistic

Managers might say that XP glosses over complexity, or that it replaces thinking ahead with simplistic naiveté.

They are assuming that existing approaches handle complexity better and let you think far enough ahead. Most approaches we have seen other than XP simply don't. They deal with complexity by trying to figure it all out up front. You draw pictures, create documents, try to cover all the bases, and do your best to anticipate everything. The problem is that you're guessing. Pretty pictures are no substitute for experience.

XP is simple, not simplistic. It recognizes the reality that things change, that you cannot plan for everything. XP says to do things in a way that lets you respond quickly and well to emergent reality.

The Planning Game helps us identify items with the biggest risk and tackle these first. Planning is so important that we do it regularly, based on real experience and a working system, not once based on our best guess when all we have is theory. In addition, two sets of eyes see all production code, which minimizes the number of times you're blind sided. Because there is collective code ownership and we have tests for everything, we are able to move our best developers to the problem areas that need their expertise, without leaving the rest of the project in the lurch. And so on.

XP forces a team to find real problems sooner, without having to guess at what they are. It reduces the number of blind spots. Its rapid feedback allows it to be simple without being simplistic.

Before assuming too much, ask the manager why he thinks XP is simplistic, and what additional practices are necessary. Ask what it is about those practices that will help you accomplish what the other 12 practices do not. In particular ask why those additional practices will produce results faster. Often managers misunderstand what XP practices are.

We find many managers believe more documentation is needed to help current and future developers understand the system. The chapters on communication and testing (Chapters 9 and 13) can help you overcome this objection.

Pair Programming Is Too Expensive

"We can't afford to pay two people to work on the same thing!" This is pure money risk. Fortunately, it just ain't so.

Research has shown that development time does increase with XP by about 15%; however, these costs are offset by higher design quality, reduced defects, reduced staffing risk, increased technical skill, and improved team communication and morale.[1] It is economically more feasible to program in pairs.

Two Heads Learn Better Than One
by Roy Miller

A few years ago, I worked on a series of projects for a single client. The first project was a tactical effort designed to throw together a reporting solution that would let our system limp along for a release until we could "do it right" the next time.

---

1. From A. Cockburn, L. Williams. "The Costs and Benefits of Pair Programming." Reprinted in *Extreme Programming Examined*, by G. Succi and M. Marchesi. Addison-Wesley, 2001. Refer your manager to this paper. Better yet, give your manager a copy.

The learning curve was steep, and the people on my team (including me) had very little experience with relational databases.

I had always been a fan of collaborative work. I knew from experience and training that two people attacking a problem together could produce better output faster than two people working alone. I thought programming would follow the same model, although I hadn't heard of the concept of "pair programming" at the time. So, seeing the mountainous learning curve my team had to climb, I decided we would pair at least part of the time to spread knowledge around. This was not a popular decision. The leadership of the project often told me that I wasn't using resources efficiently. But we got work done, and the effort was a "quick and dirty" tactical one, so I got away with it.

During development for the next release, my team grew, but many of the people on the team had very little relational database experience. We were developing a data mart with all of the business rules built into stored procedures in the database. The one person on the team who knew the most (Jason) was getting married two months before we were supposed to deliver. Everybody else had to get up to speed fast, or we would miss the deadline. Project leadership still didn't like the idea of two programmers working together, but it was the only approach that would solve the knowledge gap. We had the people who knew what they were doing pair with the people who didn't. It worked. We were productive while Jason was away, and we delivered a great system on time.

Our personal experience tells us that the economic feasibility goes up as group size increases, assuming the other practices of XP are in place. This is because the communication overhead is proportionately much lower than with traditional approaches, while the quality of communication improves.

Even if pair programming is more costly in terms of development time, it is still better to program in pairs. The toughest part of programming is design, and that happens at the keyboard, not just in an architecture picture. Would you trust your design to one person? That is what you are doing if you don't pair. You are building extreme dependence on your "stars." Even worse, you are counting on your less experienced developers to implement that design without significant checks on their work.

Without pair programming, you open the door for more bugs to make it into later testing and into the released product. You are meeting all the prerequisites for code that's hard to maintain. Is it better to have someone verify the code as it is being written than to depend on unchecked code? Suppose you actually produced the documentation of this code at some point. Why is it too expensive to have a second set of eyes on the code but not too expensive to have a developer take the time to produce unverified documentation of the lower quality code? How can you be sure that the documentation accurately represents what is in the code even for some moment in time? If documentation is generated from the code to keep it up to date, it doesn't tell you anything the code can't tell you, so why do it? Ask the manager to be as picky about existing practices as about pair programming. An honest manager will quickly discover that traditional practices increase project risk much more than pair programming does.

You might not pair all the time. There are tasks, such as exploration or even some debugging, that might make sense to do alone at times. But pairing should be the norm. Anything else is too risky.

I Can't Afford a Full-Time, On-Site Customer

If you want to move at full speed, you can't afford *not* to have a customer available to answer questions for the development team immediately, whenever those questions come up. We don't know of any research that's been done in this area, but we've been on many projects. When developers have to wait for answers, two things tend to happen:

1. The project slows way down or grinds to a halt while developers wait.
2. Developers get tired of waiting and guess at what the requirements are.

The first costs money by delaying the realization of value from the project. The second costs money because developers often guess wrong and have to redo lots of work, producing still more delay.

Jim Highsmith told us

> . . . Customers don't know their requirements until later in the project or they may modify them considerably based on what they see. This turbulence and uncertainty causes frequent changes and without daily contact, the team can be working on the wrong things. One of the suggestions that I give people is that we are not talking about a "full-time" customer representative, but a "frequently available" customer representative. We are trying to get maximum value from their time. I'd rather have the right person available an hour a day than either the wrong person full time or the right person one day every other week.[2]

Ask yourself a basic question: Do you want the developers to give you the software they *assume* you need? We suggest you save yourself the financial and

---

2. E-mail correspondence with Ken Auer, March 2001.

psychological pain. Put a customer at the disposal of the development team, preferably on-site.

Look at the alternative. A study recently showed that the typical requirements document is 15% complete and 7% accurate.[3] That stinks! If we rely on the requirements spec, we will fail. If we accurately guess how to fill the holes 50% of the time, we are only 57.5% complete and 53.5% accurate. Do you feel better yet?

It will often be difficult to have a customer on site or available all of the time, but that is no reason to ignore the problem. Even if we do all the other XP practices well, without direct customer input we're still guessing to fill the holes.

XP Is Too Informal

Managers may take issue with XP not having lots of documentation. They may claim that XP is an excuse to code like a cowboy—that it's hacking without documenting. They might also think that because XP stories aren't formal they don't give programmers enough information.

The most common source of the informality objection is a bad experience in the past. Most managers have been burned before and have no desire to repeat the unpleasant experience. But they throw the baby out with the bathwater. They assume that formal documentation will increase their chances of getting accurate results. Nothing could be further from the truth.

Lots of documents do not make software better—cleaner code does. The only way to keep code clean is not to clutter it up with unnecessary stuff and to scrub as you go. XP lets you concentrate on doing both. Build only what the stories for the current iteration call for. Refactor mercilessly. In a private, anonymous e-mail somebody told us:

> *I cannot tell you how antiproductive tangled and unclear code has been for me. With documents that could replace a forest at my disposal here at [my company], I am so discouraged to find the code a tangled mess ("ball of mud"). It seems to me that management uses documentation as a means of control over an area they fear the most—software that they can't understand in its native form. This is an illusion, since the devil is prowling in the details. Some love to cover it up with fancy PowerPoint slides and PDF documents. But as an astute manager here once said, "You can't compile PowerPoints."*

---

3. J. Highsmith. "Adapative Software Development." Presentation at OOPSLA 2000.

Certainly, it is useful to have a presentation or short document that provides an overview of the system (the XP practice of metaphor fulfills this function). There is a huge gap, however, between the value gained by creating and maintaining this document, and the value of creating and maintaining all of the other more detailed documents that may follow it.

Using stories instead of detailed specs is no excuse for being lazy. We still have to get all of the requirements. We just don't need all of the details for ones that won't be implemented soon. Experience tells us that these will be completely different later anyway. Remember that a story is a commitment to have a future conversation to flesh out the details. You need to verify the details of any story before you implement it, so we defer the detail gathering until then. XP requires that you produce all necessary documentation but discourages production of unnecessary shelf filler.

By the way, why is an approach that encourages us to write tests before we code less formal than one that makes us write documentation before we code? It's often important to question the value of formality and focus on results. If the formality we are familiar with gets us the results we want, why change? The only reason to change is if informality gets us the results we want faster, cheaper, and more reliably. We would choose running tests over paper documentation any day when we are looking for reliability. If reliability doesn't matter, then all that's left is faster and cheaper. We're going out on a limb here, but we'd venture to say that producing formal documentation does not make the process faster or cheaper.

Be Wary of "XP-Lite"

Sometimes there is no formal resistance from a manager. The manager simply states that XP sounds interesting, but the organization can't afford to try it now. "Maybe after we transition the existing system to the new platform," or some other future milestone the manager might suggest.

At this point, you may be tempted to pick a few XP practices and implement them rather than the whole ball of wax. Maybe having more tests, or programming in pairs, or using the Planning Game will help flatten the curve you're currently on.

Be careful. Bringing in a single practice that is most likely to have an immediate positive impact can make people more receptive to the next practice you'd like to introduce. On the other hand, it might make people think XP is just a bag of practices that can be chosen at random. We have seen that XP is much more than the sum of its parts. All of the pieces work together to produce something amazing.

Many people have had success introducing XP one practice at a time. We recommend that you introduce it in chunks, several practices at a time, and don't let more than a week or two go by before introducing the next chunk. This way, people will recognize how each of the practices supports the others. If you do it one at a time, your project could end up way out of balance.

If your developers think that by no longer writing documentation and by programming in pairs once in a while they are doing XP, gently point out that they are missing the value of feedback. Then provide the feedback: "they are playing to lose." This is not reducing risk. This is not playing to win. This is rationalization for not writing documentation. This is the reason people came up with heavy methods. XP is not an excuse to stop doing things you don't feel like doing.

You should certainly be smart about your timing when introducing practices. The end of a project might not be the best time to introduce a full-blown Planning Game. You probably don't want to pair your database guru up with someone who can't spell "database" a week before delivery. You certainly don't want to refactor too much without first having a critical mass of tests around the stuff you are refactoring. But we can't think of a time during development where writing a unit test before writing new code would be a bad thing. We don't know when the customer shouldn't be in charge of setting priorities.

If you are satisfied with having your process "stink less" and not being as far from the best as you used to be, introduce a new practice every year. If you want to play to win, don't play around.

The Tipping Point
by Michael Feathers

As a programmer, it was easy for me to get excited about XP. On XP teams, programmers have the opportunity to work under nearly ideal circumstances. They are able to do what they like most, programming, but without many of the anxieties that are associated with traditional development.

Today, XP is definitely on many managers' "radar screens," but in the early days, most of the interest was in the programming community. This shouldn't be too surprising; Kent Beck is a programmer, and the practices he integrated into XP were developed by programmers. XP is an answer to the question, "How do we, as programmers, establish a win-win relationship with business?" XP is a good deal for programmers, but can you get management to play?

A few years ago, I was called in to do a week-long XP course for a small Web development company who'd recently decided to use XP for a project of theirs.

I was excited about the course because they were interested in using their current project as exercise material. Moreover, their customer would be attending.

What I discovered during the first few days of training was that both the managers and the customer had heard about XP, and they were eager to have their team try it. But the programmers were completely new to many XP ideas, and they did not seem as enthusiastic. On the first day, they sat opposite the manager and the customer and asked few questions. During the break, I discovered that the customer had had bad experiences with the same team in an earlier project. Delivery was late, and the final product was buggy. Although the customer was enthusiastic about XP, at times his frustration was apparent.

Securing the involvement of the programmers over the course of the week was tough. Pairing with them tended to brighten them up a bit. One of the most important moments in the course came during a Planning Game exercise. We chose to go through the planning process for the first iteration of their actual project, but the programmers did not have a historical basis for their estimates. We took some time to do some exploration and consider how some of the stories might be implemented, but then an interesting thing started to happen. The customer started to reduce scope unilaterally. Each time a programmer asked a question, the customer made his requirements narrower and narrower until he had the bare kernel of what would be needed to make money with his Web site. It became obvious that he was concerned he would not get what he wanted. He dealt with that fear by tossing in the towel on many requirements.

When the programmers started estimating, the customer became very frustrated. He started to ask the programmers if they could reduce the estimates any further. Red in the face, he started to ask the programmers whether they thought that programmers over in Silicon Valley could do any better. I held back a little. Would anyone on the development side speak up? At that moment, one of the programmers said, "You've already seen what rushed software looks like. These are our estimates. Let us do this work, with these estimates, and we'll have better estimates for you next time." The customer capitulated. He understood.

I was very happy at that point. The programmers were stepping up to the table and it was important that I hadn't done it for them. There was a chance for a good healthy relationship.

Since that time, I've worked with and been in contact with quite a few teams who have decided to move toward XP. It appears to me that there is a "tipping point," a point at which teams have a vastly better chance of continuing with the process. That point comes when development pushes back. When development isn't able to push back, the process goes out of balance. In some cases, programmers start to underestimate, code quality goes down, and the team slides toward disaster. In other cases, the team just falls away from the practices early, caving to pressure.

XP requires a real balance of power between business and development. It can be hard to achieve. If you are a manager, you have to know when you can't push. Sometimes, it is as simple as making sure that you aren't the customer. Find someone else to play customer and have that person and the rest of the team report to you. Manage the relationship. And, by all means, make sure the developers can hold their ground on estimates. Let them push back.

There is a "tipping point." I know it when I see it and it is a giant leap toward sustainability.

_____

Chapter 5

Developer Resistance

Developers will resist XP because they might not see the advantages. Focus on the environment fostered by XP to overcome developer objections.

Developers Are Different

Developers are born with a "geek gene." They are certainly different from managers. Some can play both roles well and shift transparently between them, but those people are rare. Developers love to write code—it's why they get up in the morning. Typically, the more they know and the better their code, the more they get paid. They derive their security from knowledge and ability.

People drawn to software development (like us) often would rather communicate with a machine than with people. Most of them were labeled smart at a young age. They spend years in school learning lots of details about how to tell machines what to do, which the rest of the world finds about as entertaining as watching grass grow. They complete programming assignments alone, since getting help would be cheating. When they graduate, they get paid big salaries. After a few months on the job, managers realize that developers don't play well with other people. Duh.

XP goes against deeply ingrained programmer habits by forcing these folks to interact with people most of the time. Developers resist.

If you are a manager, this chapter can help you overcome developer resistance. If you are a developer, this chapter can help you overcome resistance from your peers. This chapter also will show you how you are likely to resist XP and help you evaluate whether your resistance makes sense in the long run for you and your company.

The Developer Perspective on Winning

In our experience, nothing overcomes developer resistance like focusing on the environment fostered by XP. Use the geek gene to your advantage. Keep in mind what developers care about:

- ✧ They want to develop software, not write documentation or spend all day in meetings.
- ✧ They want to be proud of the software they develop.
- ✧ They want to have fun doing their jobs, not feel like they are undergoing surgery without an anesthetic.
- ✧ Once the software is released, they don't want to get stuck maintaining it forever, or go through hell to change it when they have to. They want new challenges, not just the same old challenge of having to figure out what unnatural act they can perform to patch the old code.

Unlike managers, developers don't particularly care about the economics of a flat cost curve, but they do care about the pain associated with a steep one. Having an environment that avoids that pain is how developers define "winning." If you want to be heard by developers, couch your responses in terms that will appeal to them. If a given approach does a better job of producing that environment, it beats all comers.

Here are the most common developer objections and how you can address each. We hope the rest of this book will reinforce the points made here.

XP Is Too Simplistic

Sound familiar? Managers said the same thing, but for a different reason.

XP challenges the perception of developers that no one understands what developers do and can't do it themselves. This is true to some degree. But it shouldn't be true because of the process developers use. XP takes the magic out of the process and lets it live in the code, where it belongs. The magic is in the results. You get to enjoy your time, rather than loathing having to come to work.

XP gets out of a developer's way because it produces no unnecessary documentation and lets some developers focus on designing and developing good code.

XP is not simplistic. It is simple and uncluttered. Some aspects of the discipline aren't easy for developers (such as pair programming), but it has the best chance of any approach we have ever seen of fostering a rich environment for programmers.

Often, when experienced developers object that XP is too simplistic, what they really mean is, "I've learned other ways to do software and my career has advanced because of it. I don't want to go backward. And besides, I'm not as good at programming as I once was because I spend most of my time doing higher-level things." Very few of these people actually think the "higher-level things" they do are as fun, or that the processes they use to do those "higher-level things" are efficient. They are often scared that what they've gotten good at will be seen as less valuable.

You need to point out that many of those skills are still needed. The experienced developer's ability to "do architecture" is still needed. He needs to help find a metaphor and make sure people are focused on how the pieces fit together. He just needs to do more of it via verbal communication and interaction. Instead of being frustrated that people don't understand his architecture and that there isn't time to make it work, XP can free up the experienced developer's time to communicate the architectural issues and to assist other developers. As a bonus, the experienced developer's hands-on technology skills will increase.

XP Is Genius-Friendly
by Ward Cunningham

There was a time when a coding genius would have to hide from a project to get genius work done. Not so with XP. The genius hangs with the team, taking task cards and pitching in on others. This way a genius gets a good feel for just what sort of invention can be absorbed. To get along, the genius avoids lording superior intellect over others. He or she wouldn't say, "I had that idea yesterday," even if it were true. So what fun is this?

The fun begins when a deep problem surfaces. The whole team feels simplicity slipping away and is distressed about it. Genius gears start working. Should the necessary flash of insight fail to come, the genius just keeps pitching in and making sure that the code stays clean enough to absorb insight that might be just around the corner. The genius knows this wait and enjoys it.

Then finally the light comes on. The genius is first to connect the pieces that solve the problem. So what then? Cry "eureka"? No way.

The genius says something like "I'm thinking we need to spend more time looking at the interaction of *x* and *y*." Then the rest of the team has a chance to try their hand at genius. If they are wise enough to look at *x* and *y* they will probably see just what the genius has seen and get to bask in the warm light of an original "Ah-ha."

The thing that is really great about this interaction is that it is really safe for the genius. If there is an error of logic, it will be gently exposed without casting doubt on the genius. Also, if there is resistance to the insight, the genius gets to explore it before showing all the cards. Finally, the genius is appreciated by people who now know what genius is like. (Remember, they just had a eureka moment themselves.)

So what is all this about XP making everyone just a cog? XP is truly genius friendly. And, in case you have any doubt, just think about how the above would work when everyone is a genius. Heck, maybe they are.

Originally posted by Ward Cunningham on *Wiki*, http://c2.com/cgi/wiki?WelcomeVisitors.

I Won't Like Pair Programming

There are two things behind this objection. First, it is uncomfortable for developers to work with others. They've never done it before. Programming is perceived as a lone wolf activity; XP says you should hunt in packs. Second, whether they want to admit it or not, developers aren't particularly fond of giving up their place in the sun. With no individual code ownership, they believe it is harder to be the hero. This is a developer pride problem rearing its ugly head.

The way to handle this objection is to focus on the benefits of pair programming. Emphasize the knowledge sharing, the improved code quality, the increased morale. Then suggest an experiment where you do all programming in pairs for a couple of weeks. At the end of the experiment, you can decide as a group when it makes sense not to pair. We've found that programmers start to like pairing, and see the benefits, after about the first week. They start to communicate better and to feel more human. During the second week, they normally start to hit their stride.

A study conducted by Alistair Cockburn and Laurie Williams found that 90% of people who tried pair programming liked it.[1] Our guess is that some of

---

1. A. Cockburn, L. Williams. "The Costs and Benefits of Pair Programming." Reprinted in *Extreme Programming Examined*, by G. Succi and M. Marchesi. Addison-Wesley, 2001.

the other 10% could be won over by identifying what it was about the experience they didn't like, and by making adjustments before a second attempt.

When the trial period is over, ask the developers what parts of pair programming they are still struggling with. Then give them a simple choice: Work through those issues as a team or give up. Be sure to put it this way. It is both truthful and motivational. Developers hate to quit on a problem.

Perhaps you've read the Dr. Seuss book *Green Eggs and Ham*. The nameless skeptic in the book refuses to try green eggs and ham because he is convinced he will not like them. He eventually does try them and likes them very much. You might face a "green eggs and ham" team who refuses to try pairing because they are sure they will hate it. If no one on the team is willing to try pairing, you've got two choices. If you think you work with people who are afraid of trying anything new, you can leave. If you have some sort of authority, you might find a creative way to force the team to try pair programming. For example, decree that the most critical portions of the system must be developed in pairs. This will make pairing more attractive. State that any code written without a pair will be subject to formal code reviews. Developers hate being subject to reviews, and they hate doing reviews even though reviewing has proven to be a huge contributor to software quality.

Several studies have shown that code reviews are the biggest contributor to software quality, even above testing. This is amazing considering how poorly we execute code reviews. Usually a bunch of people who haven't struggled with the problem get to pick apart those who have. Certainly they are supposed to provide only constructive criticism, but it is very difficult for the person whose code is being reviewed not to be on the defensive and it is difficult for the "gurus" in the room not to find something to pick on (to establish that they are smarter than everyone else).

In our experience, most of the benefit of a code review is attained by the first person reviewing the code. We think there are two main reasons for this:

1. Before a developer presents code for review, he conscientiously cleans it up so as not to look bad.
2. Most of the things the developer missed because he was engrossed in the problem can be seen by any other competent developer looking at it with a fresh, critical eye.

Among other things, pair programming offers these benefits in a less intimidating and more productive way. You don't have to do as much code cleanup because you are always conscious that someone else is viewing your work.[2] You don't have to be defensive, because the constructive criticisms come a little at a time. When you just "hack something to see if it will work" you can simply communicate to your partner that this is what you are doing. Your partner will then remind you that you have to go back and clean it up. You also get to learn from each other and discuss the value of certain approaches as peers rather than as someone who is being interrogated.

Pairing is critical to success. It also is a healthier way to develop software. This is a case where you might have to practice a little tough love for your developers' own good—make them try to.

XP Is Weird

We are the first to admit that some parts of XP sound a bit odd to classically trained programmers. These tend to have the greatest shock value:

- ✧ You write tests before you write code to exercise the tests.
- ✧ You let the design evolve to fit changing requirements.
- ✧ You program in pairs, often sharing a single keyboard and mouse.

If you're like the authors, you didn't cut your teeth in an environment like this. It takes some getting used to. The way to handle the "XP is weird" objection is to focus on the freedom XP can give developers to concentrate on writing code. That is what they love to do, after all.

Writing tests before writing code feels weird at first, but it is similar to what developers have always done. When you write code, you start with some functional requirement and then map that to code somehow. The code is in your head for at least an instant before you write it down. Stop! Now write a test that will verify what you expect that code to do. Then write the code to make the test work. When most developers stop to reflect, they find that doing things this way forces them to think about design and then to verify it quickly. This may seem to slow them down at first. In fact, when they are first figuring out how to write tests it probably does. But it doesn't take long to see the benefits. They should work through it!

The results are phenomenal. Their code will be simpler, because they only had to write enough of it to get the tests to pass. They don't have to be afraid

---

2. When you throw in collective code ownership, others will end up reviewing and fixing the things that escape the pair over time, too.

of other people changing their code, because they can run the tests for validation. Having tests gives managers confidence that they can let developers move on to greener pastures. And tests also serve as good documentation, killing two birds with one stone.

The best way we have seen to overcome this resistance is to start writing the tests yourself even while other developers refuse. Every time you experience one of those "thank God, I had the tests" moments, talk about it. Pretty soon you will be test-infected.[3] The infection will spread.

Letting design float with changing requirements feels odd, too. People often ask us if we're nuts. We prefer to think we're realistic. Designs will need to change whether we accept that reality or not. XP just makes that normal. The design doesn't fall on the floor, it simply spreads out. Rather than doing it all up front, you do it "just in time."

The results of incremental design are amazing. Changes in requirements aren't cause for mass suicide. Designs reflect reality instead of theory and guesses made months beforehand. On the other hand, this is not an excuse to ignore design.

Evolutionary Design with XP
by Ken Auer

A recurring problem we've seen in several systems is the need to abstract a "persistence layer" to keep the system as simple as possible. As soon as you realize that more than one object is calling the database, and that embedding database connectivity into your code is making it "complex" (which may or may not be before you write a line of code, depending on your experience), it is time to consider separating a persistence layer from your domain layer.

We've seen the benefit on one project where the database was switched on us twice due to business negotiations gone bad. Due to our good design, switching the database out (and adjusting the persistence layer) could be done without having to change many of the other objects. The point is that we didn't need to spend months designing the persistence layer to figure that out.

On another project, we needed to convert one key object to XML. After asking ourselves what the simplest solution that could possibly work would be, one of the developers did a quick Web search and found a free product that

---

3. K. Beck, E. Gamma. "Test Infected: Programmers Love Writing Tests." http://members. pingnet.ch/gamma/junit.htm.

The bottom line is that feeling awkward is normal when you're doing something new. Think of it as learning to ride a bike. When you started you stunk at it, and probably fell off once or twice. After you got the hang of it, it felt natural.

XP Doesn't Give Us Enough Information

Developers don't like to create a lot of documentation (or any, we suppose), but they do like to have enough information to act on. They don't want to fly blind. Nothing hurts quite as badly as working like a dog to deliver something nobody likes. We hear often that XP sets you up for failure by not providing enough design documentation and by depending on stories instead of comprehensive specs.

When you join an ongoing project, your first day typically follows the same pattern. You walk in and somebody hands you a functional spec, a technical spec, and/or a detailed design document. Nobody ever reads these and they're hopelessly out of date you're told, but here they are. This is no better than having no documentation at all. Often, it's worse.

Code as Better Documentation
by Ken Auer

Several years ago (pre-XP) I went to help a group who had lost a developer due to a family emergency. When I got there, I was told that the team was a day or two away from delivering "Phase 1." Since the chances were that I couldn't get up to speed fast enough to help with that, the team suggested I should begin thinking about the next version of the system. They handed me a document to help me get up to speed, but told me that the code didn't really follow it.

After almost two days of reading, I still wasn't done, but a cursory scan of the rest told me that it wouldn't help much. I asked if I could review the Phase 1 code instead. The rest of the team was still busy, so they agreed. I discovered that their code was built on a framework that another group had built for a different application. There was little documentation on that framework, but an occasional class comment explained some of the trickier parts and the code was clear enough that I could figure out the rest. On the third day of reviewing the prototype and doing some experiments to explore how the team might approach things differently, I overheard the morning panic meeting that happened to be held in the middle of my cube set. A developer was talking to the project manager:

DEVELOPER: This bug is a bear. It would be nice if we could do something like X, but that would take some time.

ME: Excuse me, but I couldn't help overhearing. I think there is a feature of the framework that already does X. After you're done with the meeting, I'll look at it with you and we can make sure.

DEVELOPER: Cool. Well, if Ken's right, then we can knock that one out today and I can look at some of the other bugs that should be easier.

I was right. The next day at the meeting a few more hairy bugs came up. This time, they called on me directly and asked if I knew of framework features that could help. Again, the features were already built in and needed only slight modification.

The documentation wasn't helpful at all. The developers on the team were fortunate enough to have some decent code from the other group to build on, but they never "read the code." Since the framework they were sitting on didn't have much documentation, they never tried to understand it. Somebody showed them how to do something with it, and they forged ahead. If they had taken two days to read the code instead of reading the documentation, they probably would have been done with Phase 1. The code was up to date and pretty well factored, and it provided something useful to study. The documentation provided almost no value. It certainly provided less payback than the months of time and money put into producing it.

XP does not recommend that you don't produce documentation. It just says you should not spend time creating *unnecessary* documentation. You need to figure out what that is. Our recommendation is to throw out preconceived notions of what is necessary and assume you don't need it. Then, when somebody wants something ask why it's needed. If they "need to understand something," offer to explain it to them. If they still need documentation, consider it.

Unless there is some external requirement (e.g., in a regulated environment), we do the simplest thing that could possibly work for documentation:

✧ Stories, tasks, the developer-customer discussions around them, and the acceptance tests supply the only specs you'll ever need.

✧ The system documentation is mostly in the code and the unit tests, which always tell you how the code works today.

✧ Short answers to FAQs can be found on a Web-based project repository.

Necessary Documentation
by Ward Cunningham

WyCash found documents useful. The most maintenance oriented was a Wiki-style database of frequently asked questions. It grew to 30 or 40 pages. We also wrote an occasional technical memo when it seemed appropriate. I'd guess we had 10 or 20 of these. I think WyCash was around 300 classes so that suggests the ratios of 1 Wiki-Faq page per 10 classes and one technical memo per 20 classes.

Specs are never comprehensive. In fact, until you have clear, consistent acceptance tests, they are far from exact. Remember the study of requirements documents we mentioned in Chapter 4. These documents tend to be woefully incomplete and inaccurate. This is the big lie of doing big design at the beginning of a project. You simply can't think of every last detail, and if the requirements aren't complete, the chances of the design being adequate are slim to none.

It is better to admit that the requirements are vague from the beginning and to work on the details in the form of acceptance tests as they are needed. That's really the hard part. It may seem impossible in some cases until you have something half-working. This is how it happens anyway, but usually the customer and developer expectations are all out of whack. Customers think they'll get the implementation of the whole spec at once, but developers prioritize it and work on it sequentially. The developers will most likely have different priorities than the customer, so the wrong people are prioritizing. If you make customer prioritization the norm, both groups will have the same expectations. We identify all the big pieces (stories), we prioritize them so that everybody knows what we're working on and why, and we flesh out the details when it comes time to do each one (tasks and estimates).

Our initial estimates are no more unreliable than the requirements, since they are at least 7% accurate. Those estimates will improve as requirements are specified in unambiguous acceptance tests. Until then (and beyond), we should work within reality.

Tests and code are a better system documentation than anything else could be. They are also the most efficient source of accurate documentation. If you're trying to learn a new part of the system, you eventually have to go from words to code anyway in order to really understand what's going on. Why waste time on the overhead of keeping paper updated?

Acceptance Tests Track Requirements Coverage
by Ken Auer

Earlier this year, I was a guest at the Extreme Tuesday Club in London (http://www.xpdeveloper.com). The first question I got was something like, "How does XP map requirements to code?" Here is the (paraphrased) exchange that followed:

ME:	Why do you need to map it to code?
ATTENDEE:	So you can see how the requirements are met.
ME:	The requirements are met when the acceptance tests pass.
ATTENDEE:	Yes, but what if the requirements changed?
ME:	Then the acceptance tests changed.
ATTENDEE:	Yes, but how do you know what change in the requirements caused what change in the code?
ME:	Why do you need to know that?
ATTENDEE:	To make sure that the requirements are met.
ME:	The acceptance tests do that. Look, you are assuming that there is a requirement to map requirements to code. I'm trying to build a product that meets the requirements. Why would I waste time doing all of this mapping? Customers don't want a map of requirements. They want the requirements met. Of course requirements are going to change. So we need a new test or set of tests and they have to pass.

The discussion shifted focus significantly after that.

XP gives you enough information to do your job as well as you can, without distracting you with too much.

Encouraging Extreme Habits
by Kay Johansen and Ron Stauffer

During 1999 and 2000, the two of us worked on a development team at a startup company where we introduced most of the XP practices. We avoided resistance by setting up a nonthreatening environment that encouraged XP and by setting policies that included a degree of tolerance around the pure XP practices. By the end of the project, the team's buy-in to XP was good, the team had grown from two to six developers, and we shipped a major release on time without working overtime.

The two of us became XP infected and were the ones that drove the implementation of XP on our team. We both had reasons for wanting to improve the way we delivered software, having had similar past experiences working long hours on poorly defined products that shipped late and buggy if they shipped at all. We were both more than ready to try something new.

At the beginning, we were the only developers at the company, and we spent several months trying pair programming. We found this practice so valuable that it encouraged us to try more of the practices, such as test-first programming and refactoring. Kay was able to attend XP Immersion* which greatly increased our understanding of the practices and how they fit together.

At the same time, more developers were being hired, and one was adamantly and vocally opposed to the idea of pairing. We wanted to try XP more than we wanted to argue about it, so instead of trying to overcome this resistance, we asked for our own team. We were told that "couldn't possibly" be done, as there weren't enough developers for two teams, but we persisted (with different levels of patience).

Eventually we did get our own team, consisting of developers who were at least not opposed to XP. Still, the new members of the team hadn't tried the XP practices and remained somewhat skeptical. Again, rather than tackle the resistance head-on with persuasion or enforcement, we set policies that encouraged developers to follow an XP practice but allowed them to substitute an agreed-upon next-best alternative. For example, we enforced code reviews for any code that was not pair programmed. This was agreed to and highlighted the advantages of pair programming, as several team members began to remark that they found code reviews less effective—a discovery they made for themselves by trying both methods.

---

* Find out more about XP Immersion at http://www.objectmentor.com.

The idea of stand-up meetings raised a few eyebrows (five meetings per week?), so we worked on making the meetings as pleasant as possible. We never stood, for one thing. Instead, to keep the meetings short, we designated someone each time to keep a timer and terminate the meeting at 15 minutes. Add in treats at every stand-up, and we never encountered any resistance!

To motivate test-first programming, we set the policy that all code changes in the business logic must be supported by test cases; but changes that were purely user interface did not have this requirement. This was actually because we hadn't figured out how to write test cases for the UI yet, not from any attempt to avoid resistance, but it worked pretty well. Restricting the requirement to business logic changes was reasonable enough that everyone agreed to it, and since developers chose their own tasks during Iteration Planning, it was possible (although difficult) to avoid writing test cases at all. Just the fact that it was theoretically possible to avoid writing test cases made them seem less onerous. Those who did write the test cases enjoyed the added benefits of being able to refactor and the confidence that they were shipping better code. Seeing the code base improve over time rather than degrade was a big morale boost for several of the developers.

Although some team members thought having requirements written and estimated on cards was humorously "low tech," no one resisted having a customer at the Iteration Planning meetings assigning priorities to tasks and then rethinking the priorities based on developer estimates. After the first Iteration Planning, the benefits of frequent communication with the customer and having well-defined tasks were apparent to all. Everyone had known the frustration of trying to work from poorly defined, constantly changing requirements, and of having far too much work assigned than was humanly doable. Seeing the customer deliberate over which tasks to include and which tasks to postpone gave developers the feeling that their work mattered enough for someone to take the time to understand the issues and cost/benefit tradeoffs involved in adding each feature. Team members who later worked on projects without iterations and cards said they much preferred having the sense of completion and accomplishment provided by completing a card and ending an iteration.

In summary, we feel the project was a success. We were able to make significant improvements in the functionality and quality of the software and the operation of the team. We hit our dates, allowed last-minute feature changes, didn't work any overtime, brought two junior developers onto the team and up to speed quickly, and created a team that really enjoyed working together. We attribute the lack of resistance to XP to our setting every policy as something everyone on the team could agree to—not what they might have chosen, mind you, but something they could and did agree to. Having agreed to it, and then having tried it, the benefits became self-evident.

Of course, we don't recommend blindly applying subsets of the XP practices. We were careful in the practices we selected and the compromises we made. To the rest of the team, the practices were presented in a coherent chunk, not introduced one at a time. We do think that succeeding with XP is all about doing the practices, even if you tailor them for your particular circumstances, not about trying to persuade people to do "pure XP." It is through doing the practices that our team became persuaded; we didn't foresee all the benefits of XP ourselves until we began doing it!

Chapter 6

Having the Right Attitude

*Pride goes before destruction, and a
haughty spirit before a fall.*
—Proverbs 16:18

*No project succeeds without trust. You can't have trust without absolute
honesty all the time. You can't have honesty without humility.*

You have to take a leap of faith to begin doing XP. The challenges of resistance
are nothing compared to maintaining the proper attitude while you're learning
and doing XP.

XP will not work in an environment where bravado and spin are the norm.
You need to nip these in the bud. The best place to start is by setting an example
yourself. This takes more courage than many people can muster.

Honesty and Trust

Lying kills trust. Without trust you might as well not do XP. Customers and
developers need to be absolutely confident that everyone is telling them the
truth all the time.

XP is not about diplomacy. It assumes (and demands) brutal honesty all the
time. The practices make it harder to lie than to tell the truth. It forces transparency on a scale most people aren't used to, and they often rebel against it.

XP forces developers and customers to be honest with one another. Take
planning. Many people criticize XP for not planning ahead like many heavy
approaches do. The problem is that those approaches are predicated on guesses

about the future. That isn't telling the truth, no matter how good your guesses turn out to be. The unvarnished truth is that we don't really know what the future holds. Planning in XP is based on admitting what we know and don't know at every step. We put together a rough project plan based on rough estimates of rough requirements (stories). So does everyone else. If they don't tell you so, they are lying or naive.

We usually put a detailed plan together only one iteration ahead. Planning further ahead is a fruitless exercise in reading tea leaves. The effort to do so will cost you time now—and time later verifying your plans, revising your plans, or explaining why you aren't hitting your plans. The more profitable of these options is revising, or more accurately, refining your plan based on the increased knowledge you'll have when you get to that part of the rough plan. Reality won't conform to the plan, so keep it simple and easy to change. Keep iterations short so that developers and customers can get frequent feedback on how things are going. That's honest.

XP also forces developers to be honest with themselves and with other developers. If you are writing code in pairs, at least one other person will see every boneheaded mistake you make. If a mistake happens to slip through, somebody will find it eventually, thanks to collective code ownership. The preferred physical environment for XP has few or no walls, so people can see you struggling or goofing off. At daily stand-up meetings people get to hear and ask what you've been up to. Being dishonest as an XP developer is like stealing cookies from someone else's cookie jar while they're watching. They'll see you do it and the crumbs are still in the corner of your mouth.

Requiring honesty does not mean XP rejects tact. You should still respect your coworkers. But XP demands brutal honesty all the time. The truth is going to have to be dealt with eventually. Ignoring it dooms you to failure, either in results or perception.

Dishonesty Doesn't Work
by Roy Miller

I joined a project for a bank in Canada after it had been going on for almost six months. The technical team for Release 2.0 consisted of four very experienced architects, and me. The first release focused more on business issues—the technical side was "quick and dirty."

From the first day, it was clear to me this was a project in trouble. The new senior architect in charge of Release 2.0 joined the project the same day I did, so we were both trying to figure out what was going on and what had happened in the past. The technical architect who had been on the project the longest (call him Bob) filled us in. The technology side of Release 1 was a mess, despite his efforts to help right the ship. The business side of the project was equally bad. On top of this, the client organization was dysfunctional and had no clue where to go. My company's on-site team wasn't much better. Strong personalities and political agendas interfered with any kind of honesty and progress. The new lead architect and I thought Bob was exaggerating, until we had been on the project for about a week. If anything, he was generous.

After a couple of weeks, the new technical team got to attend the all-hands status meeting. Everybody on the team (about 25 people) sat in a circle in a conference room. As we went around the circle, each person gave an update about where his team stood. Every single person said things were proceeding nicely. We on the technical team sort of stared at each other, wondering how people who were arranging chairs on the deck of the Titanic could think things were fine. Thinking maybe we still didn't understand the situation, we gave our updates by saying something like, "We're still trying to figure out what's going on."

It never got any better. We struggled valiantly for three months before the client cancelled the technical initiatives for Release 2. To the end, everybody at the status meetings said everything was fine. They simply denied reality.

Humility

One of the guys at our company said on a recent XP project, "I love XP! I feel like an idiot every day! When I wasn't doing XP, I thought I was brilliant. Now I know I'm not, but I don't care because I've learned so much!" We thought about getting T-shirts made that said "Join the Extreme Programming Software Studio™ . . . Feel like an idiot every day!" We haven't done it yet because we aren't sure how many others would see the splendor in the statement. Go figure.

You won't last long in a brutally honest environment without being humble. Other than quitting, it is the only reaction that makes sense. Your mistakes, weaknesses, selfishness, and pride will be put on display. You can get humble real fast, quit because you hate embarrassment, or stay brazenly arrogant and be sacked by your team. This is a tough choice for many developers.

Developers are smart people in general. The ones with a reputation for being experts will have the hardest time getting humble. Often, they'll do whatever they can to avoid it. Ironically, the reputation they are guarding will dwindle as they begin to be seen as arrogant. Work will get done without them.

When they choose to participate, they'll be behind everyone else. The rest of the team will get frustrated with having to catch them up all the time.

Everybody on an XP team should feel like an idiot regularly. That's healthy. Instead of paying lip service to the phrase "nobody's perfect," we realize it every day. On just about any team we're on, we find that we often have much more experience than others on the team. But not a day goes by when we don't make mistakes that are caught by our pairs. When Ken coaches, he sometimes says apparently contradictory things. He can't count the number of times he's had to admit he was actually inconsistent. He has never regretted that. The result is always positive. Everybody learns. Sometimes, they learn that Ken can be an idiot, too.

This whole humility thing may seem ludicrous to those who listen to us and other XPers talk about how great XP is. But, please recognize the difference. We personally realize that we make mistakes and they are going to be found out. That gives us confidence that we are doing great work. Fewer mistakes go unnoticed. And we are moving faster and more confidently than we ever have before. We may not be moving faster and more confidently than *you* ever have before, but we've seen the difference it has made for us. It's quite remarkable and you cannot deny that we have noticed a marked difference.

Sweet Freedom

We think disciplining ourselves to be honest and humble is worth doing for its own sake. But even if you're not into building character like that, developing honesty and humility is still great because they give you the freedom to maximize your potential.

Here is a stereotypical discussion between a developer and a customer in a traditional environment:

CUSTOMER: I want everything yesterday, and I don't care if it kills all of your people to get it done!

DEVELOPER: Well, that's a lot of stuff. Do you really need it *all*? Isn't there some subset that's more important that we could focus on first?

CUSTOMER: It's *all* critical. If we don't get it all, my butt's in a sling.

DEVELOPER: I hear you. We are in this together. We'll get it done. You can count on us.

A month later:

> CUSTOMER: You didn't deliver! I want this stuff *now*!!
>
> DEVELOPER: There were some unexpected speed bumps. But I hear you loud and clear. We are in this together. We'll get it done. You can count on us.

This is rubbish. The customer is lying to the developer. Not everything is a number-one priority; that's being lazy. The developer is lying to the customer, too. He's committing to something that's ludicrous, and he's doing it with a straight face. When he fails (no surprise, really), he learns nothing and makes the same stupid promise again. The customer acts like he believes him. It's a big game of charades.

Here's a real-world example of a similar conversation with the customer on the Ken's largest XP project to date. The team was close to a release date, and was under tremendous pressure when the following exchange happened:

> CUSTOMER: I know you just got the relative date thing working by typing in a plus or minus followed by a number, but I'd really like to be able to specify *today* by typing in a zero.
>
> DEVELOPER: That's not going to happen. You said you wanted a plus or minus. That would be a new requirement, and it would push the end date out.
>
> CUSTOMER: (angrily) Don't tell me that's what I wanted! I wanted a zero from the beginning and you talked me into the plus or minus because you said it would be easier to do.
>
> DEVELOPER: Calm down. I'm sorry I used my words poorly. It wasn't what you wanted, it was what you agreed to.
>
> CUSTOMER: Okay. It's what I agreed to. Don't tell me it's what I wanted.
>
> DEVELOPER: Again. I'm sorry. I should have said it was what you agreed to.
>
> CUSTOMER; Well, how much longer would it take to make it work with a zero?
>
> DEVELOPER: Well, let's talk about it calmly. Okay? (pause) I don't remember what I told you originally. The issue was that a *T* for today or a *Y* for yesterday wouldn't work for internationalization. A zero would work theoretically, but it's ambiguous and

could be interpreted as the beginning of a valid date. As soon as you type a plus or a minus, there is no confusion and we can shift into relative mode. That date widget we are using from the third party has some really raunchy code and it wasn't easy to get it to work with the plus and minus, but writing our own date widget at this point would be foolish. I don't think it will be difficult for users to get used to typing a plus or minus for *today* even though it isn't intuitively obvious. Of course, neither is plus or minus for that matter. We're going to have to teach them to use them, so I don't see that it will be more than one sentence in the user manual to teach them how to use plus-zero, minus-zero, or just plus or minus to get *today*.

CUSTOMER: Well, maybe not. But how much would it cost to make it work only when you type a single zero and tab out of there?

DEVELOPER: Well, now that I've been in the code and pretty much figured it out, it might be a little easier. But this isn't the same as keying off a plus or minus because when you type in a zero, you don't want to switch to relative mode. If you wanted a T or some other character that wasn't a number, that would be a piece of cake and I could do it for you right now. But I can't think of any other characters that would be more intuitively obvious that wouldn't cause problems for internationalization. There's also a lot of hairy testing to make sure it works for all the ways you can get to the point of one zero followed by a tab. I don't think it would take more than a day, but I'm not so sure there won't be some other gotchas in there.

CUSTOMER: Hmmm . . . I still think I want the zero, but I'm not sure.

DEVELOPER: Well, we'll just leave it out for now. If you are sure you want it, let us know and we'll put it back into the remaining list of things that still need to be done.

That is honesty and humility in action. Which scenario would you prefer? We prefer to be free to tell the truth. If everybody expects this, and does it, everybody wins. If either side doesn't, you will crash and burn.

Notice that this exchange wasn't perfectly smooth, but brutal honesty made the discussion realistic. Would "Yes Ma'am, the customer is always right" have gotten us a better result? We don't think so. What if the customer had said, "Look here, it shouldn't take you more than a couple of minutes to make it work with the zero. So make it work!" We would have said no.

It's not just about honesty and humility between a customer and developer. It's also about interaction within a development team. In a typical status meeting, there is a lot of finger-pointing and responsibility shifting. Nobody is communicating with anyone. No problems, interpersonal or otherwise, get solved. Everyone is defensive, caught off guard, or continually ignorant without any hope of catching up. After the meeting, everyone returns to their cubes and gets deeper into the jungle without an escape plan.

We prefer a supportive environment where everybody is learning, no one gets left behind, and nobody is a prima donna, no matter how talented. If you have an environment like this, you feel like you can do anything. If you don't, prepare for battle.

When you're honest with others and with yourself, you have no choice but to be humble. When you are humble, you are teachable. When you are teachable, you learn. When you learn, you can use what you learn to achieve great things. That's winning.

Part II

First Things First

We have now set the stage. Either you've already tried an XP experiment or you have the tools you need to try one. Sooner or later, you'll take the plunge and start doing XP for real. When you do that, you have to know what to do first, why, and how.

In this section, we talk about which XP practices you should focus on first. The other practices are important and will come into play—you can't get the synergistic experience of XP without them—but they aren't what you should start with.

For each of these essential practices, we specify why we think it's essential. We summarize how to go about doing it. Then we describe the best way to *start* doing it, since these practices are probably the most foreign to you right now.

We also describe our own experiences and those of other pioneers, to help you avoid problems or at least know how others have made it through the problems.

By the way, our confidence in being able to explain and execute these practices in any environment is much higher than it is for the remaining parts of XP. We might go so far as to say that if you are not doing *all* of these practices in roughly the way we describe them, you shouldn't tell anyone you are doing XP. We won't be nearly as dogmatic about the remaining parts.

We start with two chapters that introduce the bare essentials, followed by a chapter that illustrates why these practices are pointless without communication. We then introduce the six practices we've identified as critical starting points:

- ✧ Separating business and technical (planning and estimating)
- ✧ Small releases and short iterations
- ✧ Testing first (unit testing, that is)
- ✧ Pair programming
- ✧ Refactoring
- ✧ Continuous integration

We follow it all up with a call to stay on process.

Chapter 7

The Bare Essentials

*If I had eight hours to chop down a tree,
I'd spend six sharpening my axe.*
—Abraham Lincoln (1809–1865)

*Nail down the essential XP practices first. Without these, the others don't
matter. If you get them, that sets the stage for implementing of the others.*

In August 1914 Ernest Shackleton embarked on the Imperial Trans-Antarctic
Expedition, intending to be the first to cross the continent on foot. At the time,
he was one of the most experienced Antarctic explorers in the world. He prepared well and took 27 experienced men with him.

By January, only 85 miles from their intended harbor, their ship *Endurance* was locked in the ice in the Weddell Sea. The ice pack imprisoned the ship
and her crew for 9 months before slowly crushing the *Endurance*. Before the
ship sank, the men salvaged as much as they could and took to the ice. Shackleton knew that they would have to spend an indefinite period of time living on
the floes. There was only one thing to do.

Shackleton gathered everyone for a somber stand-up meeting. He told
his men that they were going to walk out of there alive. To do that, they
could carry only what they absolutely needed—the bare essentials. That
meant only a few pounds of personal gear. He told his men that no article had
any value when weighed against their ultimate survival. When he finished
speaking, Shackleton took out his gold cigarette case and several gold sover-
eigns, and without hesitation dropped them on the ice in the middle of the circle of men. His men all followed suit. Coming out alive was more important

than utlimately worthless baubles. The amazing ending to the story is that not a single man perished.[1]

Developing software isn't like crossing Antarctica, but the odds against success are similarly daunting. Don't believe it? Consider these sobering statistics from over 200 projects in various industries from 1997 to 1999.[2]

- ✧ 40% were late by an average of 67%
- ✧ 30% were over budget by an average of 127%
- ✧ requirements volatility was roughly 22%
- ✧ 47% of the projects couldn't find their original numbers

Maybe we don't change our ways because these stats aren't as bad as facing death on the Antarctic ice, but they shouldn't be ignored. We hold onto things we like and then wonder why we fall so short of success. Surviving and winning require that you follow a principle of XP: Travel light.

The First Step

Appeal to your boss' individual desire to win. Meet with your boss to talk about what his goals are. Tell your boss that you've been examining the way you've been working and that you think you could be doing a better job of helping him meet his goals. In order to do a better job, you need to be perfectly clear on what his goals are and what he needs you to produce over the long term. Emphasize that once you're clear on those goals, you want to examine everything you're doing to make sure that you're making the best use of your time to help him meet his goals.

Your boss will probably be a little surprised and focus on a short-term goal or talk about political and interpersonal office pressures. We will almost guarantee you the first words out of your boss' mouth won't be "attend as many meetings as possible and produce lots of documents that nobody reads." So go ahead and ask him for his goals.

Once he tells you what he wants, hold him accountable to it. Whenever your boss asks you to do something that seems contrary to his goals, ask whether that thing has become more important than meeting the originally

---

1. A. Lansing. *Endurance: Shackleton's Incredible Voyage*. Carrol and Graf Publishers, Inc. 1959.
2. J. Highsmith. *Adaptive Software Development*. Presented at OOPSLA 2000. Data comes from Michael Mah of QSM Associates.

stated goals. If it has, gladly do it. If this becomes a habit, find a good time to talk to your boss about it.

Nine times out of ten, when you ask your managers what they want most from you and they see you sincerely trying to give it to them, they'll be thrilled. Both of us have managed people. Starting here, two out of two managers surveyed want nothing more from their employees. If you work for a manager who says otherwise, you might want to consider seriously looking for a new manager.

Once you've had this meeting with your manager, all that's left is to start doing the essential practices of XP on whatever part of the project you can, while being sensitive to your boss's other pressures.

The XP Essentials

None of the XP practices matters a bit unless you have one team committed to producing great results. This means that both the business and development sides of the project must be committed to working together to win. Once you have that collective attitude and commitment, the practices become important. Fortunately for teams and organizations new to XP, the practices are not all equally important in the beginning. All of the practices reinforce each other, so they all are important ultimately, but certain practices are more important than others *when you start*. These are the essentials:

1. Planning and estimating
2. Small releases (and iterations)
3. Testing first (unit testing)
4. Pair programming
5. Refactoring
6. Continuous integration

You may not get the rest of the project moving with you, but doing these things on even a subset of your project will get you going in a positive way and soon people will start noticing the difference.

You can add any of the other XP practices when you get started. We suggest not doing that for at least a month if it in any way hinders you from concentrating on the basic six. Usually adding the other practices will help, rather than hinder you. You'll have to make the call. We suggest even more strongly making an extra effort to be incredibly cheerful and friendly. This should not be hard if you are really doing nothing but XP.

Here is where the courage comes in. Abandon everything else that is not part of doing XP.

Maybe you're thinking, "Surely, you can't mean everything we are currently doing. We still need to attend the XYZ meetings. And, of course, Sam needs to finish the design document he has been writing since he is already 70% complete. . . ." Nope. We mean everything. Tell whomever you can that you are going to put everything but the essentials necessary to meet your boss's goals on hold for a while because of your tight schedule. Then there is a lot less risk in experimenting with XP because you won't be under a microscope. After a month, if missing something really hurt you, you can retrieve it—you didn't leave it 50 miles back on the ice. After all, how will you know how fast you can travel if you don't unload everything else?

If doing this will get you fired before the month is out, do just enough not to get fired. The first week will be the scariest. After that, you will probably be so productive that people will start noticing the productivity and start following your lead.

Stripping Down to the Essentials
by Ken Auer

Once I stood in for another developer when he had a family emergency. Well, when the emergency was over, the other developer who had been out (I'll call him Joe) and I overlapped a week in order to make a smooth transition as I handed the reins back to him. On the day he got back, Joe spent most of his time with me to find out what I had done in the previous five weeks. By midday, Joe was quite impressed. "You sure have been busy while I've been gone." Over the next two days, I didn't see Joe other than in fleeting moments. We arranged to have dinner together the following night. At dinner, our conversation went something like this:

ME: Where have you been the last few days?

JOE: You know, all those meetings.

ME: What meetings? You've just been back for a couple of days. What are you doing in meetings?

JOE: Now that you mention it, I've noticed that you don't seem to be in any of those meetings. How did you manage to avoid them?

ME: Simple. Whenever Ralph (the manager, not his real name) asked me if I could attend a meeting, I'd say, "Sure I can attend, if you think that's the best use of my time. You had asked me before to get X done, but if you want me to push that out, it's your call." Most of

Ken likes to drum a basic software development mantra into people's heads: "Make it run, make it right, make it fast."[3] These core practices are what it takes to make XP run in your organization. Once you have these in place, you can make it right by adding the others to get the full, synergistic XP experience. Maybe you will even find a good reason to add something else you used to do (or some variation of it). Once all the practices are reinforcing each other, you can refine XP within your particular context. That's making it fast.

If you make it run first, you will be better equipped to overcome resistance that you are likely to face when you're trying to make it right and fast.

You can probably get away with "acting weird and being into that XP stuff" for about a month without getting too much resistance, as long as you don't try force it on everyone else or break commitments to others without permission. At the end of a month, you should have enough results to begin defending yourself if attacks come. But more likely, you will find others interested in joining you and still others spending their time defending themselves.

Picture this. After asking your manager what he wants most out of you, you are successfully tackling it with XP and seeing good results. You have a great attitude toward your boss, your morale is going up, and it's starting to get contagious. Your boss has heard about some of the cool side benefits of having the tests. You are moving faster than ever, partially because XP is helping you and partially because you are not doing a lot of other things that are less productive. One of your resistant colleagues seeks out your boss to complain. Think about that. He's complaining that you're playing to win.

---

3. We've had many people tell us who said this first. There is virtually no way to verify who was first, so we just thank whoever it was, and recognize it wasn't us.

Remember the XP Values

When you're starting out, there are a few rules to keep in mind that will make things much easier. These rules are based on the values of XP:

- ✧ Simplicity
- ✧ Feedback
- ✧ Communication
- ✧ Courage

Think Simply

Roy came to XP from a large consulting firm. He was used to a methodology that came on a CD, because that was the only medium it would fit on. On his first day working at RoleModel, Ken wrote a test and asked Roy to write a little code to make it pass. Roy spent four hours on the problem and came up with something ridiculously complex, and he had a headache. Seeing his pain, Ken came over and helped him refactor. Within 30 minutes, Ken had an elegant solution with about one-third the code. Yes, Roy felt stupid.

People have forgotten that the simplest solution is probably right. When you are taking your first steps with XP in the real world, nothing could be more important. XP is an answer to the question, "How little can we do and still create great software?"

Simplicity is easier than complexity in the long run. Certainly, coming up with the simplest thing that could possibly work takes some skill. Most often, though, the barrier that keeps us from doing this is a predisposition to doing complicated things. Maybe this makes us feel smarter.

Be a child again. Kids often don't know the complicated way to do something. They just assume the simple way will work, and they go for it. XP requires you to do the same thing. Just do it and see if it works. This is especially true when you start. Try the XP practices and see if they work. If they don't, respond just enough to make them work. Simple.

Get Feedback Early and Often

XP works only when you're getting lots of feedback all the time. You can't steer otherwise. Pay attention to the feedback you get, especially when you're starting. XP is based on some fundamental principles that don't change, but it has to be adapted to fit its environment. Changing it is not only acceptable, it's required.

The Value of Reflection
by Ken Auer

When introducing XP at a client, we spent the first few days in a group working through some of the practices together. We'd start every day by asking what concerned people the most, what they were most uncomfortable with. Around lunch, we'd ask if they were making progress in the areas that made them uncomfortable. Before people left at the end of the day, we'd ask them again.

When Duff and I first did our three weeks of mini-XP, we started each day discussing what we were going to try to do, based on our current understanding of XP, and what we were uncertain about. We also reflected on our XP implementation several times during the day. We always ended the day reflecting on what we had done well and what we could be doing better.

These discussions covered everything imaginable. We talked a lot about how to test and how to pair. Most of the time, we negotiated to consensus on the things we weren't sure about and then just tried a couple of things to see how they worked. In general, we assumed simplicity and deferred arguing. We learned at a great pace, and we got good at it faster than we thought we would.

Just about everyone we've talked to who started XP and stuck with it reflected a lot on what they were doing for the first few days or weeks. It didn't stop then, it was just less intense after a while. Listen to the feedback you get from your fellow developers, managers, and customers. Squeeze all the lessons out of that feedback that you can. Apply them as soon as possible.

Iteration Retrospectives
by Frank Westphal

If you start improving your software process, XP is not the finish line— it's a starting line. The single best step toward adopting XP we took at Channel One was holding a retrospective at the end of every iteration to tune and adapt the XP process to the locale.

Our team made it a special ritual to stop and reflect on its process before proceeding with the planning workshop for the next iteration. Reliving history in a retrospective was as simple as the discussion of some simple questions:

- What worked well?
- What problems were encountered?
- What are areas for future improvement?

The stories shared during this discussion became part of our team's tribal knowledge and tradition. Each meeting provided a chance to look forward, to shape the future, and to design a change about what we had to approach differently next time.

I suggest promoting iteration retrospectives to another recommended XP practice to implement the principle of local adaptation and to enforce the unwritten value of constant learning. If you're doing XP, you'll be playing with your process all the time. If you're practicing XP exactly the same way after six months, you aren't practicing XP.

Communicate

Success is directly proportional to communication. Talk with people about XP in your environment. There is no better way to learn. If you are paying attention when applying XP, it will change somewhat to fit your context. Without communication, these changes are impossible.

Most problems with projects can be traced back to at least one communication problem. Fortunately for geeks, you can't really do XP without communicating.

XP forces all parties to communicate by employing practices that can't be implemented without communication, such as pair programming. If you didn't at least communicate with your partner, you'd have to be mute all day, which is hard even for geeks. And your stand-up meetings would be really weird.

Be Courageous

You had the guts to try XP. Have the courage to see it through. Don't give up when things get tough. That is too easy. Play to win.

Chapter 8

Exception Handling

Plurality should not be posited without necessity.
—William of Ockham

Assume the practices of XP will work. Don't come up with elaborate schemes for handling exceptions before you encounter them. When they come up, handle them as simply as possible.

People who have difficulty believing XP will work often list off a bunch of exceptions:

- ✧ How do you pair if you have an odd number of developers?
- ✧ What if the customer won't write stories?
- ✧ What if the customer won't write acceptance tests?
- ✧ What if management refuses to set realistic delivery schedules?
- ✧ What if management doesn't believe your estimates?
- ✧ What if management refuses to let you pair program?
- ✧ What if the cost of tea in China doubles?

How do you handle these proposed exceptions without just ignoring them? Ignore them until they can't be ignored. Then handle them as simply as possible. That is the simplest thing that could possibly work.

Handling XP Exceptions Like Code Exceptions

Writing code is easier if you can count on the methods you are using not to throw exceptions. You can just invoke the method and expect a certain result. This lets you proceed with confidence. In fact, we have found that programming goes better when we assume exceptions don't exist. We find out soon enough if we're wrong. Then we handle the exception with the simplest approach that could possibly work. This almost always works.

If we went to the other extreme, we would be afraid to write any code until we knew how to handle all of the possible exceptions and all of the exceptions in our exception handlers. That way lies madness.

Implementing XP in an organization that's not used to it is the same. Assume there aren't any exceptions to handle. The practices of XP are simple, although not always easy. It has been called a "lightweight" methodology because none of the practices requires a lot of ceremony or training. Each is simple to implement and gives the results it advertises. Assume they work.

When you find an exception, handle it as simply as possible without turning it into something completely different that misses the point. Don't come up with an elaborate scheme of exception handling that turns XP into a heavyweight methodology. Just handle the exception. Figure out the best way to keep it an exception, rather than a rule.

Here are just a few exception handling routines we've used.

An Odd Number of Developers

All production code must be written in pairs. What happens when you have an odd number of people? Find a "maverick" task for the single programmer to work on. Spikes and research are good candidates.

Odd Pairs
by Ken Auer

On one of the first pair programming days at our first big XP client, we had an odd number of people. Since all production code has to have two sets of eyes on it, we knew the solution was *not* to let someone write code alone. So we tried a couple of things. We tri-programmed for a bit, which worked for a while. To some of the novices, every line of code was new and exciting. But after a while, that got old. So I let the two novices continue on their own while I went to check on the other pair. They were doing fine, so I went and read the manual for one of the physical components (the serial port) of the system we were working on.

When I had a clue about where to start on the serial port task, it was almost three o'clock and one of the developers had to go pick up her daughter at her day care center. Imagine that—one pair stopped what they were doing and another one formed. Cool.

Sometimes, there are unavoidable instances where production code has to be written by one person. Suppose the hard part of a problem is solved and both developers in the pair know exactly what's going on. When one party gets interrupted by someone else, or by nature, the other developer might take the next few steps without a pair. When the partner gets back, the driver explains what's happened. If the driver went too far, he has to undo it. If not, the pair can move on.

Does this ever backfire? Absolutely.

The Danger of Coding Alone
by Ken Auer

One day, I was pairing with Duff. During the day, the pairing was interrupted four times. It went something like this.

I was pulled away for a couple of minutes. A few minutes later, I came back and took the keyboard. Within moments, I was confused. A method I was trying to invoke wasn't there. I knew it was supposed to be there, because I had written it earlier that day. I was speechless. Duff saw this and asked what I was looking for. I told him that there used to be a method there that I was counting on, but I couldn't find it anymore. Duff said he deleted it because nobody was calling on it except the test, so it wasn't necessary. I told him I had put it there earlier as the first part of the task we were working on because I knew I needed it in order to make the task work. Duff replied, "Oops. Man, you leave me alone for two minutes, and we've just lost ten minutes."

An hour or so later, Duff went off to relieve his bladder. While he was gone, I browsed a couple of methods looking for one that we might be able to use when Duff got back. During my browsing, I noticed some superfluous code in one of the methods, so I changed it. Duff returned and we finished our task. All the tests in the related test suite passed. I suggested we integrate. Duff

> suggested we run another related test suite, just to be sure we didn't break anything. I claimed we didn't have to, since we hadn't touched anything that would have affected that other suite. Duff said, "Well, just humor me." Red bar! Duff incredulously stated, "How could that test have failed?" I sheepishly told him I had an idea.
>
> Similar scenarios happened two more times that day. We went four for four. It was quite comical. We haven't stopped doing little snippets of code when we are interrupted, but now we are a little more mindful of showing each other what we did while the other was away.

Most of the time when you have an odd number of people, there is something that can be done safely by one person. When that person is ready to roll, it is often possible that another person can find something safe to do as an individual. If not, think of something or tri-program for a little while.

As long as pairing is the rule, and exceptions are few and far between, you'll be fine. In fact, the problems that come up when you make too many exceptions will become obvious, and you'll discover your own limits as long as you are honest and humble.

The Customer Won't Write Stories

For some reason, the customer at one of our client sites has a tough time picking up a pencil or keyboard and writing stories. However, the customer doesn't have any problem telling us what she wanted. We write down what we think we heard and ask for verification. This is nothing to panic about. We need user stories. The customer won't write them down. The simplest thing that could possibly work is that we write down user stories based on customer input.

If you can get the user to verify the stories, you end up with roughly the same results. The point is that the customer is still the one identifying the business requirement and setting the priorities. The customer just has an assistant, which happens to be you.

The Customer Won't Write Acceptance Tests

This is essentially the same problem as a customer refusing to write stories.

If you can't get the user to write the acceptance tests, do your best to write the tests and get the customer to verify them. By verifying them, the customer is signing off on them. If the customer refuses to verify the tests and won't offer you an alternative, he has indirectly verified them. Eventually the truth will come out and somebody will try to fix it. If not, at least you've got a set of tests you can run to verify you are building something, which is better than what you had before XP.

Management Sets Unrealistic Schedules

If your leadership sets an unrealistic deadline, explain that you don't think it's possible and offer a date or scope that is possible. In the meantime, say you'll do what you reasonably can to meet the schedule. The more realistic schedule will come closer to matching reality.

The big concern here is that management may blame XP for the missed schedule. One strategy is to ask what is expected in the next month. Estimate how long you think that will take to get those items done by breaking them into small chunks, just as you'd do with XP. Do what you can and estimate how much the schedule is off. Then point out the discrepancy and ask whether you can try a different approach for the next month.

As long as management offers unrealistic schedules, reality will keep hitting them in the face. Eventually they will either stop setting unrealistic schedules, lose their job, you'll lose your job, or nothing will happen. The only bummer is option three—you lose your job—and that might not be as bas as it seems.

If your management begins setting realistic goals, that's the best situation to be in. You can run the project according to the more realistic schedule you set.

If you lose your job, this can be a blessing. You will have a good excuse to leave an unreasonable organization. This might have happened even if you had never tried XP.

If your management continues to set unrealistic goals, you probably are in an organization with no accountability. In this case, you can look for another organization to join, or you can take advantage of the situation and do the job well. If you do, your team will stand out as people who actually do what they say they are going to do, and others may follow. At least your integrity will remain intact.

Unreasonable Questions, Unreasonable Answers
by Jim Highsmith

In New Zealand a few years ago, I had a senior IT manager who—when faced with a recalcitrant, unbending, unreasonable request from a client

---

department—would just say okay and move on. He knew his development team couldn't make the date and didn't push them to do so (he informed them of the date and encouraged them to attempt to make it, but was clear that it wasn't an expectation). When the project was late, he'd just say oops, and move on. Some people just don't want an honest answer, but here was a case of a good manager who didn't pass the unreasonableness along to his development teams.

One of the reasons we get in trouble is lack of courage when a customer walks in the office and asks, "How long will it take to do X?" It's easy to say, "Oh, that sounds like a three-week or three-month project." We often create our own problems. Everyone knows there is no data here, so the customer can argue that we have the wrong answer, because there is a real possibility that we do. Even a two-hour Planning Game session can provide a common basis for negotiation, whereas the "instant estimate" is fraught with danger. Courage!

Management Doesn't Like Your Estimates

Ask management if it knows something you don't that will help you get the work done quicker. If it does, great! If not, tell it you are sticking by your estimates and tracking each one. You would be delighted to find out that you were too conservative.

Otherwise, see *Management Sets Unrealistic Schedules*.

Management Won't Let You Pair

When management won't let you pair, try using another word that doesn't trigger the corporate gag reflex.

In his submission to Ken's "Refining the Practices of XP" workshop at OOPSLA 2000, Dan Rawsthorne conveyed how he did a lot of "mentoring" because "pair programming" was not acceptable in the high-ceremony DOD project he was on. Mentoring, good. Pair programming, bad. You may have to be creative to explain who is mentoring whom at times, but try it.

The Cost of Tea in China Doubles

There are lots of exceptions that can crop up. We'll leave how to handle those up to your imagination, but follow a general rule: Ignore each exception until you know you need to handle it, then keep it simple.

Chapter 9

Can We Talk?

Most conversations are simply monologues
delivered in the presence of a witness.
—Margaret Miller

If you aren't communicating well, XP won't work, no matter how many of
the practices you try to implement.

Let's look at an XP value that can get lost in all the talk about the mechanics of
XP. Ward Cunningham put it best:[1]

Don't write if you can just talk.
Don't talk if you can just point.
Don't point if you can just do.
And know when you can't.

Success on any software development project is directly proportional to
communication. One of the brilliant things about XP is that it forces developers
to communicate in order to get anything done. If left to their own devices,
most developers wouldn't talk much. XP makes not communicating unnatural.

Think about the person with whom you have the most intimate communication. Do you ever produce a document for that person so they know what
you've been up to? How about a weekly status report? Do you send an e-mail

---

1. W. Cunningham. Private e-mail exchange with Ken Auer. 2001.

when they are in the same building? When you're concerned about how they're doing, do you schedule a conference room, invite a lot of other concerned people to come, and then intimidate them into committing to doing more in less time?

We hope not. People in the same room talking to one another have the highest bandwidth of direct and indirect communication. "Ken's got that look again. What am I doing wrong?" "Bob, you look frustrated. Is it with me? Do I need to slow down?" "We're stuck. Can anybody help?" Somehow, programmers and their managers think that they can improve on that communication by using formal processes or technology. That doesn't make sense.

XP uses four things to force and facilitate face-to-face communication among the people involved in developing software:

1. Pair programming (and switching often)
2. Stand-up meetings every morning
3. Planning (essentially, talking to the customer and to each other a lot)
4. A team atmosphere and environment that encourages impromptu communication as the first line of defense

Pair Programming

We discuss the mechanics of pairing in Chapter 14. What's important to note here is that pairing makes programming an exercise in constant communication, both within and among pairs. It does this in two ways:

1. By replacing most written documentation with oral history and explanation
2. By disseminating information through the "pairvine"

The traditional theory holds that, if you have everything documented, losing people is less of a risk, because new people can come up to speed quickly. Documenting also should keep everyone on the project in sync with what's going on, thereby maintaining design consistency.

In practice, this doesn't work. On every well-documented project we've ever seen, the pace of production was lethargic, fixing a problem took forever (unless rules were broken), and the design was notoriously complex and confusing. New people didn't come up to speed quickly because the documents were outdated or incomplete. If new people wanted to find out what those documents meant, they had to talk to people anyway.

- -

I Thought I Needed More Documentation
by Jeff Canna

Being new to XP and having been a programmer for roughly 15 years, I joined a four-iteration old XP team. I very much wanted to become a productive member of this team quickly.

My background was working against me. On all of my other projects, I gleaned useful information from documentation written when the project began. While the details in that documentation always were out of date, the overall metaphor usually matched. Having skimmed the documentation, I would pull details from the code, mostly by skimming comments. I had to change my work pattern.

I was now working on a project with no documentation, which had code that was almost completely uncommented. My crutches were knocked out from under me. I very quickly became frustrated. I was completely dependent on other people to do the simplest tasks. It seemed I had no way to become a productive member of this team. I felt the lack of documentation was getting in my way. I started pushing for documentation, just a little.

After many discussions, including an XP workshop at OOPSLA, I came to realize that the documentation I was after would only be relevant to a new person on an existing project. In the two-year time span that this project has been under development, only one other new person had joined the team. Additionally it turns out that my perceived lack of productivity was exactly that, perceived. The customer was very happy with how quickly I became productive after joining the team. As such, there would have been no gain from the effort of creating the extra documentation I thought I needed. In fact it would have hurt the team's velocity, which would have made it a net loss.

Document only what you need to document when you need to document it. Spend the rest of the time asking the code and talking to other people.

It seems that one of the curses of heavyweight processes is that they treat people as commodities. Not surprisingly, this usually results in people who blindly follow a process and aren't allowed to think effectively. It looks very much like the nameless horde in that famous "1984" commercial Apple Computer used to debut the Macintosh. It strikes us as asinine to have a small group use their brains to document an approach to the problems they think they have, and then have other groups use their brains to interpret what the first group wrote. Maybe they'll have a few cycles left over for programming.

We would rather encourage people to use their brains and collaborate to solve real problems. Pairing does that by having people spend their time in the code. When new people join, they learn by pairing with folks rather than by being handed a document when they walk in the door. Pairs rotate frequently. That means code knowledge gets passed around, as do development lessons, tricks, and so on.

Sharing Knowledge Through the "Pairvine"
by Ken Auer

I had used VisualAge for Java for quite a while. Wherever I went, I was pretty much considered the "VisualAge guru" even though I had no formal training with the tool. Because of my experience with VisualAge for Smalltalk, I understood the foundations of the IDE. But there were features particular to VisualAge for Java I still didn't know. One day, Duff asked me a question about VisualAge I couldn't answer, so he went off to study the on-line help a little bit. While he was doing that, he learned of a great feature: using CTRL-space to fill in method names automatically after typing zero or more characters after a period.

I was out the next day. When I got back, I was pairing with Karen. I had the keyboard and was just about to type out a long method name. Karen told me to stop so she could show me something. She hit CTRL-space. The least experienced programmer on the team taught "Mr. VisualAge" how to use this powerful feature. The next day, I was pairing with Andy and he asked, "What's the name of the method I need here?" Ready to show off my new trick, I took the keyboard and hit CTRL-space. Andy said, "Oh yes, of course." Surprised, I said, "You already knew about CTRL-space?" He said, "Sure, I think it was John who showed me yesterday." Within three days, everyone on the team had learned the new trick, including a person who would have missed any kind of formal announcement had it been made. No one had to put together an e-mail describing how to use the new feature. No classroom required.

If you switch pairs frequently, most of the verbal communication necessary to avoid surprises and to disseminate knowledge will happen. We're not making that up. Now, for the real kicker. If you add stand-up meetings, we predict that more than 90% of that communication will happen. Some would say 100%, if things are really clicking.

Stand-Up Meetings

Nobody will know everything all the time. That means everybody will require some outside knowledge at certain points. Pairing is the first step, but if you don't know the details of what other pairs are doing, how can you know what they need to know? And how can you get knowledge that you don't have when you need it? The answer is the stand-up meeting.

Trying to plan who will need to know what and when is a fool's errand. You don't know everything yourself right now, and you don't know what you'll need to know tomorrow, because the problems will be different by then. Everybody else is in the same boat. The trick is to communicate a little about what everyone knows, and find out what they don't, on a regular basis. That way, people on the team can identify who has the knowledge they don't have. That is what a stand-up meeting is all about: It is a chance to connect the people who have knowledge with the people who need it. If you do it on a daily basis, the chance of missing the opportunity at this important rendezvous goes way down.

In fifteen minutes (or less, depending on the size of the team) you can

- Get a sense of the trouble spots
- Identify who might be able to help
- Communicate surprises to exploit or prepare for
- Make sure you are starting the day right

Replace your regular meetings with stand-up meetings. Get everybody together in one place and stand in a circle. Go around the circle and have each person share what he did (or discovered) yesterday that might affect others, what progress he made yesterday, and what he plans to do today. The only discussion allowed is the asking of questions that have simple answers. Longer discussions should be taken off-line. It's as simple as that.

We do stand-up meetings every day on all of our projects. It's a habit, and it's amazing what gets done. Late last year Laurie Williams brought a few of her students to be "flies on the wall" for a day. She stuck around for our stand-up meeting, but had to leave shortly afterward for another appointment. She interrupted Ken just long enough to say, "I hate that I have to leave. This has been amazing! The number of issues that were raised and addressed in such a short period of time in your stand-up meeting is phenomenal."

And Ken thought we were having an off day.

If it's so obvious that you should have stand-up meetings, why don't people do it all the time? There are several reasons:

- There may be problems getting a quorum.
- People with the most knowledge might not share in the meeting.
- People with the most knowledge might try to share it all in the meeting.
- People might go into elaborate detail.
- It might be difficult to find a place to stand up together.

If you have trouble getting a critical mass to show up, examine whether you've communicated the reason for the meeting. If you haven't, do it. If people are still skeptical, ask them to humor you with a one-week experiment. They will be addicted in short order.

If people with knowledge seem reticent, identify why they won't open up. Many times, the ones who think they'll get the least out of the meeting will be the ones most likely to resist. They might feel threatened because they feel their knowledge gives them status, or scared that it will be revealed that they don't know as much as others think. Try encouraging them by acknowledging their importance and asking them to share. If that doesn't work, ask your manager to encourage them.

Stand-up meetings are supposed to be short. If people drone on, stand-up meetings get long. Express appreciation for shared knowledge, but remind people that the meetings are supposed to be short. Direct people to each other for more information, but tell them to take detailed discussions off-line. Thank them in advance for being available for off-line discussions. Ask people to answer only the three important questions:

1. What did you do (or discover) yesterday that might affect others?
2. What progress did you make yesterday?
3. What do you plan to do today?

To develop the habit of being brief, you can interrupt long-winded speakers, but yield them some extra time when you suspect that there are a significant number of people who want to know more. These folks are typically searching for significance. Once you've given them the floor, they'll be less prone to take it unnecessarily.

If you can't find a place to stand up, ask management to rearrange your space. It's not a lot to ask. Stand-up meetings don't require a conference room.

If rearranging the space simply can't (or won't) be accommodated, ask someone in management if you can use his office while he tries to find a more convenient place. Make sure management understands that scheduling a meeting room daily for a 15-minute meeting blocks other people from using that space. It's also wasteful to make people travel five or ten minutes to get there. As a last resort, you could try meeting in a hallway. It's not ideal, but it usually keeps people from rambling, since they don't want to disturb others. It also sends the message that it's more important to communicate than to travel to meet or to be comfortable.

We would go so far as to claim that the stand-up meeting ought to be the thirteenth XP practice. We're certainly not advocating an explosion of practices. The existing 12 are great. But we've talked to so many people who claim to be having trouble implementing XP who aren't doing stand-up meetings. We don't experience most of their particular difficulties because we address issues in our stand-up meetings while they're only emerging concerns. We also think that the need for stand-up meetings is not as explicit as it should be in the XP literature, or more people would be doing them as an essential part of the discipline.

Planning

Planning in XP is very different from the way it's done in other methodologies. This is a good thing.

Heavyweight methodologies tend to replace communication with formality and documentation. This is most obvious with regard to planning. Various groups on the project develop their own bottom-up estimates of work based on their understanding of the requirements and of how they relate to the rest of the world. They develop complex lists of dependencies and milestones. They have status meetings, disseminate status reports, and make contingency plans in case something goes wrong, and still get messed up.

Big Plans Are Not Communication
by Roy Miller

I worked on a huge project at a nationwide bank in the United States. At one point, between Release 1.0 and Release 2.0 , it seemed like the management team spent almost two solid months planning. The plans were so complex that you needed degrees in finance and logistics just to read them. It seemed like all the possible bases were covered (they better have been with all that detail).

The problem was, the project struggled constantly to keep its head above water. All of the elaborate plans were effectively useless for keeping everyone informed and maintaining control. Even worse, we all had to keep working during the two months when the plans changed every day. They continually pulled in other members of the team, the folks actually doing the work, to help with various aspects of the planning. There was a lot of talk, and a lot of direction changing, but work still had to be done. Past a certain point, people stopped paying attention to the plan and tried to do what made sense to them. That's what happens most of the time anyway.

The reason heavyweight approaches fail is simple. There is a lot of talking, and certainly a lot of paper, but there isn't much communication. They say, "Make the plan, then follow it religiously. All will be well." But there's something rotten in Denmark. Requirements change. Your bottom-up estimates that you worked so hard to make absolutely right turn out to be wrong. The complex dependency charts are missing something.

The only solution is to increase the bandwidth of communication. Planning in XP requires constant communication. Documentation is minimal (some note cards are about all). Customers have to talk to developers and vice versa. Everybody has to listen. If they don't talk and listen, they will have no clue what to work on next.

Atmosphere and Environment

XP requires an open, group workspace to be effective because stand-up meetings, planning, and pairing still aren't enough communication. Perhaps you're getting the point that communication is paramount. Stand-up meetings and pairing cover only about 90% of the communication that has to happen to keep the team humming. Often, people run into trouble in the middle of the day. If it is their nature not to interrupt others, or to avoid asking for help, they'll probably wait until the next morning's meeting. That's suicide. This will kill your velocity.

People on your team need to start forming the habit of looking around at their teammates whenever there is a break in the action. If they see frustration, concern, anxiety, strange behavior, or simply lots of silence and little typing, they need to help. They might help by offering to work with them or by asking for help on a different problem. That could break the logjam.

When emergencies happen, everybody needs to be within earshot. For example, if someone accidentally deletes something that everyone is using (hey, it happens), he can say, in a louder-than-normal voice, "Team, we've got a problem. I just deleted the project files by accident and I need help recovering." Or maybe somebody at the integration machine can't integrate their stuff because the existing tests don't run. "Team, we can't integrate. We're getting a resource error. Can the last person over here help us out?"

Everybody on the team should be behaving this way—looking around, helping out, keeping people out of ditches, asking for help when *they* are the ones in the ditch, letting people know vocally about emergencies that might affect them. You can't do that with walls in the way. An open workspace where everybody can see and eavesdrop on everybody else is critical.

Don't Fence Me In
by Tom Kubit

I worked at one company that really understood the value of an open work area. In the past year and a half we have occupied a couple of different spaces. Prior to implementing XP, the environment for developers was like most development shops: each developer either had his own office or cube, and people rarely worked together on development tasks.

When XP was started, however, we changed the development area. The company had recently discontinued their OEM printer manufacturing and therefore had an abundance of space to use for the experiment. We moved the entire development team into the "Java Factory," which was simply a slightly modified manufacturing area consisting of cement floors, a couple concrete block walls, and a couple of temporary painted plasterboard walls (see Figure 9.1).

It was great! Everybody on the team loved it. Each workstation was set up in the middle of a large folding table, which gave us plenty of room for pair programming. There was lots of space, and the cement floors made it very easy to roll your chair from one workstation to another when somebody needed help or a fresh pair of eyes. The tables were easy to move around and we did just that a number of times to facilitate things like internal classes and separation of multiple projects. Finally, we didn't have to worry about wrecking the walls, so we stuck up signs, posters of "code smells," design drawings, whiteboards, you name it. It was an incredibly collaborative and supportive environment.

Due to other circumstances, we had to give up that space after a while. The area we were moved to was a cube farm with eight-foot walls. The first things to go, even before we moved in, were the interior walls (we left the outside ones

FIGURE 9.1 The Java Factory

to provide a boundary between us and the other areas). We kept the desk furniture, and with the walls gone, the monitors and keyboards didn't have to be shoved in corners, like they did when the walls were there. We could actually use the old cube desks and set them up to be pairing friendly. We also made sure there was room for some rolling whiteboards and the all-important snack table. It looked like Figure 9.2.

FIGURE 9.2 The new space

> I think we all miss the factory environment because it was so unique, but when we had to move we knew just how essential having this open area was, so we made the changes we needed, and it has worked out very well.

If you have to live in cubicle land, you can still create useful workspace. If the people you are working with are not close by, make sure people know that this is keeping you from being as productive as possible. If it can be done, remove and/or rearrange the cubicle walls. They are supposed to be moveable. Don't let cubicles be an excuse for not communicating.

Limited Space Shouldn't Limit You
by Ken Auer

In the first days of an early XP project, the team had to do all of its work in cubicles that were barely big enough for one person. The only place the monitor would fit was in the corner. The keyboard was on a shelf under it. To reach the mouse or trackball, you had to reach under the desk, and your hand had about an inch of clearance. We worked that way for the first three months of the project. It was awful compared to anywhere we've worked since. But that's the space the client supplied and we made it work. We'd yell over the cubicle walls. A couple of people outside the project but in the same vicinity were disturbed once in a while, but they didn't complain too much because they realized how crammed we were and gave us a little leeway.

It was hard to find a place to hang a whiteboard, so we bought some static cling whiteboard sheets and put them on the sides of the cubicles. Almost none of the conference rooms had whiteboards, either. I've never seen so few whiteboards in a corporate environment. Even when there was a whiteboard in a conference room, it was usually very small, and it was hard to find dry-erase markers.

When the client extended our contract they found a small room that had been abandoned and let us move up there. The project manager found some old desks that were being scrapped that didn't have any drawers so two people could fit their legs underneath. We arranged the room with the desks facing the wall at first because we didn't think we'd be able to arrange them so we could face each other. It kind of worked, but people would bump into each other in the corners.

Getting the room outfitted with whiteboards was not in the budget, so one of the people in the group went to Home Depot and bought four mylar boards for $80 and submitted it as an expense. In a week or so, "facilities" showed up to screw them into the wall. We probably had more square feet of whiteboard in that 300-square-foot room than were present in the rest of the nearly 300,000-square-foot facility! I know we had better communication.

Then, after a few months, we rearranged the furniture to three sets of two tables facing each other. This made rolling chairs from place to place a bit difficult, but we could see each other without having to turn completely around. It improved communication and lessened the amount of chair collisions when people weren't intentionally moving them.

Eventually, the client rearranged the original space, taking down all those cubicle walls, and we moved back there. Tight, but a massive improvement over the original layout (see Figure 9.3).

FIGURE 9.3 Our studio is extremely spacious compared to this, but this works

Programmers are like plants: All we need is sunlight, fresh air, food, and water in order to thrive. Why can't we get them in most places they want to put us?

When you can get better space, go for it. In Chapter 14 you'll see some pictures of our Extreme Programming Software Studio. We ran all of the wiring under the floor to the middle of the room and arranged six custom-made pairing desks in the form of an H so we could all see each other without having to turn more than 90 degrees. We added small shelves for books so we can grab whatever we need to work. One wall of the room serves as semiprivate space and other rooms are close by for more private times when needed. The full kitchen is next to the studio. We have windows you can actually open to get fresh air. The floor plan appears in Figure 9.4.

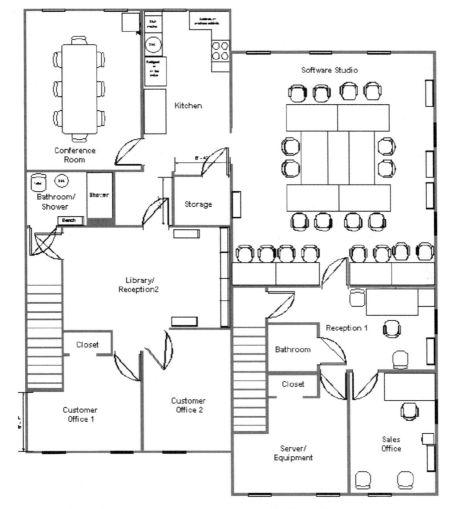

FIGURE 9.4 Extreme programming software studio floor plan

Don't forget whiteboards. Alistair Cockburn has pointed out that the most efficient form of communication is two people at a whiteboard.[2] Good ones can be expensive and you might have problems getting the capital outlay. In our studio, most of the walls are covered with whiteboards. After pricing whiteboards we went to Home Depot and bought mylar paneling for about $20 a sheet. Each sheet is 4' × 8'. We bought 10 of those and a bunch of tubes of liquid nails. Some parts of the wall could not accommodate a 4' × 8' whiteboard. Saber saws came in handy there. Now we have whiteboards everywhere you turn and it cost us less than $300 plus a bit of manual labor.

It Doesn't Stop There

There are a lot of other XP practices that encourage communication, too. We just outlined the ones that are predominant. If you are doing all of these and you find that there still isn't enough communication, then you might have a legitimate reason to consider adding some more practices.

Communication doesn't just take place among developers. You can improve your development process immensely by getting your developers communicating to each other via the means we've stated here and others, but that is only part of the equation.

Remember that the entire project is one team. Communication is vital between business and development if you are going to play to win. We tackle that in the next few chapters on planning.

---

2. A. Cockburn. "Selecting a Project's Methodology." *IEEE Software*, Volume 17, Number 4, 2000, pp. 64–71.

Chapter 10

Planning Roles and Reality

*. . . and you will know the truth and
the truth will make you free.*
—John 8:32, New American Standard Bible

We won't always have everything under control, but we can avoid foolishness with a few simple rules and tools.

Planning the XP way formalizes and reinforces the separation between business decisions and technical decisions. It lets customers and developers learn their respective roles and teaches them how to talk to one another. This is essential to your project success.

In traditional projects, planning is seen as laying the rails for a project train to follow. XP planning is like driving a car – you determine an initial course, and you steer all along the way. If you don't have to steer, planning is done; if you do, planning is an ongoing process.

How XP Planning Is Different

Most planning approaches we've had experience with have made at least one of the following assumptions about planning:

⬦ We should gather all the requirements first, then plan.
⬦ Only certain members of the team should plan—planning requires special skills and is more of a management thing.

- We should first talk to our customer and management, then plan, and then present the plan.
- Planning is expensive, so we should do it as infrequently as possible—simply track things, have status reports, and meetings in between.

We have tried each of these. They don't work, because they're unrealistic. You will never know all the requirements up front, and they'll change anyway. Top-heavy planning produces confusion. Merely listening to your customer and management at the beginning of the planning process, without having them intimately involved during planning, will guarantee that they don't entirely buy into the plan you produce. Large, infrequent adjustments don't work—you'll go too far before you realize you're on the wrong track. Status meetings between big planning sessions make it too easy to lose sight of where the project really is.

There must be a better way—a more realistic way. A realistic approach would

- Allow for incomplete requirements in the beginning and changing requirements over time.
- Involve all team members in planning, but make roles clear, which forces the people involved to fill those roles consistently.
- Require almost constant communication among all parties involved.
- Make planning a very frequent thing and relatively inexpensive and get rid of busywork that can show false progress.

This is what XP planning is like. It is the only consistently realistic approach we've ever seen. Realistic planning is the only useful kind.

How to Steer

Most other approaches we've experienced begin with planning. Lots of sub-teams scope out what they're supposed to do, create bottom-up estimates of work, and then people above them create "the plan." When it's time for a new release, there may be some additional planning. You might call this approach "big planning up front." It doesn't work very well.

When you're driving, the only way to steer is to make frequent small adjustments. Making big adjustments few and far between will put you all over the road, or in a ditch. Planning is the way we *steer* a project. As the project unfolds, we learn about how our guesses were right or wrong. As we learn something, we need to change to reflect the learning. That's why we plan. XP builds that kind of adaptability into the development process by making frequent planning.

In XP, we plan at several different levels. We plan for the next release in Release Planning (usually a few months). We plan for the next iteration in Iteration Planning (usually two or three weeks). We plan for each day in our stand-up meeting. All of this planning lets us make multiple small adjustments as we learn. That's the only way to drive.

Out in the Open

Most other approaches require people to do lots of stuff that makes them look busy. The problem is, that stuff isn't helping the project make real progress. Attending status meetings and updating project tracking documents doesn't make software. This busywork lets a project show progress, but that progress is false—very little is really getting done. This is not always intentional, sometimes projects just get buried under a mountain of paper and lose sight of the fact that they're stuck.

XP planning makes it almost impossible to obscure the reality of where a project really is. There isn't much paper to hide behind, intentionally or by accident. With everybody communicating on a daily basis about the status of a project and everybody able to see and hear what other people are doing and saying, it's hard to misrepresent what's going on.

Requirements Are a Dialogue—Not a Document

The study of typical requirements documents we referred to earlier in the book showed that it isn't cost effective attempt to make the documents better or more complete.[1] This is a communication problem. It results from a fundamental misunderstanding about what it means to gather requirements. Requirements are not requirements until someone translates a desire into something that has to be in the system. Requirements evolve as the team learns and as business priorities and desires change.

When you gather requirements in order to plan and estimate what the team is going to build, you have to do three things:

1. Identify the fundamental desires of the project
2. Break those desires down into small, significant user stories
3. Identify the detailed acceptance criteria (e.g., acceptance tests) necessary to verify that the required user stories are implemented completely

---

1. J. Highsmith. "Adaptive Software Development." Presentation at OOPSLA 2000.

The most efficient and effective way to do this is for businesspeople and developers to work together. Software developers would be much better estimators if their customers handed them a comprehensive and perfectly accurate set of clearly-defined, easily-parsed, and executable acceptance tests at the beginning of any project. If this could be done perfectly, developers could be left to themselves; until it can be done perfectly, developers and businesspeople have to work together.

As we mentioned earlier, a dialogue between two developers at a whiteboard can be the most effective means of communication. A businessperson and a technical person manipulating story cards on a table is a close second. The critical enabler for this kind of communication is everybody knowing his role in the process.

Learning Roles

At an XP leaders' retreat, someone asked Kent to boil XP down to its essence. The first thing out of his mouth was, "Separating business and technical decisions." We agree. This is most prominent during the planning process of XP—when developers and customers actively learn and practice their roles.

Business decisions are those that determine how money is spent, in the hope of getting a profitable return. Technical decisions are those that determine what approach should be taken to meet a business goal, and the estimated cost of proceeding with that approach.

Someone needs to take on the responsibility of making the business decisions, and someone needs to take on the responsibility of making the technical decisions. We call the entity that makes the business decisions the "customer." This can be an actual end user (highly desirable), a product manager, a committee, or someone else. Whoever it is must be identified clearly and must take the role seriously. Just as importantly, everyone else must take that person, or those people, seriously in that role. For simplicity's sake, we refer to the customer as singular here.

We have also simplified the discussion of the business side of a project by focusing on the customer. In reality, there is a management team involved as well. We assume here that the management team has already determined that a given project is important, that it has devoted resources to that project, and that there are one or more people assigned to the team as customers. When those things are true, developers and customers can begin interacting in the way XP prescribes. Until that is true, it will be tough for any XP project to gain the support and nurturing it needs to be successful.

We call the entity that makes the technical decisions the "developer." Again, this can be an individual (in rare cases), a team of developers, or several teams of developers. The developer may or may not include people who don't write code directly. As with the customer, the developer must be identified clearly and must take the role seriously. Just as importantly, everyone else must take that person, or those people, seriously in that role. For simplicity's sake, we refer to the developer as singular here.

The developer must provide the input the customer needs to make informed business decisions. The customer must provide the input the developer needs to make informed technical decisions.

These roles are crucial to XP. Customers decide what gets done and in what order. Developers decide the approach to getting it done and estimate how long it will take. Confusing these roles is the cause of many problems in most processes. That is why XP brings them to the forefront. XP works when all of the players respect their separate roles. Getting to that point, however, is not always easy.

The Customer

There is a fundamental difference between defining requirements and making business decisions. The two are *not* the same.

The customer must, at the very least, suggest stories and prioritize them as input to the process. The customer cannot really make business decisions until he knows what implementing the stories is going to cost. But the customer can't know the exact return the functionality described by the story will generate, nor the exact cost of the story; the customer can only make a best guess. It is not the customer's job to determine the cost.

In a simplistic view of the world, the cost is what a developer says it is. In reality, cost also includes the customer's investment of time and effort, communicating the story and analyzing the options the developer presents for delivering the story. In most cases, the story starts out vague. The hardest thing for many customers to learn is that concrete estimates based on vague requirements aren't very reliable.

Therefore, customers have to recognize that getting reliable estimates takes time and conversation. The best way to handle this is typically with an Exploration Phase at the beginning of a project (see Chapter 11). If a project is already in progress and the developer understands the general requirements well, you may just be able to get a good enough handle on a project with a Planning Game, followed directly by Iteration Planning (see Chapter 12).

Fundamentally, the customer is responsible for making the business decision, no matter what. Do not compromise on this, but there is a lot of room for variation in how this happens. Whether the customer does all of the talking, writing, and describing is less important than whether the customer makes the final call about when the developer implements the story, and the details of when the implementation is acceptable.

Each customer has strengths and weaknesses. Some customers are better than others at expressing stories. Some express stories in excruciating detail, and some are more comfortable giving a very vague description and letting the developer figure out all the details. Sometimes the developer knows the domain better than the customer. Sometimes the customer represents an existing installed base of end users, and sometimes the customer has only a hypothetical end user.

To help your customers learn their role and understand the purpose of the dialogue, focus on getting the stories (or even just a good name for the story) on cards and having the customer prioritize them. This gives the customer practice in specifying what the system is supposed to do and in prioritizing business value for the developer. When the developer asks for clarification on something, the customer gets practice in refining stories. These exercises force customers to learn how to talk to developers honestly as partners.

Customers are certainly allowed to ask questions about estimates that seem out of line, but they should refrain from questioning all estimates. The customer can respectfully ask why a particular story would be so difficult to implement. The answer and resulting dialogue can clear up misunderstanding and even suggest a simpler approach. But in general the customer should trust that the estimation process will be self-policing over time, and that developers generally don't pad estimates. When the developer tells the customer that something has to fall off the plate in order to satisfy the customer-established priority of stories, the customer has to tell him what falls off; there can't be any bickering. No fair "holding their feet to the fire" to get more in less time. That's against the rules. It's also unrealistic.

Finally, to make the customer role work well the "gold owner" and the "goal donor" must be lined up completely. The "gold owner" is the one who is paying for the development. The "goal donor" is the entity defining the stories. In a perfect world, these are the same person. In the real world they rarely are. Getting the gold owner and the goal donor to agree on project direction, priorities, and resources is sometimes the most challenging part of software development. We aren't always successful at this and you won't be either, but expect problems if the gold owner and goal donor are not "lined up."

The Developer

The developer is responsible for two things:

1. Making the best possible estimates so that the customer can make the best possible business decisions
2. Delivering functionality that reliably meets the requirements implied by the most important stories to date

The developer is *not* responsible for using the latest technology possible, or delivering on the second most important stories. The developer *is* responsible for informing the customer of the impact that taking shortcuts might have on future stories.

The developer must learn enough about what the user is asking for to estimate the time it will take to implement, possibly in qualified form. The developer may not feel comfortable making an estimate, but he must at least come up with a ballpark number. If estimating is especially hard, the developer should ask for a *short* period of time to explore and return with an estimate. Many customers don't like estimates greater than a few days. If the customer doesn't like the estimate, the dialogue continues, it doesn't stop. This is *not* a take-it or leave-it situation, at least not yet.

When a customer does not like an estimate it is usually for one of two reasons:

⟡ The customer thinks the value of a fulfilled story is not worth the cost. Perhaps the story is less important than initially indicated, or a simpler version of the story may provide most of the value at a fraction of the cost.

⟡ The customer does not realize the complicated nature of the story or the impact doing it quick and dirty will have on other parts of the system. This is an opportunity for education. The developer should offer to explain to the customer (off-line, if there's a crowd) what has to be done to implement the story. Often, the developer can just pick the one or two of the trickiest things to explain. The customer may recognize the complexity or decide that the developer has a better handle on it. Sometimes, when the developer is explaining why a story is difficult, the developer may even realize he was overcomplicating things.

A developer cannot assume a given feature is necessary unless the customer says it is. If the customer doesn't put it on a card and prioritize it, it doesn't exist. If the developer doesn't understand a requirement, he should ask the customer. If a developer has spare time, he should ask the customer what to work on next. If the developer runs out of time, he should ask the customer what to defer. When in doubt, ask the customer. Then follow instructions.

If the developer sees a hole in the customer's thought process, he should simply point it out as politely as possible and then discuss it. After all the issues are laid out, the customer might disagree. The developer should recognize that if the customer is wrong, the topic will probably come up again. This is not the time to start a battle—there are stories to address.

A Tool to Introduce Reality

Everybody needs at least one CASE tool. The best CASE tool is found at office supply stores everywhere and it comes in a variety of sizes, colors, and designs. Cardboard-assisted software engineering (CASE)[2] is done with a stack of index cards. The resulting product may not look as polished as the pretty diagrams produced by your favorite software-backed tool, but the positive effect it can have on your project is quite remarkable. Index cards, when used correctly by a trained professional, have the power to make both business and technical people face reality. It does not have the power to make them *like* reality or deal with it rationally, it just makes them face it.

Reducing Chaos with Cards
by Ken Auer

The client was under a lot of pressure to raise its next round of capital from venture capitalists. They only had a few months worth of money remaining. It seemed pretty obvious to the founder and to me that the framework I was working on for them was the foundation of the client's long-term future.

In the first few weeks of my engagement at the company, my task was to learn the prototyped version of the framework and some of the technologies it was exploiting as well as to recommend where they should go with it. After doing so and spending time in discussion with the founder I could see that the framework needed to be tightened up. The principals agreed to this, and the direction had been somewhat clearly set before they left for a three-week trip to California for a series of shows, sales calls, and fund-raising efforts. It was agreed that I would work with Duff in XP fashion while they were gone.

---

2. Thanks to Keith Braithwaite at the Extreme Tuesday Club for this acronym.

Those three weeks were considered Iteration 1 even though the client didn't call it that. We had to create our own stories based on what the client had said before leaving, and we broke the stories down into small tasks (at the time, we were confused over the difference between a story and a task). We made great progress, and it was clear that the footings for the foundation were laid. Not only had we accomplished a tremendous amount in those three weeks, but we had gotten quite good (relative to where we started) at XP. We had broken down the stories into very small tasks and estimated them before we started them. We paid attention to how well we estimated and were getting pretty good. And we had a lot of candidate stories to share with the customer that we felt would be needed to finish the foundation in the next few iterations.

So, even though this wasn't full XP, things worked relatively well. Stories basically came from the customer, gathered over several weeks. We had estimated that in three weeks we could demonstrate the stories, and we made the technical decisions necessary to implement them. Looking back, the problems that happened next were fundamentally caused by an unclear distinction between business and technical decisions, poor communication, and falling away from the process.

The principals came back from California and were ready to meet a few days later. By this time, Duff and I were ready to propose doing XP exclusively until we got proof that we shouldn't. The principals were thrilled with what we produced, but felt we'd be better off working on our tasks by ourselves, because they "couldn't afford to pay two developers to do one thing—it's just not realistic."

We accepted this for a while, but three problems became obvious very shortly. First, we saw our quality going down and our work getting harder to sync up. Second, communication with the principals kept getting worse. They usually just gave us directives to add things or change things. When I asked for clarification, I usually just got more directives. Third, scope was all over the place and the system was changing out from under everybody. The principals were still doing some development at the time, and they were making changes in the wee hours of the morning. We pointed them to the documentation they had insisted I produce, but suggested that pairing might be a better way to go. They responded by getting upset, reminding us that they had said no to pairing before. They also warned me to watch my hours, because money was getting tight.

It was pretty frustrating. After three to four weeks of increasingly poor communication, I came up with a plan. We would make cards. I put everything I was asked to do on index cards in the smallest chunks I could imagine and estimated each one in days to complete. Most of the numbers ranged from half a day to two days. The ones I wasn't clear on due to some ambiguity had significant question marks next to the number. I had between 40 and 50 cards. Duff started making his own set of cards.

At about the same time, the principals said that they could only commit to about 200 more hours of work. I took advantage of the opportunity. I told them, "I appreciate your limited funds and would like to be sure you get the best out of these 200 hours. I've been writing down all of the things you've asked me to do and it adds up to a lot more than that. Can we get together sometime in the next couple of days for an hour or two after normal business hours to prioritize the tasks? That way we'll both know exactly what we are expecting and aren't expecting." They agreed.

The meeting started out pretty amicably. Duff and I provided the cards. I explained that each card just had a sentence or two about each thing we had been asked to do, and explained the numbers. I said that estimates didn't include any time for communication with them or any other "overhead," so they might want to multiply by a fudge factor of 2 or so to figure out how much we could actually get done. I asked them to sort out the higher priority items first to narrow down the list, and then prioritize those.

The poor principals, who were already overwhelmed trying to keep the business running while trying to raise funding, were even more overwhelmed. After weeding out cards that weren't urgent, they still had about 40 cards to sort out, most of which they felt had to be done in the next two months or sooner. We worked through the ones with question marks, attempting to clarify what was being asked for. Often it was simple. Sometimes they needed more time to think about it. Occasionally our estimates were challenged. On one or two occasions it got ugly.

The bottom line was that, in a few hours, we had a plan that everyone agreed to. Some tasks had been reassigned. We also had a few action items. One of the principals would keep a master list of the tasks, and if others were added, they would have to say explicitly where that task fit in the list of items and what would slip out.

We wish we could say that communication immediately improved, that XP got accepted, and that we all lived happily ever after. It didn't happen that way. However, for the next two months, everybody did a pretty good job of living in reality, whether they were happy about it or not. We did well at hitting our estimates, and the principals acknowledged that as a good thing.

About a year later, the founder called me up and asked forgiveness for how he had treated me. He shared that the work we had done, especially the work Duff and I did together, had stood the test of time, and he had grown to appreciate it more and more. Did they become an XP shop? No. But they hired us to do some more work and didn't have an issue with us doing it in XP fashion.

Those little cards are pretty powerful when a team of people who aren't communicating well employ them. It turns out this is true even on a larger scale, when communication isn't bad. Getting stories on cards and having customer and developers talk about them can work wonders. In our experience, it certainly produces better results than any formal requirements document does.

Verifying a Release Date
by Ken Auer

At a large XP client, we realized over time that there was a disconnect between the goal owner and the gold donor. The development team's management owned the budget, but the requirements were coming from a marketing organization. They identified a single person to play the customer. They were excited about being able to "steer," and we made sure that she knew that each new turn might come with an additional cost. The problem was that they lost track of reality. We had to get them back. We used cards to do it.

We released our iterations internally. At the end of each iteration, we reviewed what we had and planned the next iteration. People liked progress, but the demonstration of what we did often generated new ideas that weren't really in the original plan. The customer would ask for something new and we'd give them an estimate. Most of the time they would say, "OK, it's worth N days." Sometimes the new stories shifted out an entire iteration. All of the old stories were kept around, but nobody was really checking whether they were still necessary, or whether the estimates on them were accurate or not. After a while, it was clear that we weren't going to hit our initial date, and a little heat was coming from the gold owner.

We pointed out how many new things had gotten into the iterations. No one from the marketing side seemed to be that concerned about an end date. We asked management, "Is there a date we need to target for shipment of Release 1.0, or do we keep on adding everything they ask for until they stop asking?" Although there had been no firm commitment to the market yet, the gold owner did feel that they should set a target date and stop spending more than they needed to. After a pow-wow with marketing management, we heard "March 2001." All we needed to do was re-sort all of the stories and figure out what went in the release.

We planned several days for the big "recommitment meeting," and got it scheduled. Beforehand, the customer and the project manager went through the list of stories to make sure they were all still relevant and to add stories that hadn't been captured. On the first day of the recommitment meeting, we went through the stack of story cards to make sure everyone understood the point of each story. People asked questions when they had them, but many stories passed without explanation. For about a fifth of the stories, someone would recognize an inconsistency with a previous story or an overlap. Every once in a while, we added a new one because of issues that were raised. After the better part of the day, we felt we had a pretty comprehensive list of remaining stories, over 200 of them. It was clear that we wouldn't get all of them done in the three or four iterations we had before we had to get it to system test (the highly regulated environment made this hand-off nonnegotiable). Time to prioritize.

We started at the top of the pile again and asked the customer to categorize the stories as "high" (we didn't have a marketable product without this), "medium" (a significant portion of the market wouldn't buy the product without this), or "low" (nice to have). She could ask for clarification to help her make her choice or break the stories up into parts. For example, we had a "user must be able to configure the system" story. It was clear that this was a high, but we could get by with allowing the user to configure only a couple of pieces of the system necessary for it to physically work in the user's environment (a smaller story). Then we'd make the remaining things the user might want to configure a new low priority story.

If the categorization the customer made didn't make sense to someone on the development team, the developer could challenge it. It was possible that the development team didn't understand it, or the customer had a different picture of what it meant than the developer did, or that the customer wasn't thinking clearly. After a challenge and the ensuing discussion, the customer still had the final word about what category the story was in. This took the better part of another day.

At the end, the project manager said, "Okay, now we estimate." I interrupted with, "May I make an observation? We could certainly pass these cards around and estimate each one of them in small groups, but I think there is something important we should not ignore before we do that. I'm holding about 50 high-priority cards in my hand. We've all heard what they are, and there are very few one- or two-day stories in here. Let's say that the average story size in here is six days, which I think might be conservative but is probably in the right ballpark. Do you all agree?" Everybody nodded or gave some other form of affirmation. "So, if it's in the right ballpark, we're talking about 300 days worth of stories. Over the last few iterations, we've been pretty consistently hitting around 50 days per iteration. Therefore, the chances are slim to none that we can hit the target date even if we only stick to the highs."

The project manager asked, "So, are you saying we shouldn't estimate them?" "No," I responded, "I'm saying that we shouldn't fool ourselves into thinking that there is any way that target date is realistic, especially since we've already been told we can't add any more resources to the project. And I've heard the customer say that she didn't want to settle for just the highs in release one but wanted to get at least a good chunk of the mediums before it got out there."

There was a lot more ensuing discussion. The point is that there were some people living in a fantasy world, or at least hoping that the reality wouldn't unfold. Once they had the stack of cards in front of them, they were all living in the same reality. The goal donor and the gold owner were forced to realign. The date was shifted out a few months. As I write this, we are pretty close to the new date and have just about all of the committed stories completed.

How the Roles Work with Multiple Projects

Some folks work in an environment where software isn't neatly divided into software projects, each of which has its own team. Instead, they have a suite of products that are often customized for their end users. The software team is expected to meet the various project life cycle demands (prototyping, maintenance, development, etc.) of multiple projects simultaneously. There is probably no single individual who can prioritize, in detail, the cross-project demands.

Individuals who work for such companies are all too familiar with the "feudal state" environment that occurs as different project managers compete for the software group's resources. In this environment, how might an XP group of programmers help its company see the value of XP practices? How could it run the Planning Game, where the business role, a role outside of the software department, becomes prominent?

You might imagine that the roles would break down in this case. With multiple customers making demands on developers, there's no way the developers can sort things out and give everybody what they want. That's the point. Developers cannot sort things out. The multiple customers have to. XP says that the customer on a software project has to speak with "one voice"—it doesn't say there must be only one customer.

If multiple customers are making demands on the same developers, the customers have to get together to sort out their demands. Not everybody can get everything he wants—the developers can do only so much in the next iteration. There has to be some compromise. The customers have to talk together, negotiate, and come to a common conclusion they all agree with. Perhaps each customer gets a number of votes and you schedule the cards with the most votes in the next iteration.

There may be other approaches. Use your imagination. But whatever approach you use must be consistent with the roles we've described in this chapter. That's the guiding principle.

The Senate Game
by Travis Griggs

It's Thursday morning. Planning Game day. Got some work to do this morning. I fire up the trusty old Web browser. Navigate to the Wiki, the story card section. There—down at the bottom of the page—is that story card one of the service techs told me they were going to put up. Click. Well . . . there's a little bit of a story there. We'll go have a talk with the service tech.

I'm in the service tech's office now. Cooter's his name. I talk to Cooter for a while. We discuss his terse request for more features. Ah . . . I discover what it is he really wants. We talk a bit more. I make a suggestion. "If we add a button that does such and such, will that satisfy the customer?" Yes. Cooter likes that idea. So do I—it's testable. Back to the pen (bull, that is) and my trusty Web browser.

The Wiki page gets edited. The story is a little more complete now. I add a list of tasks. I note that the pair coding across the pen could probably service an interrupt from me, so I butt in. They pull out their trusty Web browsers ("Have Browser Will Travel"?). We talk a bit about the card. We kick around some estimates and arrive at one. Edit the page again with the estimates (time and risk).

Time to roust the troops. I rip off an e-mail to prospective game players reminding them that today is the day. I offer to rotate out with one of the pair for a while. We enter programmer bliss of actually coding for a bit.

I feel a bit drowsy from lunch, but I've got things to do! I have to print all of the story cards. I print them in order from the last Planning Game's priorities. There are two new cards, too. Then I update the executive summary. It's a condensed synopsis of all of the story cards. I print 10 or more copies. I grab the goodies I brought in. I reach for the software shelf—timer and poker chips . . . .

It's two o'clock now. Planning Game time! A typical conference room with chairs around a long table. The software geeks and boss are here. Here come the various product managers. Then the service entourage (their boss, the guy who answers the phones, and the trainer). The applications guy flops down in his chair. Who are we missing? One of our super-techs. Quick dash down the hall; he's on the phone, but he'll be along ASAP. Back to the room.

Start already! I call them to attention. We welcome them, invite them to eat some goodies. I recount our experiences of the last two weeks, including having finished one of the story cards. A question about the final implementation is asked. One of the other software geeks pipes up and gives an answer.

We have two other story cards that we're actively working on. I give a little status for each. One's almost done. The other's about half way. I explain (vaguely) a compromise that we had to make in the implementation of the second. We had checked with the card originator; everybody else seems to be okay with this.

We go to the next phase. The room grows quieter. The players are reading through their summaries, refamiliarizing themselves with all of the cards (there are about 30). Occasionally a muted request for a full card is made; it's dug out of the pile and passed on. Mumbled conversations are starting around the room; looks like everybody's up to speed.

Now, each player gets a chance to say their piece about the current set of story cards, which ones they think are important and why. I ask for a volunteer to start. The service boss goes first. I start the timer. He soliloquizes for a bit. He finishes before the timer goes off. We proceed around the room. Only once does the timer reduce one of them to sputtering and begging for more time. We do not acquiesce.

Now comes the real meat. The story cards have been laid out on the table, in order from last time's prioritization so that they match the flow of the summary. Each player is given a stack of poker chips. The players stand up, all of the chairs are pushed back, voting begins. Each player roams around the table, dropping a chip on this card, another on that card, quite a few on another card, indicating which cards they would like to see get immediate attention. Eventually, each player has spent his wad. We're almost done.

The chips per card are tallied. The cards are sorted. The top six or so are written up on the whiteboard. We adjourn. I'm almost done now. The master Wiki page is updated to show the new priorities. An e-mail goes out to all players (both those that came today and other interested parties). It summarizes the new priorities, as well as movement of cards relative to the last game. Back to bliss. I offer my services to one of the other software geeks; we go write some tests.

At first the Senate Game went really well. People enjoy making a game out of their work, doing something new. The software team received rave reviews around the company; formerly they had received the opposite. All four XP values were in play. The idea was new and brave. The meeting format and goals were simple. A lot more communication was happening between all parties. Business people were getting feedback on their desired features.

Over time though, the process began to degrade. People became bored with the game and began quibbling about the details (how many chips they got, how they could be used, etc.). As disillusionment set in, the mood became dismal. The senate game moved from being everybody's favorite to one that all dreaded. Ultimately, it was suspended.

Was the Senate Game a failure? No and yes. The Senate Game is about communication. It is an attempt to get the business counterparts to do more of it. That's always a good thing. However, the senate game is just a means to an end, a catalyst.

Where we failed was in allowing the Senate Game (the means) to become the center of attention. Ultimately, you want to separate your team of software programmers from having to make decisions about which card to do next. Ideally, it would have been an XP-minded customer who would have seen the need for and started something like the Senate Game. But in this case, the software team attempted to jump-start the process for them. We failed because we did not extricate ourselves from the process (after it was demonstrating success) and let the process evolve to better meet the business needs. Not doing so prevented the business states from ever really taking ownership of the goal.

When Roles Are Clear

So far, we've talked about the cards getting people to face reality in the middle of a project and the importance of people being true to their roles. When the roles are clear and you are just starting out it may work differently.

If everybody understands their roles and has realistic expectations about how planning works, you can concentrate on talking about the system features that the customer needs. You can move past arguing about unrealistic expectations. When you reach this point, you can produce some amazing results in a very short time.

Bigger and Quicker Than Expected
by Ken Auer

A long-term RoleModel client had previously used us mostly for prototypes and sanity checks while they were exploring entering some completely new markets in the healthcare industry. They had spent a long time exploring a lot of different angles to entering the new market. It was tough to wait while we were all confident that the longer they waited to start something, the better the chances that someone else would beat them to it. Finally, one day the phone rang.

"Ken, I think we might finally be ready to go forward. Can we spend some time talking about what we want to do and come up with a plan to get there?" I responded, "I've been waiting for this long enough. I'll make it work. Thursday is the only day I could do it this week. If that doesn't work, we can try to juggle my schedule next week." He answered, "I'd really like to get going on this. I can meet you Thursday afternoon. At least we can get started. Even if we don't finish it, we'll at least have a better feel for it."

The setting was perfect: The client and me at the studio with others to draw on if necessary, and a $1 shrink-wrapped CASE tool.

I cut open the tool and gave the client a 15-minute training course in the Planning Game and in using the CASE tool. The client said, "I think I get it, but I'm not sure what kinds of things you want me to write on the cards or what granularity of detail you want me to write down." I said, "I'll tell you what. Why don't you start by describing the things you want the system to do. I'll take notes by writing stuff on the cards and ask you for clarification as we go."

In the next couple of hours, we talked and recorded about 40 cards. I then asked him to prioritize. Then I attempted to put ballpark estimates on them. Asking for some clarification on some of the stories, I quickly realized that some would take quite a while, so I asked how they might be broken down further into "minimum necessary functionality to demonstrate the capability," "functionality necessary to really add value," and "nice to have." I could put rough estimates on most of them, but there were a lot of questions about the possible user interface approach.

So I called a couple of the other guys in and we discussed some user interface issues. The client seemed to want a Web interface. We discussed a couple of approaches to that and raised some performance concerns due to the environment he expected the users to be working in—on the go with a basic portable and intermittent connection, often via a phone line.

We ended up with about 60 cards with numbers on them, a few of which were big unknowns. We adjusted for the big unknowns by adding a couple of eight-craft unit (similar to an "ideal engineering day" from *Extreme Programming Explained*) cards that said "revisit X," since we suspected that the first thing we tried would not be sufficient but would uncover issues. I asked him how fast he would want to move in terms of how much they could spend per month. He said, "I'm not sure, but let's go with $X/month". "Okay, how long do you want each iteration to be: two, three, or four weeks?" "Let's go with four. You know our company. There's no way we could respond to something you produce any faster than that."

"Okay. That means you get 12 craft units per iteration. The numbers are on the cards. Start with Iteration 1 and pick the cards you'd like to tackle first. Once you've got 12 craft units, start Iteration 2, and so on."

In about 15 minutes, he had 13 piles (the thirteenth being only partially full). Based on some of the things he had deferred in our earlier discussion, I told him that he might want to be conservative and assume the whole thing would take 18 months at that pace. He could shorten it by picking up the pace, but he probably couldn't make it under 12 months without losing a lot of efficiency if he could get it shorter than that at all.

The client said, "Wow. This is a lot bigger project than I thought. And you are pretty confident in your numbers?"

I responded, "As sure as I can be without getting into a lot more detail. Based on my experience, I'd say we're not off any more than 50% to get something out that does all that you've asked for in some way. That's why I suggested figuring 18 months, even though we have just over 12 iterations here. But let's face it, we're just guessing at what this is really going to look like. We should probably work on the first two or three iterations and we'll have a much better clue."

"Would what we put in those first three piles be enough for you to show it to someone and get some real feedback?"

The client enthusiastically responded, "Yeah. I'm pretty sure it would. I'm pretty excited about that. I was hoping we could get something to show people in three months, but I was doubtful that it would be possible. That's really good. It might make the whole project easier to swallow if they know that they can have something to shop around in three months."

I asked, "Okay, where do we go from here? (Tongue firmly planted in cheek.) Can we start Monday?"

The client chuckled, "I wish. But I think I have enough to go on to present this to some people next week. Let me write down the stories and the time frames. I'll turn it into something more polished and present it to some senior management people. I was real impressed with this process, but I don't think they'll give me that much money if I come into their office with nothing but a handful of cards."

I said, "Go figure."

He chuckled again. "But really. I can't imagine any other process I've seen giving me this much information in this short amount of time. It's pretty powerful."

I agreed. "Yeah. It's powerful because it's simple and there are no smoke or mirrors involved."

By the way, they still haven't gotten the funding for that project, but they were back the next month to scope out a different project in half a day. They learned a lot from that one, too.

The Xtreme Hour

Several years ago, Peter Merel came up with the concept of the Extreme Hour. The idea was to get people to experience many of the concepts of XP in a way that tied all those concepts together. The original version of the Extreme Hour was posted at http://c2.com/cgi/wiki?ExtremeHour. Many people have used it since at various events and with their own variations.

You can do this with people whose natural roles are business or technical, or a combination. The ideal seems to be a mix, with the business people playing the role of development and the technical people playing the role of business. That way they get to walk an hour in each other's shoes. The point is usually made whether you mix them up this way or not.

At the end, ask them what they've learned. Here is what a VP of IT operations at a large multinational bank told Ken:

> *I learned how important it is to have more collaboration and to spend more time communicating. I also learned that when I ask for something, I should specify testing parameters whenever possible. In an environment like this, I can clearly see the confusion that vague requirements cause and how hard it is at times to figure out how to do something even when the requirements are clear. It has to work with all of the other requirements, and often they seem to be contradictory or at least difficult to implement such that both requirements are met.*

Would you like to hear someone in your management chain say something like that? Ask them if they've got an hour or two to learn about the development process.

Running the Extreme Hour
by Ken Auer

Recently, we've been making pretty good use of the Extreme Hour at Role-Model Software. We've modified it from its original form slightly, but it fundamentally is the same.

First we divide the participants into groups of 6 to 10 people. One group plays the role of the development team, and one plays the role of the business team. We (RoleModel) monitor the clock and play the role of the market. Each group is tasked with building a product from concept to delivery in one hour. (Really they just deliver a picture of the product in one hour). We ask them to build a robot lawnmower that will "define and dominate the high-end retail sector of the automated grass-cutting market." At the end of the hour, the teams try to sell their product to the market at a lawn and garden show. If the business team is smart, they will ask questions of the market sometime during the hour.

We then tell the teams they have one hour to plan, schedule, develop, and quality assure the initial release of the product. The hour is broken up as follows:

10 Minutes—User Stories and Architectural Spike

The business side splits into stakeholders and QA. As the stakeholders write the story on an index card, the QA people write at least one test (on the back of the card) to determine whether the story is implemented acceptably. For example, if the story says, "must cope with obstacles," a corresponding test might be, "We put a soccer ball on the lawn. Can it mow the grass underneath without damaging the soccer ball?"

In the meantime, the development team explores the technology and develops an "architectural spike," experimenting with ideas that might work and estimating. Basically, they draw a prototype of a robot lawnmower without knowing the detailed requirements. If they are smart, they'll pay attention to how long it takes them to draw certain features.

10 Minutes—Estimate Priority and Scope

Stakeholders sort stories into three piles: must have, costly to lose, nice to have. They begin a discussion with the development team and QA, describing the stories and tests, which are probably not all completed yet. The development team then estimates the amount of time in craft minutes they think each story will take, starting with the must haves. If they think a story will take more than 10 minutes to implement (usually because it is too vague, like "must be attractive"), they can ask that the story be broken down into smaller parts or clarified. At the end of the 10 minutes, they should at least have a guess at most of the stories.

5 Minutes—Initial Commitment Schedule

The development team commits to a number of craft minutes per iteration. They are told that all development must be done in pairs—the other developer will help make sure the development doesn't break other parts of the system—and are given a hint to consider using a load factor of 3. If they have four developers, that means they have 40 potential individual minutes, and 40 ÷ 3 yields approximately 13 craft minutes that they could confidently deliver in an iteration.

The business team then defines two iterations worth of stories based on estimates. QA may come up with additional tests during this time. They must know by the end of the 5 minutes what they expect to work on and shoot to deliver in Iteration 1.

10 Minutes—Iteration 1

The developers determine whether stories can and/or need to be split into multiple tasks. Individuals take tasks and find a pair to help them draw the response to the story or task on the master picture. QA people determine when each pair has passed the test(s). In the meantime, the stakeholders may talk to the market or otherwise create additional stories and be available for questions. Note that as developers add to the master drawing, they may have to refactor some of the old features to make the new features fit. If they do, the old acceptance tests need to be reverified.

5 Minutes—Iteration 2 Planning

The entire team examines what developers really got done in Iteration 1 and adjusts expected velocity (how many craft minutes actually are expected to be completed) based on recent history. The business team redefines what should be in Iteration 2. The developers can adjust estimates based on their experience and changes made by the business side. QA may use this time to add missing acceptance tests. At the end of the planning meeting, the development team needs to know what to work on and the business team needs to know what to expect.

10 Minutes—Iteration 2

The developers determine whether the stories can or need to be split into multiple tasks. Individuals take tasks and find a pair to help them draw the response to the story or task on the master picture. QA people determine when the drawing has passed the test(s). In the meantime, the stakeholders may talk to the market or otherwise create additional stories and be available for questions. Note that as developers add to the master drawing, they may have to refactor some of the old features to make the new features fit. If they do, the old acceptance tests need to be reverified.

Business can start thinking about how to present their expected product at the upcoming show.

5 Minutes—Release and New Commitment Schedule

The business team determines whether they have an external release. Is it marketable? Assuming it is, they prepare for the big show and determine what they might want to advertise as coming in future releases, based on estimates of remaining stories and projected velocity if development continued.

The Big Show

Assuming there is time, the market sees the exhibit of each group and determines whether it will buy any of the products. We usually play the role of a skeptical buyer who questions every claim. If QA did a good job, something usually sells.

Chapter 11

Project Planning

*Vision without action is a daydream; action
without vision is a nightmare.*

—Japanese Proverb

*Just because we won't know everything ahead of time doesn't mean we
should blindly start in a direction without a clue where we're going or how
long it will take us to get there. We will get better by refining things. To do
that, we have to have something to refine. So we plan and estimate quickly,
and then get busy reducing our risk by taking action.*

Without a direction, you can't begin to implement XP. If you don't plan, you
will have no idea what to code today, or tomorrow, or next week.[1] That means
the programming piece of XP won't matter. A great system metaphor (or any of
the other practices we talk about in Part III) without a roadmap for making it
real is worth about as much as sock lint.

It would be foolish to begin a trip without having an idea of how long it
will take and what roads will get you there. It would be almost as crazy to take
two hours to chart your course for a one hour trip. It might not be so crazy to
take two hours to chart a course for a trip across the United States. For most
trips it makes sense to take just enough time to chart out a reasonable course,
take a map with you in case you need to determine an alternate route, determine a reasonable starting time and a best guess at an ending time, then get in
your car and go. You never can know for sure when you start driving whether

---

1. For more on this, see K. Beck, M. Fowler. *Planning Extreme Programming*. Addison-
   Wesley, 2001.

you will actually arrive at your destination at the appointed time (or at all). But the risk seems reasonable, so you go.

Planning a project is like charting a course. We really don't know exactly how long each leg of the journey will take or when we'll hit annoying detours or opportune stops, but we have a rough idea. If something causes us to vary significantly from our original course we may decide to come up with a new course for the last few legs of the trip.

The rest of XP is like driving a car along the charted course. We make small adjustments to keep ourselves on the road, and we do this even if we are a little behind or ahead of schedule. When it's clear we're significantly ahead or behind schedule, we call ahead and let the person waiting for us know. If we're behind, the person waiting might tell us not to bother finishing the trip or tell us to ignore a stop along the way or suggest a short cut or agree to meet us part way. If we're ahead of schedule, the person waiting might ask us to pick up something else along the way, slow down and relax, or encourage us to arrive early. If, after driving a while, it doesn't seem the course we chose is going to get us to our destination in a timely fashion, we might pull off the road, check the map, and come up with an adjusted course.

Charting the Course

When we drive in the United States we tend to rely on maps and roads, especially for long distances. It's not too hard to chart a course from a known starting point to a known ending point. With a few simple rules, you can plan a course, estimate a time, and hit your estimate within 10% to 20%, barring major catastrophes. If you have a reliable car, it's just not that hard to get to the destination in a predictable manner. If you have made the trip before, your margin of error will go way down.

A few years ago, Ken had the pleasure of going to West Bengal, India. Predicting anything there was difficult. Traffic jams would occur at any time for all sorts of reasons, especially in Calcutta, where it was often more efficient to walk. Most vehicles were unreliable. Punctuality was virtually nonexistent. If Ken was told his escort would pick him up at a certain time, there was a good chance that the escort would show up two hours later.

One day, Ken was to take a trip to a remote village, "several hours northwest of Calcutta." He didn't have to chart the course because his escort had it all under control, at least as under control as things could be in that part of India. The escort had never been to that particular village before but had lived in West Bengal quite a long time. There was nothing to be concerned about.

When they finally left their place of origin, the trip was a nonstop series of unpredictabilities. Cows blocked roads. Torrential rains had created small ponds in the middle of the major thoroughfares. The major thoroughfares were often barely wide enough for a single car, yet traffic moved in both directions. In the middle of one town along the way, elections were being held and the communist military in the region were all over the place as well as seemingly everyone who lived in or near the town. (Ken's still not sure whether the military was trying to create or control the chaos.)

There were no roadmaps. At most intersections, which were frequent and in somewhat random patterns, there were no street signs. The driver would call out to whomever he saw on the street and ask which direction he should go until at least two people confidently pointed him in the same direction. This sometimes took a while. Sometimes, one or more of them would get in the car for a distance. About 15 minutes of the total travel time was moving at a comfortable speed on a relatively smooth road. The rest of the time they were either stopped or bouncing in the car.

Most significant software projects are more like a trip through West Bengal than a trip to a known address in the United States. You still need to chart a course, but don't fool yourself into thinking that the trip won't be filled with unpredictabilities. Be ready to make constant adjustments along the way.

You'll always be wrong about the future, even if you get the major events right. Unfortunately, you're measured on how close to right about the future you were. The further off you are, the more trouble you'll be in with those who are doing the measuring. There is no way to fix this situation. The only thing you can do is go with what you know for sure:

- Time keeps moving, so you can predict that a particular date will arrive in a certain number of calendar days.
- Before that date arrives, if everyone involved agrees to dedicate a certain number of days to a particular set of tasks designed to solve a problem, you can make progress toward the goal.
- If you don't apply effort toward achieving the goal, you won't be any closer to it by the time the date arrives.

So chart a course. Reality won't ever match your course exactly, so don't spend too much time on it. Specify the target, estimate the effort, then execute the effort. At every major intersection, check your time and double check that you are still going in the right direction. Determine whether there is a smoother road you can take.

As you travel, take notes regarding how well you move during the unpredictabilities. Explore what you can do to predict them better and navigate them more successfully. Identify the patterns so you can leverage your experience next time you see one. This is common sense, but we've noticed it isn't that common. "Ready! Fire! Aim!" isn't as backwards as it sounds.

When you plan a trip, you need a map and a feel for how fast you can travel over various roads. Then you identify and estimate each leg of the trip. If there are legs of the trip you've never traveled before, it might be wise to do a little more research on them. If you don't, you can simply identify them as high-risk parts of the trip and take your chances.

When you plan a project, you do the same thing. The map and the "feel for how fast you can go" is the data in the customer's and developers' heads. Use the Planning Game to identify and estimate each leg of the trip (the stories). If some stories make you uncomfortable, it might be wise to do a little more research on them. Alternatively, you can just make your best guess and take your chances—that's a business decision.

We have found the best way to plan a project is in three parts:

1. An Initial Planning Game
2. An Exploration Phase
3. A Release Planning Game

The Planning Game

The Planning Game is the key technique we use to create a project plan. One of the refreshing things about XP is that it isn't unnecessarily formal. Planning is a back-to-basics affair. If the name "Planning Game" sounds too informal, call it something different. RoleModel's marketing literature calls it a Project Planning Workshop. Call it what you want; it's the first tool we use to plan a project, and we may use it several times thereafter to refine the plan.

There are really only a few differences between an Initial Planning Game and a Release Planning Game:

❖ The Initial Planning Game is often used before the development team has been identified and assembled. A single customer and single developer can do this, although having extra help is a good idea, too. In the Release Planning Game, all of identified developers and customer representatives should be there.

✧ The Initial Planning Game should be done as soon as possible, in the gestation period of a project, when it is still just an idea waiting to become a project. The Release Planning Game should happen after you have explored enough to be able to chart a course in which you can feel somewhat confident and have all the resources available to begin the course immediately.

Other than that, the amount of attention you pay to detail is the only real difference.

In a Planning Game the customer(s) and the developer(s) sit in a room together. All you need are some pens and some note cards. Since a lot of communication has to happen, whiteboards and markers are good to have, too. Then the game begins. It proceeds very simply:

1. The customer writes stories on note cards.
2. The developer puts estimates on each of the cards in some unit of measurement.
3. Based on some predetermined level of resources, the developer identifies approximately how many units of measurement (M) can be completed in each N-week iteration (where N is typically between one and four, inclusive).
4. Customers sort the cards into piles of M units or fewer, in the order they'd like to see them implemented.

That's the basic description. You can find more detailed descriptions in other books. It's so simple even a child can do it; unless of course you are trying to do something that is real and people are measured by how well they execute. Then it's a little more complicated. The practical details behind each step follow.

The Customer Writes Stories

The customer starts talking about what the system needs to do. Somewhere along the line, it is good to get the stories on a card. Sometimes a lot of stuff happens on whiteboards or other media before a story takes shape.

What's the difference between a story, a use case, a functional requirement, a system goal, or anything else that will lead to work? We've heard many descriptions of the differences, some from people who have never been on an XP project. As we've seen it applied effectively, we can confidently define a story as: *The simplest thing that can possibly work to make everyone in the room agree that they have a placeholder for something that needs to be done.*

Officially, customers write stories on cards. In reality, it doesn't ruin the game if someone else *writes* the cards, especially at first. If the customers are not comfortable writing the cards for whatever reason, you can help them get over their fear. Often writing something down feels too much like committing to it, and no one wants to do this prematurely. The thought process goes something like this: "Nobody used to see what I wrote until I wordsmithed it and was pretty confident. I don't want to put something so vague on an index card. Somebody might hold me accountable to their interpretation of it and say that it came from me." Cards in someone else's handwriting feel safer. The comfort level seems to change over time. Some developers we know have learned to move the pile of blank cards and pen simply closer and closer to the customer until, one day, the customer writes a card.

On the other hand, it's vitally important that the customer *owns* the cards. Before the end of the game, the customer will have to sort the cards out. If the customer doesn't like what's on the card it doesn't have to be included in the plan. He can make another one. So how the cards get captured is not important; what cards you end up with is.

Stories may also be captured in some electronic form(s). Do this if it provides value. It provides value if it reduces the stress of someone in the room, especially when first getting started. It may also provide value later when people leave the room and would like to look at the cards or present them to someone who isn't used to their simple beauty. But when we are charting the course, there is nothing that can replace the cards. Create cards even if you only use them in the Planning Game. There is probably very little value in capturing them in electronic form before the game is over. There may be tremendous value in agreeing to capture them in electronic form as soon as the issue is raised.

Concerns about only having cards are raised out of a possibly justifiable fear of the unknown. Over time, as people become more comfortable with the cards, you should question whether you need to continue capturing them electronically. How have the electronic versions been used? In those uses, would using cards have been better? The answer should become obvious and will not be the same for all. The electronic version will not be more useful when you are initially sorting things out.

Developers ask clarifying questions. The customer answers them. If the developers think there is a story missing, they can suggest it, but only customers write (or at least validate) stories and they can reject suggested stories entirely if they want to. That's step one.

The Developers Estimate

Kent has suggested, in *Extreme Programming Explained,* that customers sort by priority and developers sort by risk. This can provide value, especially when there are a lot of cards, but it isn't always necessary. It depends on what you are trying to get from the Planning Game. If you are constrained by a predetermined target date, initial sorting might cause the less important stories to drop off the end of the plan, so making an estimate on them (especially the high-risk, unnecessary stories) can quickly be identified as a waste of effort.

Often during the Initial Planning Game, you are just trying to get a ballpark estimate. As described in Chapter 10, a half-day Planning Game can give us a ballpark estimate. In fact, at RoleModel we usually insist on spending no more than a day on the Initial Planning Game. This is usually enough to get a ballpark size of the project, and usually uncovers enough things that have to happen outside of the conference room in smaller teams that it doesn't pay to continue until some further action is taken.

People think programming is expensive. It is not nearly as expensive as having a group of highly paid professionals sit in a room refining guesses without any new information entering the room.

The most useful pre-estimation sorting is when the customer sorts the stories into three piles based on business value:

1. Necessary for the system to be viable (must haves)
2. Not absolutely necessary, but valuable (want to haves)
3. Not necessary (nice to haves)

Then the developers begin to make their estimates. Estimating doesn't need to happen in this order, but people usually care more about the estimates for the first and second priorities.

At RoleModel we call the units of estimation craft units. A craft unit is basically an ideal engineering day as described in *Extreme Programming Explained,* but we believe that what we do is more of a craft than engineering. When we start a new project, we assume we can get one craft unit every one-half-person week. We've heard of other people using person-weeks as a unit. Use whatever unit you feel comfortable with. Just remember, you are trying to get a feel for the size and direction of the project. Stick with the analogy of planning a trip. You wouldn't plan a trip in inches or seconds, so use something bigger than minutes or hours. As you start tracking how accurate your estimates are you may wish to revise the units you use.

Once you decide what units to use, it's not simply a matter of putting numbers on cards. Solid thought and some verification of what is being estimated should back those numbers. Usually a lot of dialogue ensues. Depending on the number of people in the room, you might want to break into groups. It's usually good to do at least pair estimate (two developers in order to get a sanity check and a verification of the conversation that led up to that number). Conversations could be short or long before developers feel comfortable making an estimate. The following is an example.

DEVELOPER 1: On this *administrator needs to define users* story, could you describe what you are going to need defined about the user?

CUSTOMER: It's pretty basic: name, password, security level.

DEVELOPER 1: What do you mean by security level? How many different levels are there?

CUSTOMER: Hmm . . . well, there needs to be an administrator level, a technician level, and a clerk level at the least.

DEVELOPER 1: Are there others? Are they strictly hierarchical? In other words, can a technician do everything a clerk can do plus some other things, and an administrator do everything a technician can do plus some other things?

CUSTOMER: I believe so. Does it matter?

DEVELOPER 1: It makes it a lot easier to implement if it is.

CUSTOMER: Is it hard to change it later if it's not hierarchical?

DEVELOPER 1: It would be a pain.

DEVELOPER 2: You know, it seems to me that there are really two stories here. One is defining the users, and one is providing security on the functions in the system. What we choose as far as hierarchical versus something like a role and privilege-based system matters more in securing the functions than it does in defining of the users.

DEVELOPER 1: Yes, that's true. I was assuming they were all under this same story.

CUSTOMER: You geeks are losing me. Explain to me what you mean by the two stories and what you mean by this privileged role thing.

DEVELOPER 2: Roles and privileges. The idea is that a user can have one or more roles. Each role has a set of privileges. Multiple roles might have some of the same privileges. Let me draw you a simple example on the board . . .

CUSTOMER: That seems a lot more complicated, but gives me more options. I'm still not sure why you say there are two stories.

DEVELOPER 1: One story is building the screen that allows an administrator to identify a new user. Whether we use hierarchical security levels or roles and privileges, we need to identify the user. Security level would probably mean you just pick a security level from a combo box. Roles and privileges would mean you might choose multiple roles for a user. The user interface would be a little more complicated. You might want to click a number of checkboxes, or have a list box of all the roles or . . .

DEVELOPER 2: (interrupting) Hey, I just realized that if we use enablers for our security, there's hardly any difference between whether we enable or disable things based on role or security level.

DEVELOPER 1: Huh?

DEVELOPER 2: Haven't you ever used enablers?

DEVELOPER 1: Never heard of them.

DEVELOPER 2: They're awesome. You use an Observer to . . .

CUSTOMER: (interrupting) You geeks are doing it to me again. Explain what the other story is to me.

DEVELOPER 2: Oops, sorry. That was kind of what we were just talking about. Once you define the user's security level, you need to apply it to the rest of the system. So when a user logs on the correct functions are visible or invisible, enabled or disabled.

CUSTOMER: Of course.

DEVELOPER 2: The point is that we can give you a system that doesn't take into account security levels. That would still allow you to add and delete users. So we could give you that story in something like two units. If we added security levels it would affect both the administrator's user interface and the rest of the system, which would now have to react appropriately based on that user's security level. If it's a hierarchical security level, it probably adds another four units. If it's a roles-and-privileges security scheme, it will probably be another unit because of the complexity of the user interface.

DEVELOPER 1: It would be a lot more than one more unit. You'd probably have to add yet another user interface to define which roles get which privileges.

DEVELOPER 2: Oh, I didn't think about that . . . Couldn't you just hard code that?

CUSTOMER: Stop the geek stuff again.

DEVELOPER 2: We could probably give you the ability for the administrator to add users and assign a simple security level, and make it so that when those users log on, all the right stuff is enabled or visible in about six units.

DEVELOPER 1: I think you're oversimplifying. You just implied a log-on screen that's simple, but it's still work. I don't understand the enabler thing, but security is always hairy. Getting all the details right on every screen will be a pain.

DEVELOPER 2: Getting the security right on the individual screens is the problem of the people working on those individual screens. We just supply them with a simple way to enable or disable, based on the current user's security level.

DEVELOPER 1: Do the people working on those other screens know that?

DEVELOPER 2: They should . . . (in a louder voice) Can I get everybody's attention? When you're making estimates on anything that involves a user interface, don't forget to take into account the amount of time to hook up security to block out certain functions.

DEVELOPER 3: If they don't have the security level, why should they even get to the screen?

DEVELOPER 2: Good question.

DEVELOPER 1: There might be buttons or menu items that allow the user to navigate to another screen. You'd need to disable them if the user doesn't have the security level to get to the next screen.

DEVELOPER 2: Yeah, what he said!

DEVELOPER 3: You have a point there . . . but your hair covers it well.

CUSTOMER: Okay, enough of the pointy-headed geek humor. Do you have an estimate for this story?

DEVELOPER 1: I think we can do it in eight units.

DEVELOPER 2: I think we can do it in a little less, but I'm okay with eight.

CUSTOMER: I like six better.

DEVELOPER 2 I'm sure you do. Let's stick with eight. I'm sure we'll underestimate somewhere else, and I'd like to have some chance of coming in on time.

DEVELOPER 1: Okay, eight goes on the card. You might want to think about whether you want another card for *expanding security scheme.*

CUSTOMER: I'll create one and put it in the *nice to have* pile.

DEVELOPER 1: Next card?

Sometimes the conversations are less cordial, sometimes more so. As the discussion occurs, some notes might be added to the story cards. For example, the proceeding conversation might end with the following added to the *administrator needs to define users* story card: "Create a simple interface where name, password, and security level are identified for users. Security level is a simple hierarchy: administrator, technician, clerk. Also need to provide log-on screen and ability for current log-on security level to enable/disable or hide/show widgets on various screens. Details of other screens not part of this story."

Breaking Down Stories

When you're charting a course, you want to be able to track and change it later. This doesn't work if there are long legs with no alternate routes. If something goes wrong, you are in trouble. This is true of driving. Ask anyone who has been stuck in traffic on a highway, miles from the nearest exit. It's true of planning. You don't want big stories with big estimates.

A rule we use at RoleModel is that stories should be small enough so that one developer (with a partner) can accomplish them within one iteration. (See *Determining Iteration Size* in this chapter.) You might come up with your own rule as to when a story is too big. It is not important to apply the rule when the customer first describes the stories, but it is when you start estimating. So, when the developer looks at a story and can't imagine it taking less than one iteration, we explore ways to break the story into parts.

One way is to ask the customer for the simplest form of the story, and then a couple of things that make it complicated. For example, if the customer asked for a story called *allow the user to add custom fields*, the developer might recognize that adding custom fields has a significant impact on both the user interface and the database. The conversation might go something like this.

DEVELOPER: Would it be reasonable to limit it to just custom text fields?

CUSTOMER: No, our competition offers that and the users are very dissatisfied with it. They want to be able to add date fields, numeric fields, multiple selection fields—basically every kind of field we've already talked about. They want to be able to add their own.

DEVELOPER: That's going to be a lot of work and impact the user interface and the database. We would basically be allowing the user to dynamically change the database schema. Most databases have very limited ability to do this, and there would be lots of side effects on existing data. We'd probably have to perform some unnatural acts to make it work. Are users going to want to query on these user-defined fields?

CUSTOMER: Absolutely! In fact, some of these custom fields are going to be more important to them than the defaults we provide. When users query based on the contents of the custom fields, it needs to be just as snappy as when they query the predefined fields.

DEVELOPER: You're posing some serious technical challenges.

CUSTOMER That's why we pay you the big bucks.

DEVELOPER: Well, I don't think there is any way we'll be able to do this in one iteration. There are too many sticky problems. How about we break it into several stories?

CUSTOMER: For example?

DEVELOPER: How about *add custom text field* as one story. That will give us the ability to let the user specify a new field, make it dynamically appear on the user interface, and make the database handle it. Another story might be *query based on custom text field*. Since I'm sure we're going to have to do something unnatural to get the field added to the database, we're going to have to do something that is just as funky to query based on it. Getting the performance up to snuff will also be a challenge. If we've mastered that, the other simple data types like date and numbers shouldn't be too hard. So we'll add another story to *add and query on custom fields of other simple data types*. If we're still alive, we'll tackle *add and query on complex custom fields*. Does that seem reasonable?

CUSTOMER: I don't care how many stories you break it into. It's reasonable as long as I get all of them.

DEVELOPER: I'm not making any promises. Prepare yourself for limitations on how many of your features we can actually deliver in a reasonable time. There's a reason that our competition doesn't provide all these features. But if we tackle it in this order, we should be able to demonstrate at least partial functionality early on, or find out we're dead in the water before we get too far. Then we'll add significant functionality all along the way.

CUSTOMER: Well, if I can get the first three stories you mentioned, my management will be happy. But I really want to make them ecstatic. So I'm counting on your brilliance to pull out the fourth story.

DEVELOPER: If we do, I'm counting on your letter of recommendation to pull out big bonuses for the development team.

There are some habits we've gotten into of automatically splitting vague but critical stories into initial story, revised story, and possibly a refined story or final story. For example, suppose a key user of a healthcare system, such as a head nurse, is going to use a screen called a dashboard as a portal to the system. We might have an *initial dashboard* story that is a high priority to demonstrate and get a feel for how the system might really work. We also create a *revised dashboard*, since it is assumed the customer will be able to demonstrate and discuss the initial version with several individual head nurses at some point. Since we expect we will provide an early access version to a select group of head nurses, we plan on a *refined dashboard* to incorporate the highly critical feedback based on actual day-to-day use in the public release. During the Initial Planning Game, the *initial dashboard* story gets put into Iteration 1, *revised dashboard* is placed in Iteration 3, and, after determining that our early access release should be after Iteration 3, the *refined dashboard* story is placed in Iteration 6.

Back to Estimating

Estimating is hard work. No wonder programmers would rather code than provide estimates. No wonder customers would rather just hand over a bunch of vague requirements and a date and hope it all comes together. But, estimating is very important work. Here are a few key things to pay attention to:

- ✧ Focus on getting ballpark numbers on the card. Don't try to make them exact—they won't be.
- ✧ Avoid getting into the details of implementation or even design, but don't ignore it completely. Instead, identify whether there are a lot of details or just a few, and whether or not you think they will be sticky ones.
- ✧ Try to limit the amount of time you spend on one card. Maybe five or ten minutes. By the time you have gotten to this point (estimation time) the stories should already have been described to a point of basic understanding. If your questions about a particular story card confuse the customer, you may have gone to the estimation phase too soon. Back up and clarify the story.

As you make your estimates, identify how sure you are of each estimate. There are several ways to do this. You might want to put something on the card to denote level of risk, such as high, medium, or low. At RoleModel, we often just put a question mark next to the estimate if we are not too confident, and two question marks if it's a total guess.

You can then move on to the next step, recognizing that there are a lot of uncertainties. If this is your Initial Planning Game, you should try to come up with an estimate of how much time it will take you to explore the uncertainties. How big should this be? That depends on how uncertain you are.

Look at the number of medium- or high-risk estimates. Identify how much time you need to improve your estimates significantly for each of them. Don't do this for every story or ask for an inordinate amount of time. Half a day is usually enough and a full day is usually more than sufficient. Add up the time it will take to explore these tasks further, and then add a significant buffer. That's one input into the Exploration Phase.

Remember, you are not looking for a guarantee, just an estimate. If the customer won't give you the time to explore further, ask what you can do to avoid getting burnt by the clearly present risk. One example is to double all of the risky estimates. The Exploration Phase is often more attractive than that. Who knows, the customer might have another reasonable alternative. But don't just give in. Point out that you want to give a realistic estimate, that you would love to find out that the high-risk items are easier than you fear, but that you can't wish away the risk.

Determining Iteration Size

How do you decide on the size of an iteration? An iteration needs to be big enough to make significant progress, but small enough so that not too much progress gets made without being reviewed. Smaller iterations are better when volatility of requirements is higher and your development team is highly productive. Larger iterations are better when the customer has a hands-off style and when your development team is less productive.

Favorite iteration sizes seem to be two or three weeks. If you don't have a strong reason to do otherwise, start with two weeks. You can always change it later. Two weeks will give you quick feedback while you are getting comfortable with the process.

How many people should you put on a project? The gold owner typically determines this. It probably has to do with what developers are available, and whether a few more can be added as needed. The general rule is to start small—say, from two to six—and add developers only when you know what you are doing. It's good to have an even number of programmers, but depending on how your team is set up, that may or may not mean an even number of people. Bigger teams are more likely to have tasks for an unpartnered person.

Make your best guess at how many units will get done based on the team size you'll have. For example, we assume each person on the development team will be able to complete two craft units per week. A team of four on a two-week iteration can handle 16 craft units per iteration (4 people × 2 craft-units per person × 2 weeks). This number can be adjusted up or down over time.

The number of developers might also be influenced by whether the spending rate at is more important than meeting a certain date. If the date is more important, the iteration size might be determined by dividing the cards that must be done by the given date into roughly even piles. Then you do your best to assemble a team that can deliver the necessary units per iteration. This is usually much harder, but it's been done, given a reasonable period to ramp up. You'd typically use this kind of sizing in an Initial Planning Game where you're still determining the constraints of the project.

Sorting the Stories

Sorting stories is simple, but it isn't easy. Once you've determined how many units will fit in an iteration, the customer has to figure out what stories end up in each iteration. Other than determining how to rank the order of importance of a card, really only a few things typically come up when you sort:

⬥ **It's hard to get the number of units to fit exactly into an iteration.** The three most important stories may be estimated to take a total of 14 units and your iterations may allow for 16 units or, worse, 12. We suggest you err on the conservative side. Better to have a pleasant surprise than a bitter disappointment. If you have two or three iterations that are short some work, it's okay to have one that's a little over. Again, you are looking for ballparks at this point. When you get to individual iterations, it will be easier to fill gaps with partial stories.

⬥ **Deciding how many *nice to have* iterations you should plan.** The reality is, you will probably never run out of nice-to-have stories. If you do, brainstorm for a minute or two. If you took the time to write the card, put it in an iteration. If someone gives you heat about the length of the project, you can always trim the nice to haves.

Cards should typically be sorted by putting all the *must haves* first, highest risk first. High-risk *want to haves* should probably be tackled early on, too. The customer should take into account the things the developers believe are foundational or provide leverage to other stories. For example, once you get security implemented, you can just take it into account when you build each screen. Otherwise, you have to go back and retrofit all of the screens, and the screens will look less polished.

The difference between the end of an Initial Planning Game and a Release Planning Game is basically this:

⬥ The first iteration (or iteration zero) after an Initial Planning Game is an Exploration Phase, and no one should get too excited about potential release dates yet.

✧ At the end of a Release Planning Game, you should have a reasonable level of confidence about when you will have what, at least for the earlier iterations. Once the cards are sorted, the customer can identify the first potential external release as the last pile with must haves in it. The customer can also identify significant demo releases.

Exploration Phase

After an Initial Planning Game, and again in Iteration Planning on a much smaller scale, the development team explores the stories they don't know how to estimate. This is the Exploration Phase. We use the Exploration Phase to accomplish a few critical things:

✧ To lower the risk of making a bad estimate
✧ To experiment with various implementation options
✧ To increase and demonstrate our understanding of the problem
✧ To determine more accurately our velocity for implementing stories
✧ To get our processes and necessary infrastructure in place

The Exploration Phase can last anywhere from one day to two months, depending on the size of the project, how well-defined the stories are, and the issues surrounding the technology choices. If we are starting a project that is not similar to one we've done with the same team members before, the typical Exploration Phase lasts about a month if all the necessary resources (human and otherwise) are readily available.

More than one contributor to this book has pointed out the importance of the Exploration Phase. Steve Freeman said, "I've seen several XP projects go drastically late because they forgot the cost of setting up the environment. Just installing Oracle can take a couple of weeks."

As an example, RoleModel's first big XP client had an Exploration Phase of about seven weeks. During that time, we

✧ Trained more than half the team of eight in the basics of XP
✧ Installed and trained everyone in the use of the VisualAge for Java Enterprise Edition team environment and JUnit
✧ Explored the communication protocol of a proprietary specimen analysis machine with which we needed to interface, along with available libraries in Java used for serial port communication

- Trained everyone in the concept and use of the model-view-controller pattern
- Explored the creation of dynamic views corresponding to data fields on objects that could be specified dynamically by an end user
- Explored Java's facilities for internationalization and localization of text and how to incorporate it into our user interface
- Created an architectural spike that demonstrated communication with laboratory instruments, fast data entry, dynamic data field creation, internationalization of user interfaces, and printed reports

When the Exploration Phase is over, the developers move on to the Release Planning Game. Or the business side may decide it's not worth proceeding. Better to find out after spending a little money exploring than later in a development cycle.

Chapter 12

Iteration Planning

It is a bad plan that admits of no modification.
—Publius Syrus, 1st century B.C.

It will take a long time to get all the details down for everything on the project and it is foolish to think they won't change as you learn. On the other hand, you need to deal with the details sooner or later. We deal with the details of what we need to do sooner, sooner. Then we have plenty of time to deal with the details of what we need to do later, later.

We left off with a stack of cards that all need to be done for a release. This is too much to concentrate on all at once, so the customer sorted the stack of cards into iteration-sized piles, based on two things:

◇ Business value and anything else that determines priority for the customer
◇ The velocity of the development team

At the end of each iteration, the development team should have produced a system that provides the functionality described in the stories for that iteration. The initial iterations probably won't produce a system that does much of anything commercially useful (although sometimes this isn't true), but they are still important as a way for customers to gauge whether they are getting what they want out of the development process.

Of course, you won't know whether you've produced what the customer wants until the end. To increase your chances, you create an iteration plan for each iteration.

Iteration Planning happens at the beginning of each iteration. It usually takes anywhere from a half day to two days. It shouldn't take more than two days. When it's done, developers know what they'll be working on next and how long it should take.

Iteration Planning is just Release Planning in miniature. But before we go there, let's talk about plans and planning one more time.

What Plans Are

Iteration Planning is the way we steer an XP project. We use stories to sketch out where we would like to go. We defer specifying details for stories until the iteration in which we'll code them. We make small adjustments as we go.

Planning minimizes your chances of getting off track and can help you get back on. Plan like people were urged to vote in Boston once in jest: early and often.

If you don't have a map you'll get lost. If you never deviate from the map, you'll probably miss the best part of the journey and maybe sustain some damage from the potholes along the way. Thus, we come up with a plan but we're willing to stray from it.

Bryn Mawr Biology Professor, Paul Grobstein, said that being "right" should be replaced with being "progressively less wrong."[1] Being right measures your success or failure by proximity to a fixed target, set at the beginning. This encourages people to put on blinders. Being progressively less wrong measures your success or failure by charting your progress from your starting point. This encourages exploration, respect for experience, and appreciation of the value of each individual's perspective on a problem. XP planning is all about learning and then applying the lessons learned as soon as possible. We hope to be "progressively less wrong" over time.

The Iteration Planning Game

Reserve some time at the beginning of each iteration to review the last iteration's work. Be critical. Take steps to reduce business and technical risk based on what you learn and changes in the customer's needs. Then use a downsized version of the Planning Game to break the stories down.

---

1. P. Grobstein. *Science as "Getting It Less Wrong."* Unpublished letter to John Bemis, an early supporter of the Bryn Mawr Serendip Project on the Web, 1993.

This time the development team decomposes stories into tasks. The act of breaking stories down is actually a design exercise. It involves figuring out the design approach you are going to take to implement the stories, and each step is a task. How long should each task take? Two days is the maximum we feel comfortable with. We've heard others say one day or one half day. Go smaller until you are better at estimating large chunks. Add up the chunks and revise the story estimates for the customer.

It usually takes us a day or two to nail this down on more complex projects. On simpler ones, it could take half a day or less. Iteration Planning usually goes something like this:

- **Demonstration and discussion of what we accomplished last iteration.** There should be no real surprises here if your customer has been active in the iteration—it is just a syncing up of what we did and did not do. If the customer hasn't been active, you might need more time for this. *Approximate time: < 1 hour*
- **Discussion of what the next iteration should contain.** This is based on what the customer thought should be tackled next and what the designers feel should be tackled next, based on what they now know. This discussion results in a candidate list, prioritized by the customer. *Approximate time: 1–2 hours*
- **Task exploration.** People volunteer to lead the breaking down of each of the candidates into tasks (in priority order). This can take many forms, but basically we break into small groups (assuming the group is greater than a couple of people) and do it, sometimes with the customer and sometimes without. Sometimes, an individual does a quick exploration, then calls someone over to analyze what was discovered. Sometimes the customer is brought into the discussion, depending on the nature of a discovery. *Approximate time: 4–8 hours*
- **Iteration plan verification.** We have a list of tasks and possibly a list of issues that need to be resolved. We review what we think we can get done with the customer and sometime during the day we're done with Iteration Planning (or at least 90% of it). People sign up for the highest priority tasks and start them. *Approximate time: 4–8 hours.*

The approximate times are taken from experience with a pretty sizeable project of 8 to 10 developers. Your mileage may vary. Items 1 and 2 on this list should be kept as short as possible, but no shorter. These are just points to make sure everybody is on the same page. You might want to use this time to bring a few people who are not involved with a project on a daily basis up to speed (e.g., the customer's manager, the developer's manager, tech support people). If it takes longer than half a day to get through these things, you probably aren't communicating enough during the rest of the iteration.

Once you know you are all on the same page about what you would like to accomplish in the iteration, it's time to explore.

Task Exploration

Typically developers who volunteer to break a story into tasks think they understand how to approach it from a design perspective. They should find at least one other developer to discuss the approach they would take.

Depending on the story, they may or may not need to get the customer's input to clarify the details of the story. If there is any question in the developer's mind, they should start by asking the customer to verify the developer's understanding of the story. Typically the types of stories you wouldn't need clarification on are the ones that are simple from a user perspective and complex from a technical perspective. For example, if the story is *add custom date fields* when you had previously delivered *add custom text fields*, it may already be obvious what the details are.

Whether a developer starts exploring with the customer or not, this is where the details need to come out. The conversation is at a completely different level than at the Release Planning Game. In the Release Planning Game, it might go like this:

Customer: We need a way for the end user to enter data quickly.

DEVELOPER: What do you mean by entering the data quickly?

CUSTOMER: Just the key fields, like date collected, bottle number, and patient ID. And they need to be able to go from field to field quickly. The user might have to enter data on fifty bottles, and each one should take less than five seconds.

DEVELOPER: Okay. I think I get the idea.

In the Iteration Planning Game it goes more like this:

DEVELOPER: What do you want this quick data entry screen to look like? What needs to be on it?

CUSTOMER: I was thinking something like this. (Drawing on the whiteboard.) The bottom line is that the lab technician is going to be standing in a lab with a bunch of bottles, maybe fifty, that someone just delivered. The technician wants to identify them and put them in the system. So, the technician just needs to wand the bar code, type in the order ID and patient ID, and enter the date collected, which will typically be today, and stick the bottle in the machine. After the fifty bottles are in, the technician will eventually get around to taking a seat and entering the rest of the information.

DEVELOPER: If the user needs to do it quickly, what fields can we default?

CUSTOMER: The date should definitely be defaulted to today. But if the user changes it to yesterday, we should probably leave it like that. Chances are good the whole lot is from yesterday. Typically the users create the order ID, and they just do it sequentially, so you could default it to the last one entered, plus one. I don't think there is any way to default the patient ID. Sometimes we get several bottles from the same patient, so maybe we could make the default the last patient ID typed in.

DEVELOPER: Do you want to add any other fields?

CUSTOMER: I'm sure some installations will want more on the screen, so we need to give them a way to customize it, but we need to give them the defaults. I'd bet that eighty percent of customers will just use what we give them.

DEVELOPER: Isn't view customization a different story?

CUSTOMER: Yes I guess it is, but this screen is special and we need to make sure we don't do something foolish.

DEVELOPER: So tell me what else I need to pay attention to for this story. So far, I see three tasks: *lay out quick data entry screen, provide appropriate defaults*, and *save the data*.

CUSTOMER: We can't let users enter bad data. It needs to be verified here.

DEVELOPER: What do we need to verify, that there is something in each field?

CUSTOMER: Yes, but also that the data in each field is valid.

DEVELOPER: I think I know what a valid date is, but what's a valid bottle ID, order ID, or patient ID?"

CUSTOMER: Don't forget that the date not only needs to be a valid date, but within 48 hours of the present time.

This could go on for a while, but the difference in detail here should be clear.

Whether or not you get the customer's input at the beginning of exploring a story, you should seek it before thinking you are done breaking it down. Here's an example. The story is *allow user to enter relative date in date field*. A developer thinks he understands the issue and begins to break it down into the following tasks:

1. Create a relative date object. This will act like a regular date unless someone asks for its "days offset."
2. Modify date entry widget to accept input that specifies relative date.

Piece of cake. Just to get the sign-off from the customer, he calls her over and explains the two tasks. After he does, the dialogue goes something like this:

CUSTOMER: So, I type in *t* for today, *y* for yesterday, and *t minus three* for three days ago?

DEVELOPER: If that's the way you want to do it, great. I'll just capture a nonnumeric key in the date field and I'll know it's a relative date. Are *t* and *y* the only special characters or will there be more?

CUSTOMER: Hmm... maybe *n* for now.

DEVELOPER: Hold on a second. The story is for a relative date, not a relative time.

CUSTOMER: Oh, right. Do we have another story for relative time?

DEVELOPER: I seem to remember it coming up somewhere along the line. I'm not sure if we captured it or what iteration it's in.

CUSTOMER: Actually, I think that's a nice to have. It might be pushed off into a future release.

DEVELOPER: Good. So, my job here is over.

CUSTOMER: Let me think for a minute. When you do data entry, the user types in a *y* to get yesterday. What shows up in the field?

DEVELOPER: I thought *y*. But I guess that doesn't make sense if users go back to look at the date later. They probably want to see the actual date. I was thinking about this in the context of queries. You would want the *y* to show up there, right?

CUSTOMER: Yes, because if the user saves that query, it would always be relative to the time the query is run. Like "show me all the specimens collected since yesterday." The user would run that every day when he came in.

DEVELOPER: So I was right about that part. I wasn't thinking about data entry. That's a different beast. When I save the query, I want to save the relative date, but if I enter a relative date when I'm entering data I want to save the actual date. I probably need to add another task to convert relative date to fixed date at data entry. Would it be okay to convert the relative date directly to the actual date in that situation?

CUSTOMER: You mean when users tab out of the date field, the *y* would go away and it would show up as if they typed in the actual date?

DEVELOPER: Yes. They wouldn't necessarily have to tab out. It would happen whenever the date field lost focus.

CUSTOMER: Let me think about that for a second (pause). Sure, I think that would be okay. I wonder if there are other fields we're going to have to do this in.

DEVELOPER: I can probably just set up a flag in the widget so I know when to convert and when not to. Then, if it comes up on any other screen, we can just pick which form it will take.

CUSTOMER: I don't understand what you mean by "flag the widget." But I think you just told me that you can set it up so that anywhere we use a date field, we just need to decide whether we want to show it as a relative date or actual date, and you won't have to write any more code no matter which one we pick.

DEVELOPER: You're getting the hang of it.

CUSTOMER: Yeah, right.

DEVELOPER: I'll have to add another task for that. Are we done?

CUSTOMER: I think so. Let's see, I'll need *y* or *t* or *t minus something*. Are there internationalization issues with this?

DEVELOPER: Uh-oh.

CUSTOMER: *t* and *y* aren't going to work are they? Can't we just use the first letter of whatever the word for today and yesterday are in that language?

DEVELOPER: I'm sure we could. But this might be a little troublesome. I guess we can make each language translation supply a translation for *t* and *y.*

CUSTOMER: Hmm . . .

DEVELOPER: Here is another idea. Why not just make the user specify a relative offset like *minus one, minus two, plus one,* whatever? Then we don't have to worry about internationalization, and it's one less keystroke for data entry.

CUSTOMER: How would you specify today, with a zero?

DEVELOPER: I guess you could. That would be a little tricky. I wouldn't have the plus or minus to key off of. Zero could be the beginning of a valid date.

CUSTOMER: I'm not following you.

DEVELOPER: You know what the date widget looks like now, right? It has those slashes to separate the day, week, and month.

CUSTOMER: Right.

DEVELOPER: Well, if we have a special character like a plus or minus sign, I would know they are typing in a relative date and then I can get rid of those separators. If the user types a zero, how do I know they are trying to identify a relative date or are just typing in a valid date like 01/02/2001?

CUSTOMER: I understand now. Hmm . . .

We could continue to show how this two-task, piece-of-cake story turned into about seven tasks by the time the conversation was over. It usually doesn't go quite this way, but it's not entirely uncommon either.

Iteration Plan Verification

It's not always clear when the planning ends and the doing begins. Small groups tend to finish breaking down tasks at different rates. It is not unusual for a developer or two to begin an obvious initial task before the iteration plan verification. This is not a problem as long as the team doesn't forget it should verify the big picture. Programming is more fun, and developers sometimes get lost there.

A rule we've come up with is to schedule a meeting time that should give everybody plenty of time to explore plus a buffer. We usually do this after our stand-up meeting on the second day of the iteration. The stand-up meeting uncovers who needs more time to explore. Based on that, someone might end the meeting with a question like, "Can we plan to verify the iteration at 11:00?" If there is no dissension, the time is set. If there is, come up with another time later in the day. Whoever is not done exploring by then should be close to done.

When everyone's finished exploring, get them together again and take to the whiteboard or tabletop. The tasks everyone identified are presented and discussed. The customer sits in to answer questions and to listen to make sure the developers understand the stories. If the customer hears something that indicates the team missed the point, he or she pipes up and clarifies.

If, after breaking down the stories into tasks, you find that your estimate for the iteration is going to be bigger than you had originally estimated, tell the customer approximately how many days of tasks you are over. The customer may pull out a story that is that many tasks or split a story. Now that the stories are broken down into tasks, there might be natural breaks that weren't obvious before. The remaining tasks can go into a future story, probably next iteration, but that's up to the customer at that point.

There are two schools of thought on what happens next:

1. **Do tasks one at a time.** Developers just pick the first task they'd like to tackle and work on that until they are done, then take the next task.
2. **Fill your bag.** Everyone signs up for several tasks until they are at their capacity for the iteration.

One at a Time

The complication with the one-at-a-time approach is that you need to get some sense of whether the tasks will still fit in the iteration. If you've adopted a uniform task size approach, that's pretty easy. The customer works with the developers to figure out what makes the most sense not to do. Otherwise the team should do some sort of estimation up front. Probably the person who identified the task should put a number on it and get a sanity check from others.

The disadvantage of this approach is that an estimate is nebulous and subject to change when somebody eventually signs up for the task.

The advantage of this approach is there is never a bottleneck. When you're done with one task, you take a new one. If one or two developers get bogged down on any particular task, the other tasks can still be going strong.

Fill Your Bag

With the fill your bag approach, once the tasks are laid out, the developers hold a kind of auction. Somebody chimes in to take ownership of the task and estimate it. Usually the people involved in breaking the story into tasks get first dibs because they've thought about it the most and volunteered to break it down in the first place. Other developers (not customers) can take shots at refining the estimate. Eventually, someone's bag is full. For example, on a three-week iteration, when you've signed up for six craft-units worth of tasks you can no longer bid unless you give up one of your tasks.

When the ownership estimation auction is done, everyone should have full bags. If not, the customer might suggest more stories. If there are tasks left over, the customer may wish to examine them and ask questions to determine what won't be done by the end of the iteration. The customer may suggest trading some of the remaining tasks for tasks that have already been grabbed. Usually, it doesn't take too long to nail things down.

The main advantage of the fill your bag approach is that the customer has a better idea of what will get done in the iteration and by whom. This is useful when the customer isn't available all the time If something comes up during the iteration that the customer thinks may affect the task, they will know whom to talk to. Also, this approach gives the developer a sense of continuity and an understanding of how the tasks fit into the story.

The main disadvantage of this approach is that a developer who is prone to think too much about multiple tasks will not be as focused on getting an individual task done. It could also cause that person to become a bottleneck. This can be handled easily if people who finish their tasks early take up the slack, as long as the team has the culture of "we're in this together" rather than "you slacker, I'm doing your work for you again." Of course, if this is the case, it is the attitude of the team that needs attention, not the method of distributing tasks.

In *Planning Extreme Programming*, Kent and Martin suggest only committing to the number of stories delivered during the last iteration. That's not a bad rule. We certainly take last iteration into consideration when we plan the next iteration. However, we also adjust per developer. A new developer may actually be able to contribute based on skill level, familiarity with the domain, and how much he has worked with other members of the team before. We also adjust for whatever else is going on (vacations, other known assignments, and so on) that we are confident will have an impact. We tell the customer how many units we think we'll be able to deliver based on all this.

We weren't very good early on. Sometimes we were off by 35%. However, we've gotten pretty good lately, and we seem to be within 5% to 10% of actual units delivered. This should not be confused with accuracy of estimates on individual tasks. We're getting better at that, too. See *Keeping Score* (Chapter 26) for more on this.

How to Start Planning

You'll never know all there is to know about planning and estimating, but you won't know anything if you don't get out there and do it. Remember that XP is about learning and doing it better next time. The more you plan, the better you'll get at it.

When you're just getting started, it's more important to get used to that rhythm than it is to be right. At the beginning, you won't have a clue what your team's velocity will be. Guess and refine it later. You'll do this frequently when you start. Get used to it. Don't be lazy, but don't be too tough on yourself either.

What Can Be Done in a Half Day
by Rob Billington

Starting with nothing more than a very high level statement of functionality to be implemented that month, the first task was for the team to break this down into more manageable pieces. Our intention was to write on a whiteboard a list of subrequirements, each of which could be implemented by a team in one half day. This effort was largely a failure. We did identify functional pieces that could be doled out to the pair teams, but our accuracy in identifying half-day tasks was way off. . . . We never did get to the goal of actually identifying half-day tasks reliably, but soon they were being completed in a whole day with very good consistency.

When you were learning to drive a car, steering was a tough skill to pick up. You probably swerved a lot. After a while, you didn't have to think about it as much—it started to become second nature. Planning is the same.

Remember, the goal with planning is to keep it simple. The best way to do this is keep it ridiculously short in the beginning. Give yourself lots of feedback and lots of opportunities to steer. As your skills improve, you can begin looking a little farther down the road as you drive (but never too far).

The Art of Estimation

The bedrock of planning is estimating how long work will take. Stories and tasks are great, but eventually the rubber has to meet the road. Estimation is a strange thing. It's guessing based on experience. The more experience you have in a given context, the better your estimates will be. If you've done exactly the same type of thing before on the same project, estimate that it will take that long this time around. If you haven't, look for similar experiences on the same project and estimate from them. Only as a last resort should you just guess.

That said, estimation can be tough. This is especially true when people are working with new technologies and/or in new environments. Tell people to keep it simple. Break stories down into very small tasks between a quarter day and two days. This exercise will help people do a better job at two things:

1. Breaking stories down to make sure they know what will and won't be accomplished
2. Making accurate estimates

This is equal parts art and skill. It will take a while to get good at it, but you will improve with practice. In a recent discussion, Ralph Johnson made the astute observation, "There is nothing that you can't do better the more you do it." Your estimates won't ever be perfect, but you can hone your skills. Before you know it, people will start to take your estimates and plans seriously as they get closer and closer to reality.

Velocity

Estimating is the art of determining how big an effort is required. That's not worth much unless you also can tell your customer when they'll get it. That's velocity.

Velocity tells you how fast your team can produce the stories required by your customers in a single iteration. The Planning Game and the Iteration Planning Game tell you how much everything costs. The tracker or the coach or the manager then determines the velocity of the team. There are a lot of things to take into consideration when determineing velocity, but the first is past performance. If your team delivered seven stories (or 20 story points) in the last iteration, assume they'll do the same the next time around. It's that simple.

There are several ways to express velocity, but they all answer the same question: How much can your team get done in a single iteration? The two major candidates appear to be ideal days and some sort of story points.

These are based on different inputs. The ideal days form says that your team can produce a certain number of ideal days' worth of work in an iteration's worth of calendar days. All stories are broken down into tasks and estimated in ideal days. You figure out how many ideal days you have and figure out how many tasks can fit into the iteration. This is basically a mini version of the Planning Game, except you are only filling up one pile. Tasks that don't fit get moved into another iteration.

The story points approach says that your team can produce a certain number of points (a simple way to express difficulty) in a single iteration. Then stories are given a point value. Stories fit or they don't. If they don't, divide one or more into parts somehow. The leftovers are candidates for the next iteration.

Which is better? Pick the form that makes the most sense to you and go with it. If measurements of your actual results and your estimates are close, you are doing well. If they are not, they should be progressively improving. If they are not progressively improving, figure out why not.

Kent talks about load factor in *Extreme Programming Explained*. Load factor is the multiple you use to get from ideal programming days to calendar days. If you can get 8 ideal days of work done in a 20-day iteration (4 weeks), your load factor is 2.5 (20 ÷ 8). In *Planning Extreme Programming*, Kent and Martin forsook load factor and claimed velocity is the only measure you need. We tend to agree, but we have found that until you have a track record with a team and project, you need to come up with something as a starting point. We've also found that assigning individuals different load factors is practical when those individuals tend to be under a heavier load on a regular or sporadic basis. For example

- ❖ Team leaders have to spend more time in meetings with powers that be.
- ❖ New programmers may have to spend more time learning technologies.
- ❖ Some developers might have to be on beeper duty all or part of the time to handle customer support calls.

At RoleModel, we express velocity in terms of craft units per iteration. Craft units are our version of story points. Each craft unit is equivalent to a single ideal engineering day. Using an initial load factor of 2.5, we expect each craft unit to be about one half week of a developer's time. Given these inputs, each developer can handle roughly eight craft units in a four-week iteration, or six in a three-week iteration. After tracking several projects, we have found this to be a pretty accurate starting point. We can adjust up or down based on the individual project, once we have some experience in that environment.

This approach standardizes our measurements. The size of each story is a multiple of a known quantity. There are lots of ways to express that known quantity: a craft unit, an ideal day, or half a person week. Load factor can vary by person, but we usually state velocity in terms of the team as a whole. We tell the customer our collective velocity, such as 35 craft units per iteration. When we start an iteration we figure out how many days of the iteration each developer is expected to be present, take into account other distractions to adjust individual load factors, and total up the resulting units we think we expect in that iteration. Table 12.1 shows an example of this.

TABLE 12.1 Estimate of project velocity

Developer	Days Available	Load Factor	Craft Units
Amy	15	2.5	6
Nathaniel	18	2.5	7
Ken	10	2.5	4
Joe	19	4	5
Duff	16	2.5	6
Donna	20	3	7
Total			**35**

We have also found that different types of customers can significantly affect velocity. Some customers tend to be much more disruptive and increase load factor by interrupting the planned work. For example, customers might generate multiple urgent requests each week that distract the team from working on scheduled stories. ("Could you write me up a quick white paper?") Other customers only cause disruption once in a blue moon and the load factor can actually be lowered. The sooner you recognize the kind of customer you are dealing with, the better you can avoid the disappointment of delivering less than expected.

The Last Word on Iterations and Planning

Truth always shows up eventually in any project. Iteration Planning makes that truth obvious. Developers and customers share what they've learned to be true since their last guess at what would be true. There's no room for fantasy.

In XP, there is no analysis phase, design phase, test phase, maintenance phase. There is mainly *planning,* which sometimes lasts more than a day, and *doing*. Many activities go on during both planning and doing. Developers write and run unit tests; customers write stories; and developers design, analyze, and write code. Focus shifts from time to time, but it typically just changes the mix of activities a bit, sometimes introducing new ones.

XP planning and doing follow similar patterns. In *doing*, first we write out what we want to be true (the test), then we try to make it true (the code), then we make sure we clearly understand what we have (refactor) so we can move on comfortably to the next task. In *planning*, customers state what they want to be true (the stories), then developers try to make them true (the iteration), then both make sure of where they are (review of previous iteration) so they can move on comfortably to the next iteration.

Traditional approaches require you to create a plan and then try to force reality to fit that plan. XP turns things around by requiring you to produce (and continually refine) your plan based on feedback about what actually works. Look back over the dialogues in this chapter. No standard analysis or design techniques would have uncovered the details and the potential problems any faster or any more thoroughly. But it costs less to get there via XP *planning* and *doing*.

Chapter 13

Write the Tests, Run the Tests

*Success does not consist in never making mistakes, but in
never making them a second time.*

—George Bernard Shaw

*Write unit tests before you write the code to implement them. This will feel
odd, but you'll get better with time. Soon, it will feel odd not to write tests
first.*

If you are like most of the readers of *Extreme Programming Explained,* you are
already convinced that having unit tests is a good thing. You also aren't in the
habit of writing tests before you write code. You might be thinking, "How can
I write tests before I've written the code I'm going to test? I don't even know
what the classes are going to look like yet and how they are going to evolve."

Ken used to say things like this back in the 1980s when he heard proponents of Objective-C claim that each class should have associated tests written
first. He has now confessed and repented. You need to write tests first precisely
because you don't know what the classes are going to look like yet, and because
they are going to evolve.

Writing tests first keeps entropy from destroying your code. We write
tests, then we write just enough code to get the tests to pass, no more. That is
the best way to keep your code clean.

Nothing gives you more confidence when changing code than having
immediate feedback about whether your changes broke anything. That's what
having tests does for you. Without the tests, you can't have confidence. Without confidence, code doesn't get changed, even when it needs to be.

Better still, well-written unit tests are some of the best documentation possible. They communicate the intent of the code being tested better than any written description. We can kill two birds with one stone.

Keeping Code Clean

Writing the bare minimum code necessary to make the tests run keeps you from wasting time on hooks for anticipated features. The hooks you might need later usually have to change, if they're ever used at all. But without the tests there to guide you while you write code, the temptation to design for the future is just too great.

It's Much Simpler Than That
by Ken Auer

I had to add some functionality to our criteria matching code. Knowing that someone else had recently worked in this area, I looked for the tests that currently provided the functionality. Unfortunately, they weren't there. After scolding the people responsible for writing code without the tests, I encouraged one of them to help me write the tests for the existing code. The first thing I asked was, "So exactly what does the existing code do?"

After a short dialogue, we found that there was a need for three simple tests. I asked whether all of the six classes that were present were supporting any other necessary functionality. The author of the code suggested that they were not. About 10 minutes later, we had written the three tests we needed and they had passed. As the tests were written, the original author recognized that there was probably a simpler way to accomplish the same goals. We talked and started refactoring. Less than half an hour later, we had deleted five of the six classes. The remaining class had been greatly simplified.

Now it was time to add the new functionality. We realized that this could be tested by a simple assertion added to an existing test. We added the test code and 10 minutes later all the tests passed.

The original author said, "It's amazing how much easier this is when you write the test first. It took us a couple of days to write the five classes we just deleted."

Writing the minimum necessary code the first time around ensures that the refactoring you do later isn't a complete overhaul. You can't get it perfect the first time all the time. You will refactor your code. But if you start with the simplest code that could possibly work you'll spend less time refactoring. If your refactoring turns into redesign on a regular basis, your velocity will nosedive. Moving at top speed is your bread and butter. Guard your velocity with your life.

Think of this as keeping a room clean. Roy's mother used to say that doing that is simple. Don't let the room get dirty. If you let the dirt build up, cleaning it becomes a much bigger job that you end up putting off. Pretty soon you've got an intractable mess.

Confidence

In 1955, Dr. Jonas Salk administered his experimental polio vaccine to himself, his wife, and their three sons. In a newspaper interview, he said that he did it because he knew it would work. That's courage in action. Salk himself said, "It is courage based on confidence, not daring, and it is confidence based on experience."[1]

At least once or twice during most iterations on our projects, someone sees the need for a radical change in some aspect of the system. When he changes it, a bunch of tests break. This is expected. The pair works through the failures one by one, modifying code to get each test to pass. This could take a few minutes or a few hours. Invariably, when the pair is integrating the changes one member says, "Wow, can you imagine how hard this would have been to do without these tests?!"

XP depends on courage based on confidence, not daring. Having tests to run to confirm each change in the code keeps us from being reckless. It lets us proceed bravely knowing that we can prove to ourselves that our changes work. Instead of holding lots of meetings to determine whether a change will break something else, we can just try it, run the tests, and find out.

Tests as Documentation

Well-written unit tests are less painful to produce than other forms of documentation. In fact, they're the best class-level documentation we've seen.

When you write unit tests first, you don't have to loop back and write documentation later. The tests are an inseparable part of writing the code. It's like having a certain dollar amount each month taken out of your paycheck and put into a 401(k). After a while, you just don't notice it anymore. Any speed you lose in writing tests first, you more than make up in reduced debugging time and

---

1. J. B. Simpson. *Simpson's Contemporary Quotations*. Houghton Mifflin, 1988.

reduced documentation time. This alone is a great boost to your team's velocity not to mention the increased velocity you get from having more confidence. Even if this weren't true, tests still would be worth the effort.

Tests are more detailed than descriptions on paper, without being cluttered by explanations that describe what the code syntax says. Written code documentation often wastes space saying things like, "The getMeal(PotPie) method on Shopper asks a Store for a PotPie. It casts this as a Meal and calls addToBasket(Meal), passing it the Meal. . . ." Why not just look at the code? When you have a test, you can see a discrete Assertion (in JUnit) that tests this very behavior and displays a message if the test fails.

Tests also are more useful than other forms of documentation. They give you a scenario in which the behavior of the code should work as intended. If you want to understand what a class does, for example, look at its tests to see exactly what you should expect in certain scenarios. Other documentation struggles to do that, and usually fails.

Best of all, unit tests are absolutely up to date all the time, unless you're cheating. What other documentation can claim that? We remember life before XP: Whenever we walked onto a new project somebody gave us a document that supposedly described the system we would be working on, usually in a very thick binder. As soon as they put this in our hands, they'd say, "This should help a little, but it's out of date. Come talk to me after you read it." So what earthly good was the document? Maybe it built character to put it together, but that's all it was good for.

Not all such documentation is bad. When a customer needs a written document other than code (say, for regulatory approval), you should produce it. In XP you should produce only the written documents that you absolutely need. The problem is that traditional approaches tend to substitute documentation for communication, and tend to exaggerate progress with documentation. Producing a document might be helpful at times, but documents don't run. In the end, it's the code the counts. Alistair Cockburn says

> *Written, reviewed requirements and design documents are "promises" for what will be built, serving as timed progress markers. There are times when creating them is good. However, a more accurate timed progress marker is running tested code. It is more accurate because it is not a timed promise, it is a timed accomplishment.*[2]

---

2. A. Cockburn. Quoted in "Extreme Programming." *e-Business Application Delivery.* J. Highsmith, ed. Volume 12, Number 2, 2000.

Tests are the best form of system documentation because they are the form that distracts least from producing releasable code. They are practical because they are like a virtual guru, walking you through how the code is supposed to work. They are short, not wasting words on things that are obvious. And, if a team is doing what it is supposed to do with XP, the tests are more up to date than any written documentation ever will be.

Tests as Documentation
by Ken Auer and Roy Miller

Recently, we were in a meeting with a prospective client. The client told us that he had software written several years ago by someone who was no longer with the company. He had brought in a new person to try to add some new functionality, but the new guy was having a rough time. The conversation went like this:

Ken: When we develop software, we write unit tests for the nontrivial parts of the code. We also have the customer write acceptance tests to determine whether the system does what he wants it to do. Both sets of tests virtually document the system in terms of how it really works right now.

Client: That makes sense.

Ken: We think so. But I'm curious. Do you have documentation for the existing system?

Client: Yeah, but it's out of date, and the new person working on the system really has no clue what's going on.

Ken: Based on where you stand now, would you rather have the tests I talked about, instead of the documentation you've got?

Client: Absolutely.

This guy was hurting. His company is successful, but a simple matter of poorly documented software threatens the company's ability to deliver to clients.

How to Write Tests First

Before you write code, think about what it will do. Write a test that will use the methods you haven't written yet. Assume the methods exist and use them in the test. The test won't compile (if you have to compile things in your environment). Write the class to be tested and its methods—just stubs, not all the details. Then your test should compile.

Add the test to the related test suite. Run the test suite. Your new test will cause it to fail. You don't have any implementation for the methods you're testing, so this shouldn't be a surprise. Running a test just to see it fail might seem a little strange, but it's important. Failure validates the test at this point. If it passes, it's clearly wrong.

Now write just enough code to get the test to pass when you run the test suite again. Doing things this way encourages the smallest design that could possibly work. It keeps your code simple. Yes, there will be refactoring to do later, but it will be small.

Add your test suite to the suite of tests for the entire system and run it. That may seem redundant, but it isn't.

Shouldn't We Write and Run the Test?
by Ken Auer

A few days before OOPSLA '99, a project I was heavily involved with was coming to the end of an iteration. I was trying to add a new feature to the persistence framework. Pairing with someone who was new to the project, to Java, and to XP, I took charge. I coded like a madman for an entire day, writing tons of code without writing tests first (strike one) and not rerunning the test suite for the entire persistence framework (strike two). After struggling to get the new feature to work (based on what I saw when we ran the application), I rotated pairs and tried to integrate with a new partner. We ran the test suite for the persistence framework and got roughly 30 failures. Thinking out loud, my new partner said, "Let's see, they all ran with your changes before we integrated, right?" I felt like an idiot.

Save yourself pain. Get addicted to running tests. Made a change? Run the tests. Made a change that you didn't like and backed it out? Run the tests. Integrated? Run the tests. Took a break for coffee and just got back to your desk? Run the tests.

Refactor the tests when they don't seem to be giving you the leverage you want.[3] If you notice that the suite of tests for a given class doesn't include something that should be tested, write the new test and run the suite to make sure it passes. If you need to refactor some portion of the code and you aren't

---

3. M. Fowler. *Refactoring: Improving the Design of Existing Code.* Addison-Wesley, 1999.

satisfied that the existing tests help you (maybe they don't cover everything well enough), refactor the tests first. Keeping your tests clean is just as important as keeping your code clean. Better tests give you more leverage to make things work better and to add new features quickly.

In *Extreme Programming Explored*, Bill Wake describes a simple set of steps for what he calls the test/code cycle in XP:

1. Write a single test.
2. Compile it. It shouldn't compile, because you haven't written the implementation code it calls.
3. Implement just enough code to get the test to compile.
4. Run the test and see it fail.
5. Implement just enough code to get the test to pass.
6. Run the test and see it pass.
7. Refactor for clarity and "once and only once."
8. Repeat.[4]

Bill claims this process should take about 10 minutes per test. If it takes longer, start writing smaller tests. That may be a bit short, but it's not crazy. In early 2000, Ward Cunningham stopped by RoleModel Software to help Ken's team build its acceptance testing framework. He paired with a number of developers on the team. Every person he paired with made one major observation: Ward took small steps, sometimes ridiculously small. Yet he moved like the wind.

Test-first programming is all about building confidence so that you can work at maximum speed. It only works if you test a lot, which means you have to take steps small enough to force you to test often. Test a little, code a little. Get the tests to pass. Make a change. If the tests fail, the change must have caused it. If you write a few tests, then code for a couple of days, you'll need more time to find errors when a test fails. Chet Hendrickson gave us this analogy:

> *I have a second cousin who is a master mason, and in Eastern Kentucky where I am from we do a lot of work in limestone instead of brick. If you have ever seen a mason lay a brick wall, you would have noticed that they first lay the corners of the wall and then put a string across as a level line. The mason then lays each course to the level line. The line is his unit test.*

---

4. W. Wake. *Extreme Programming Explored*. Addison-Wesley, 2001, pp. 7–8.

When you are working with limestone, you have to do it a little differently.
You put the line a foot or so up from where you are starting and then
arrange the rocks so that you come out level by the time you reach the line.
The point being that even though you are using irregularly shaped stones
you still need to know where you are in relation to level all the way up, if you
are to have any hope of being level when you reach the top. It is basically code
a little, test a little, only using limestone and a level line.[5]

What to Test

Write tests for nontrivial things that could break. We tend not to write tests for getter and setter methods. We also shy away from writing tests for methods that simply invoke another method, as long as the invoked method already has a test. You'll come up with your own cases when you don't need to write tests.

Err on the side of having too many tests. When in doubt, write one. If you need the confidence that your getters and setters absolutely will not break, write tests for them. There aren't any hard and fast rules here. Write the tests needed to instill confidence that the class will work as expected.

Very few of us like writing tests, but we love having them. It may be extra work, but it's well worth it. Until you have a lot of tests and a lot of experience getting burned by not having the one you need, it's better to have too many.

How to Start Writing Tests First

You should be convinced that you need to write tests first. You might have no idea how to do it. Relax. You're in good company. Every time we talk with people who aren't used to writing tests first, we hear things like

- ✧ How exactly do I write a test first?
- ✧ How would you write a test first for XYZ?
- ✧ Huh?

To be honest, most people "in the know" about XP respond roughly the same way. They say they can show you how to write tests before you write code, but they can't describe it to you. This is a cop out. This is not a cop out. That was not a typo.

---

5. C. Hendrickson. Comment made in a review of this book.

Asking someone how to write tests first is like asking someone how to write source code. You can't code by number. The code you write depends on a host of variables. Likewise, there is no comprehensive set of rules for writing tests. The tests you write will depend on the code you want to build to exercise the tests.

Unit tests are just another type of source code. You write them, compile them if you have to, and run them. If you use xUnit (and we recommend it), it's just like writing code that employs a small library of components, methods, or functions.[6] The only real difference is the goal.

Old habits die hard. If you aren't used to writing tests first, it feels awkward. Take comfort in knowing that

- eventually, it will become as natural as writing source code
- your first tests will stink, but that's okay
- your tests will improve with practice
- even crummy tests are better than none

The key to getting into the habit of writing tests first is to realize that you've been doing it for years, but you probably didn't know it.

When you write code, you are imagining the tests. You just haven't written them down yet. If you're writing code to compute a salary, for example you might be thinking, "Get the base salary and bonuses for a given employee from the database, compute FICA, determine the employee's tax bracket, compute withholding, compute take-home pay," and so on.

Stop. You already have imagined how the code is supposed to work. The only thing you have to do now in order to write a test first is to write a test method for the first step that assumes that step is in the code already. Write a method that calls the as-yet-unwritten method getEmployeeSalary(String employeeName). Give it a known employeeName and check that the results are what you would expect. The test will fail, of course, because the method isn't there.

Write the real code for getEmployeeSalary(). Run the test again. Fix the code until it passes all the tests. That's all there is to it.

Some things are harder to test than others. Sometimes it's hard to imagine the tests first. Keep at it. It will feel more natural in time.

---

6. You can download an xUnit framework for writing tests in Java (JUnit), Smalltalk (SUnit), VB (VBUnit), C++ (CppUnit), and many other languages at http://www.xprogramming.com.

Testing Challenges

If unit testing were just about writing tests for PC-based applications, things would be simpler. In today's multidevice, multiplatform world, writing unit tests can be a challenge. Responding to those challenges takes creativity and persistence. Responding well can increase your development confidence dramatically.

Here are some of the challenges you might have to face.

Testing User Interfaces

Testing user interfaces is a royal pain in the backside. We get asked a lot how we write tests for these things. We have lots of answers, but they all stink. The coverage we get from our user interface unit tests seems significantly lower than what we get from testing our business logic. The value received from the tests doesn't seem to be worth the effort put into writing them.

The best way to test user interfaces (UIs) is to isolate what you're testing first. Separate the user interface from the business logic behind it as much as possible. Test the business logic with unit tests, which make the UI less prone to break. Of course, that just means there is less to break, not that it's been tested adequately. Try to write unit tests for what remains in the UI (probably because it belongs there). You may not be able to test everything this way, but that's all right. It's better to have solid unit tests for 90% of the system than none at all.

We've also found it useful to test user interfaces as much as is profitable with unit tests, and then use acceptance tests to fill in the blanks.

Testing in Small Spaces

The world gets very strange when you develop software for small-device platforms. Our company has had experience developing for Motorola iDEN cell phones, Microsoft CE devices, devices running PalmOS, and an interesting platform from Dallas Semiconductor called TINI (Tiny InterNet Interface).

When developing Java applications for small devices, the device size doesn't allow enough room for all of the Java classes we take for granted when developing desktop applications, or even Web applications. This can be frustrating. Typically, it means you'll have to do a little more work to write and run tests. The alternative isn't attractive.

You can test around the small space, perhaps by testing all of the supporting code that runs in desktop applications or on a server, but that leaves gaping holes in your testing. You cannot proceed with the same kind of confidence if you do that. Junk will tend to build up in the code. The extra work you do to create testing frameworks (or to adapt them) for testing in small spaces can pay off by letting you proceed with confidence.

Creating or adapting frameworks for testing in small spaces can be done. The authors know of several examples from personal experience and otherwise.

Testing Without Reflection
by Chris Collins

We were working on a project for one of our clients, porting their framework to run on Motorola's new iDEN device platform. The main iDEN product we were focusing on was their cell phone, which contained a Java Virtual Machine. The cell phone supported the Java 2 MicroEdition (J2ME), Connected Limited Device Configuration (CLDC), Mobile Information Device Profile (MIDP) specification.

One of the problems we encountered was that we could not instantiate some of the MIDP-specific classes on the development platform. This made running unit tests extremely hard. JUnit would not run on the MIDP platform, because J2ME does not support reflection (along with a few other classes). After much discussion, we decided that it would be easy enough to port JUnit to run under J2ME.

We spent about a day porting JUnit and writing a MIDP-specific UI for it. Setting up the tests became a little more difficult because we could not rely on reflection to find all the methods that began with "test." We modified the TestSuite class to work around this. We accept an array of strings, which we use to pass in the methods we want to run. Then we write a TestCase where we override the runTest() method. Then, based on which method gets passed in explicitly, we call the test case. The code looks like this:

```
protected void runTest() throws java.lang.Throwable {
    if(getTestMethodName().equals("testOne"))
        testOne();
    else if(getTestMethodName().equals("testTwo"))
        testTwo();
}
```

This code let us run our unit tests on the target platform itself, which also made each test more reliable. After finishing the port we were able to move ahead again at full speed with our battery of unit tests.

You can freely download J2ME Unit at www.rolemodelsoft.com/aboutUs/products.htm or www.xprogramming.com/software.htm.

Testing the Web

In some ways, testing Web-based applications can be as challenging as testing in small spaces. This is because there are pieces of the puzzle that you probably don't own or don't have programmatic control over. You didn't write the Java Servlet engine from scratch, but you have to interact with it. A significant portion of the interaction with a Web application probably happens on a Web page. This means you might not have direct, discrete programmatic control over the widgets for acceptance testing.

If you are employing the practice of simple design, the problem becomes easier. In an e-mail to an XP mailing list, Steve Hayes provided the following two hints that can make testing servlets and EJBs manageable:

> *My approach in [this] environment is twofold:*
>
> 1. *Separate the Servlets into two layers—an interface layer that understands HTTP protocol (requests, responses, etc.) and an application layer that is independent. You can test the application layer independently.*
> 2. *I constructed proxy HTTP protocol objects I could use to drive even the interface layer without actually having the server running. It made testing with JUnit much easier. There may be other approaches, but this was the simplest thing I could do given my level of experience with HTTP.*

Tests Have to Run Fast

Regardless of what kind of testing you're doing, if your tests don't run quickly, you will be less likely to run them as often as you should. This will let you revert to the habit of taking large steps when you code, without verification that you didn't break anything. This in turn will slow the team down over time.

Tests Have to Be Fast
by Steve Hayes

One thing we (re)discovered is that, to be effective, tests need to run quickly. If a test suite takes two seconds to run, it's run after every change. If a suite takes five minutes to run, it's only run every hour or so, which corresponds to many changes. If you want to take small steps but move as swiftly as the wind, then you need to have fast-running tests.

This is another constraint on design—the first one XP imposes—that everything actually needs to be testable. For example, SQL statements embedded

---

in business logic won't meet this constraint because they make the business logic tests too slow. This constraint forces layers of software and the ability to plug in dummy layers for testing (e.g., in-memory database instead of SQL). It's one of the forces that makes XP software more flexible.

The trick is to write tests first, then refactor them for performance when necessary. This refactoring should be part of your project's flow—tests are code, after all. Entropy can kill your tests over time just like it can kill other parts of your system.

At Martin's refactoring workshop at OOPSLA 2000, Chet Hendrickson talked about the challenge of fast-running tests on the C3 project. He said that every once in awhile, the tests would start to take longer. The project had thousands of assertions, so even at top speed they took some time to run. Big delays were a threat to progress. They treated major test refactorings as stories that had to fit into the schedule. When they did that, the tests always ran at top speed, but the customer realized that took some effort—it wasn't free. The result was that even when their systemwide test suite was at maximum size, it took only 12 minutes or so to run.

Chapter 14

Stop the Maverick

Two heads are better then (sic) one.
—John Heywood, *Proverbs*

Force people to break the habit of working alone most of the time. If you don't, you will not see maximum productivity.

Ever try writing with your nondominant hand? Pair programming can feel like that if you're not used to it. It is one of the hardest XP practices for developers and managers to adjust to. Pairing seems a little weird, but is absolutely essential to your success in XP.[1]

Programming in pairs increases code quality because it acts like a continuous code review. Nothing keeps you honest like having somebody sit next to you while you code.

Programming in pairs increases developer speed, which reduces development time and thus project costs. XP is structured to let customers get value out of their software sooner rather than later. Money today is worth more than money tomorrow.

Programming in pairs reduces project risk. If you're a manager, that's music to your ears. If you're a developer, you're happy when your manager is happy.

---

1. See J. T. Nosek. "The Case for Collaborating Programming." *Communications of the ACM*. Volume 41, Number 3, 1998.

Code Quality

Code reviews are quite possibly the best way to improve code quality. Much of the benefit from code reviews comes from the first reviewer, so XP makes this the norm. We pair almost all the time, which means another person is reviewing our code constantly. There is no better way to ensure code quality.

Very few people like doing code reviews. The exciting part to most is creating the stuff that solves the problem. Reviewing code someone else wrote is not nearly as exciting as writing code yourself. To many, it is sort of like proofreading a doctoral dissertation on the mating habits of fruit flies. Even if it weren't quite that unattractive, code reviews don't get done with the same zeal as code writing.

Though it is true that if you don't take the time to write quality code right, you won't have time to do it over, on most traditional projects there seemingly isn't time for either one. Code reviews go by the wayside when the schedule's on the line. When reviews do get done at all, they're often cursory affairs conducted by people who are under such extreme stress they aren't able to give it their best. Worse still, the reviewers often don't know enough about the details of what they're reviewing to do a credible job of it. A crummy code review might be slightly better than none at all, but not much.

XP doesn't give you a choice. You review code all the time: It's part of writing the code in pairs. While your partner is typing, you're reviewing. If your partner does something stupid, it's your job to point it out (politely, of course). It's your partner's job to do the same for you when it's your turn to drive.

Code reviews after the fact are fine—in fact, they can help projects produce better stuff—but they are a distant second to the quality improvements you get from pairing.

The Need for Speed

American football is a psychological game. No, really. If you watch enough of it, you'll hear commentators talk about momentum a great deal. The team that's making the big plays, getting the yards when they need them, marching down the field—they've got the momentum. Despite talent and preparation, a momentum swing sometimes is enough to put a team over the top.

Momentum on a software project is about velocity. If you're chugging through your iterations producing great value for your customer, you've got momentum. If something slows you down, you can lose momentum, despite the talent you have or the preparation you put in. You should guard your velocity with your life, because your velocity *is* your life.

Two things are most likely to slow you down:

- ✧ Bad code
- ✧ Poor communication

If your code stinks, you'll move slower. Pair programming improves code quality because the code is under constant review. Improved quality means you don't have to spend as much time on clean-up or on hacks, or on bug fixes. Those things take time, sap your energy, and slow you down. They represent death by a thousand cuts for a project.

XP is a team sport. People must work together and share problems. Some people may experience short bursts of hyperproductivity when they program solo, but solo programming will slow the team down in the long run.

One other thing to keep in mind is, people can use their time more efficiently when they pair. If another person is watching you code, you probably won't surf the Web or check e-mail every ten minutes. You will feel obligated to treat your time together as valuable. You are less likely to be unnecessarily interrupted. When you code alone, you are readily available for interruption. When you code in a pair, casual interruptions will be less frequent, because people will notice that you're busy.

Pairing keeps people honest. It keeps them focused. It keeps them moving at maximum speed.

Reducing Risk

In *Extreme Programming Explained,* Kent says that an approach to software development that increases a project's chances of staying alive is more valuable than the alternatives.[2] Pair programming is critical to helping XP do that. There are times when programming solo is the right thing to do, but far more often you will pay a price for not pairing.

Mavericks Are Always Found Out
by Ken Auer

Officially, everything is supposed to be done in pairs, and we intial everything we check into the system. It is amazing how many times someone who is struggling

---

2. K. Beck. *Extreme Programming Explained: Embrace Change.* Addison-Wesley, 2000, pp. 12–13.

to make something work finds that they are working on top of some software that was checked in with just one set of initials. The person who checked that code in usually did so thinking that he was just going to make a simple change that wouldn't affect anything else negatively. He was just fixing a bug.

The tests didn't catch the problem, but eight out of ten times, a pair would have.

Once on our project, we discovered a problem enabling and disabling tabs and menu items. In order to fix this bug, one developer figured he could just knock it out. He started down a path that didn't get him to the fix. So, he decided that, since the menus were just built in one place, he'd just destroy and rebuild them every time the screen was built instead of using "enablers." Some time later, we tackled a story requiring dynamically adding items to a menu. We couldn't understand why we were getting some strange side effects. Eventually, we realized that the maverick's approach to fixing the bug had not only produced really ugly code and the strange side effects, but it also made extending our acceptance test framework to examine menu contents very difficult. We eventually got it fixed. We reduced the code and put enablers back in. The maverick had misdiagnosed the original problem. A partner more familiar with enablers would have caught it early on.

Projects fail for lots of reasons, but there are a few primary things that increase the risk of failure:

✧ Slowness
✧ Poor communication
✧ Dependence on individual heroes [3]

Pair programming minimizes these risks better than programming alone. We addressed slowness earlier in this chapter. We tackled poor communication in Chapter 9. Dependence on heroes needs some explanation.

Suppose the best programmer on your team gets run over by a truck. If you are not using XP, you can kiss the project good-bye. The only way to get past this is to reduce your team's dependence on heroes. Pairing does that.

---

3. Jim Coplien coined the term "truck number" for this concept. See J. Coplien. "Pattern Languages of Program Design" in *A Generative Development Process Pattern Language*. Addison-Wesley, 1995, p. 194.

Jim Highsmith told us:

Cross-training has always been one of those things that management wants, but there is never enough time for. And even if there were time—how do you actually do it? Pairing provides cross-training while delivering a product![4]

How to Pair Program

Pair programming is two programmers actively working on the same problem on the same machine at the same time.

There are two roles in pair programming: the driver and the navigator. The driver writes code and the navigator helps direct and look for potholes. Both are active roles. When you program in a pair, you must be engaged at all times.

When you're driving, you've got to manage the mechanics of what you're doing. "Should I use this method or that one?" You need to pay attention to what your navigator is, or is not saying. If your navigator makes a suggestion or raises an objection, listen. If your navigator isn't engaged, slow down and ask what he doesn't get. Better still, let the navigator take the wheel.

When you're the navigator, you're not just riding and admiring the scenery. This isn't "pair watching." You must actively understand everything that's going on. Ask questions. Suggest alternatives. Stay on the same thought plane as the driver. Think beyond the code mechanics, to be sure, but don't veer off on some crazy tangent. Don't distract the driver. Give him time to see his own mistakes and correct them. If the driver gets stuck, ask to drive.

Conversant Pairing
by Nathaniel Talbott

There are so many benefits to pair programming when it is done correctly. The problem is that there are so many ways to do it incorrectly. How do you know when you're doing it wrong? This was a question that rattled around in my brain when I first started pairing, until a coworker and I realized that there was a common element in the really excellent, productive pairing sessions we had. We found that a great pairing session was a conversation, and that all of the rules of discussion applied to pairing.

---

4. J. Highsmith. Personal e-mail conversation with Ken Auer, March 2001.

Say you sit down with someone to pair. You're driving and they're navigating. After coding for a while, you realize that you're doing all of the talking, and all they're really doing is nodding their head. Uh oh, this isn't a very good conversation, is it? It takes two people talking to have a discussion. So how do you fix it? Again, take it back to talking to another person. If you want feedback in a conversation, a great way to get it is to ask questions instead of just making statements. So start asking your pair questions: "How do you think we should do this?" "What's a good name for this method?" "Do you know of a clean way to implement this?" Try to stay away from yes and no questions, because they'll just beget more head nodding.

This certainly applies the other way around, too. If you're navigating (and the other person is driving) and you don't feel like you're helping or engaged, start asking questions. "Why did you do it that way?" "What are you thinking?" "Would it work better if . . . ?" Oops, now your pair is having trouble thinking because you're asking so many questions in succession. In a good conversation, there are lulls as people think about what they're going to say next. Allow the pairing session to flow in the same way.

It's amazing how much my pairing has improved since I've understood and applied this fundamental principle.

If pairing is to be effective, people have to practice filling the role of driver and navigator often, and they can't be joined at the hip with a particular pair all the time. Switch places from driver to navigator and back again with regularity. Switch pairs often, keeping one caveat in mind: don't switch pairs in the middle of a task. Ken claims that he needs to reach a point of critical mass with his partner, making sure they both know where they're coming from, where they're headed, and how they might get there. It really slows down the team if people have to switch in the middle of tasks. As long as you can see a task through to the end, knowing when to switch pairs becomes more obvious.

For all the laudatory talk about pair programming, people sometimes forget it's hard. When two people who are good at pairing write code together, the results can be mind-bogglingly great, but remember that those two people had to learn how to pair. They didn't start out being able to do it so well. Even though pairing might seem impossible for you when you start, you *can* get better at it. Your perseverance will be rewarded over time. Be patient with yourself and with others while you learn how to pair well.

Do's and Don'ts of Pair Programming
by Kevin Johnson

Software development is a social and cultural process at least as much as it is a technical process. Software development in the wild seldom even approaches the Software Engineering (be sure to pronounce the capital letters) ideal of producing programs based on fixed requirements with a linear progression of formal steps. While the traditional model of software development has been instrumental in advancing the state of the art, it fails to address the aspects of the craft that derive from the fact that software development is a process performed by humans who are part of a culture. Pair programming is one among several of the practices of XP that acknowledges the fact that humans are social beings and work best in the context of a web of social contacts and shared culture.

It's not only the effect of two heads being better than one (although they are) that gives pair programming its strength. The shared understanding of the whole system that grows naturally out of pair programming tends to produce valuable insights more often. The often reported effect of detailed or tactical thinking while at the keyboard and more abstract or strategic thinking while filling the other role is real and gives pairs an important advantage over individuals. In my experience, code written with a partner is almost invariably better by any measure you care to name than code written by either partner alone. All of these effects and more contribute to the power of pair programming.

It is probably true that not all people are cut out for pair programming. But in several years of using the practice in various environments I have yet to find anyone who could not work that way. Different pairs may find it best to work in different ways and the team relationship evolves over time. But as long as a pair starts with or can quickly establish a certain amount of mutual trust and respect, they can probably work together. There are, however, some things that work and some that don't.

Take frequent breaks. Pair programming is an intense activity. You simply can't keep it going for eight hours straight with no rest. Pair programming accelerates progress, but it's also more intense than solo programming. You get tired sooner and for that reason long hours are an even worse idea when pair programming than when running solo. Breaks can take the form of a full-scale coffee break or simply a few minutes of talking about anything *but* the software.

The backseat driver effect. It sounds strange, but the person who is *not* running the keyboard and the mouse can find the location of menu choices or a particular item in a list faster than the person who is running the keyboard. This can lead to conflict because the driver feels stupid when the backseat driver impatiently points out the proper menu choice so quickly. You need to realize that the effect is real. If the roles were reversed, it would still be easier for the one not running the keyboard and harder for the one at the keyboard. It's a fact of life and you need to learn to deal with it. Practice with the menus as well as an understanding on both sides helps mitigate the problems. Accepting guidance from the backseat driver can be useful. The backseat driver needs to cultivate patience realizing that when the tables are turned it will be just as hard for her to see the proper choice. The use of shortcut keys will also help minimize the friction caused by the backseat driver effect.

Take time to learn the tools. Pairs need to discuss the most efficient ways to use the tools just like they discuss the state of the software. Advice should be given in the spirit of helpfulness rather than competition and should be accepted cheerfully. Modern development environments are so complex that it takes a long time for anyone to learn all their capabilities. The pair will be stronger if they both spend some time learning from each other and discovering the most efficient way to use their tools.

Take time to build a shared vocabulary. Pair programming requires close communication. Before I had done much pair programming I found it hard to convey my ideas about a design to other people in real time. Written documentation is essentially useless for day-to-day work while pair programming. You need to be able to communicate face to face. "Trust me I know what I'm doing" eventually becomes unsatisfying. Developing a shared design and vocabulary allows teams to increase velocity because they can communicate more effectively. Part of the shared vocabulary can take the form of pattern names from GoF.* But the shared vocabulary also needs to encompass the business domain and the objects in the system under construction. Working in pairs almost guarantees that a shared vocabulary will develop over time. But conscious attention to the process can lessen the time it will take.

Limit design discussions. Even after some preliminary design is done, there will be blank spots that need to be filled in as the pair works on the implementation. Particularly in the early phases of a project, filling these blank spots can lead to long abstract discussions. If you find yourselves spending more than an hour debating a particular design choice, you probably don't understand it very well yet. You should pick the simplest question that could possibly provide some insight into the design problem and write

---

* GoF stands for "gang of four," E. Gamma, R. Helm, R. Johnson, and J. Vlissides, the authors of *Design Patterns: Elements of Reusable Object-Oriented Software*. Addison-Wesley, 1995.

Pair-Friendly Space

We've paired under the worst conditions (e.g., the corner of a cubicle that was barely big enough for one person) and made it work. We've also had days with the best physical conditions (e.g., a cordless mouse and keyboard, two monitors and a good refresh rate, lots of table space, comfortable chairs, both developers knowing the tools and system well), and had it be a bad session. So far, the critical success factor seems to be two people focused on solving the same task and desiring to do it together. Attitude matters much more than the physical environment. However, we'll choose the better physical environment every time.

Before you can do any of this comfortably, you have to have an environment conducive to pairing. Roy once worked on a big project (not using XP) with over fifty developers. Everybody sat in cubes shared by two people. He couldn't directly collaborate with anyone but his cubemate, and switching places with somebody was an unpardonable sin. He wasn't allowed to remove walls entirely or reconfigure them either. This didn't work. The team ended up removing panels to make "windows" in the cubes. They had to overcome too much to do what should have been natural.

Pair programming is all about communication. You may need to arrange your workspace to facilitate that. Don't be shy. If people don't have cubes next to each other, change that first. When they're all together, make sure each cube has enough space at one desk for two people to work side by side and still get their legs under the desk. Then tear down the walls. You shouldn't have any walls between programmers on the same team.

Another thing that needs to be encouraged is a standardized development environment. If one developer uses VisualAge, another uses SlickEdit, and still another uses emacs, it will be very difficult to pair program. If you can't get everyone to standardize, throw in some rules that get them over their personally tuned space. For example, suggest that in order to broaden their horizons, people must agree to program in a different environment for at least half the time for the next several weeks. Soon they may decide they can converge on a single environment. If you are a champion of XP, be the first to offer to learn another's programming environment. Point out that it is more important to work together than to use a particular editor.

We suggest adopting three rules for setting priorities in XP (and in life):[5]

1. People are more important than things
2. People are more important than things
3. People are more important than things

Don't Ignore Problem Children

Once you're pairing, switch up as often as practically possible. Don't let a bad apple spoil the barrel. If one person resists pairing or simply refuses to do it, don't put up with it. We have found playful joking to be successful in getting people over their resistance. When somebody mavericks, we scream, "Witch!" That's a humorous way to remind people of what they're not supposed to be doing. It usually does the trick. When it doesn't, the coach should talk to the rule breaker to explain the reasons behind the rules. If he still refuses to comply, bid him farewell. Here's how Ron Jeffries puts it:

What I do (as opposed to how I talk) is that when someone is transgressing rules in some way, I'll have a talk with them. Usually something bad will have happened, which lets us begin by agreeing that something bad shouldn't happen again. I relate the rules to the bad effect in an impersonal way. "The unit tests weren't run before the code was released. The unit tests would have shown the problem. That's why we insist on running them every time. We're fallible, the computer isn't." Usually the problem won't occur again. Also I watch the person and nag them a few times in a friendly way. Perhaps most importantly, I'd coach the other team members to watch out for the bad behavior when partnering. In other words, gang up on him. If it does happen again, I'll have a still friendly but serious chat that says "Everyone in the group really does have to follow the rules." Since they're programmers, they can do the math on people who don't follow the rules. If it happens a third time, I would politely but gently remove them from the

---

5. R. Swenson. Talk given at North Carolina Home Educator's Conference, May 2000.

group. If removing them isn't possible, I'd make it turn out that they didn't get to work on anything important.[6]

XP isn't for everyone. Most people who try it love it, but some don't. Find these people and help them exit gracefully, for the health of the rest of the team.

Taking It to the Next Level

All this talk about how to pair is great, but the really wondrous thing about pairing is the interpersonal relationship part, not the mechanics. Anybody can sit next to someone else and throw in two cents every so often. Many people can be completely engaged and try to make the result better. But the ones who really understand pairing know that it's about loving another person.

Yes, you heard right. Pairing is about loving the person you're pairing with. We aren't talking about romantic love. We're talking about the kind that seeks to show itself through actions. You will only get the most out of pairing if that's the attitude you have. Here's what we mean.

When you love another person, you try to see the best in him. You try to help him be the best he can be, rather than just looking out for number one. You are investing in that person's growth and coming out better for the experience. You will be patient. You will be kind. You won't be jealous of that person's success, but rejoice in it. You won't build yourself up at his expense. You'll take a back seat sometimes and let the other person shine. You won't hold a grudge when he screws up and it hurts you. Instead, you'll forgive. You will support that person when he's down and take his side when the going gets tough. In *Extreme Programming Explored*, Bill Wake quoted Harris Kirk as saying, "Pair programming asks us to accept our fallibility and continue."[7] If you're loving your partner, you'll accept *his* fallibility and continue.

As Ron Jeffries says

Extreme Programming (and leadership in general) is a work of love. If you don't respect others, you're not doing it right. I try always to let my great respect show through for people who try hard to do the right thing. And sure enough, they do try, in almost every case. The others, who are perhaps trying in some way I don't understand . . . I respect them too . . . and wish them success elsewhere.[8]

---

6. R. Jeffries. *Enforcing Methods* at http://c2.com/cgi/wiki?EnforcingMethods.
7. W. Wake. *Extreme Programming Explored.* Addison-Wesley, 2001, p. 71.
8. R. Jeffries. *Enforcing Methods* at http://c2.com/cgi/wiki?EnforcingMethods.

How should that attitude affect how you pair? It's taking pairing to the next level. You won't just contribute. You'll be humble and polite, truly respecting what the other person has to offer. You will talk so that your partner can keep up with you.[9] You will listen when your pair offers some wisdom or advice, because, hey, you don't know everything. You will be gracious when your partner makes a mistake. You will let the other person drive sometimes, even if he's junior. You will notice when your partner makes a great contribution and be his biggest fan. You will respect each other enough to know your partner's rhythm. You will speak in terms of "we" not "you," unless you're paying a compliment. You will speak in "I" terms when things get rough.

Radical? Sure. But that's taking pairing to the next level. The question of why you should have this attitude in general is the subject of another book. Suffice it to say here that it makes pairing a much richer experience than simply going through the motions.

The Inevitable Objections

In Chapters 3 through 5 we talked about resistance to XP. Most likely, the resistance you face will concentrate on pair programming. It's an easy target for knee-jerk myopia. Fortunately, you have anecdotal and empirical evidence on your side. We think the best summary of both is in an article by Laurie Williams of North Carolina State University and Alistair Cockburn of Humans and Technology.

Managers view pairing as wasteful in terms of time and money. Programmers resist it as well, because they aren't taught to do things this way and they feel it steals their individuality. Alistair and Laurie investigated these objections. Here is a summary their findings:[10]

1. **Pair programming saves money.** Pair programming increases development cost by about 15%, but the resulting code has 15% fewer defects. Based on a simple example Alistair and Laurie give, this can reduce fixing costs (in testing, in QA, or after release) by 15% to 60%.

---

9. See "Conversant Pairing" by Nathaniel Talbott at http://www. pairprogramming.com for some excellent opinions on how to do this. It is a great elaboration on what Ward Cunningham calls "reflective articulation."

10. A. Cockburn, L. Williams. "The Costs and Benefits of Pair Programming" in *Extreme Programming Examined,* by G. Succi and M. Marchesi. Addison-Wesley, 2001, pp. 223–243.

2. **Programmers like it once they try it.** Consistently over 85% of students studied said they enjoyed their work more when pairing. Professionals surveyed on the Internet said the same.

3. **Design quality improves.** Pairs produce higher-quality code, and they implement the same functionality in fewer lines of code than solo programmers do.

4. **Code quality improves.** Pairs find mistakes sooner and follow coding standards better (and learn to talk and work together better). This improves code quality.

5. **Pairs solve problems better and faster.** Pairs combine brainstorming and "pair relaying" (tag-teaming when one or the other gets stuck) to maximum problem-solving effectiveness.

6. **Pairs learn better and faster.** Pairing is basically a revolving apprenticeship. The partners alternate learning and teaching from moment to moment. "Even unspoken skills and habits cross partners."

7. **Pair programming improves team building and communication.** Pairs communicate all the time. Rotating pairs increases information flow, which increases team effectiveness.

8. **Pair programming facilitates management.** Having people program in pairs increases programmer skills faster (they're learning all the time). Everybody is familiar with key parts of the system, so the project faces lower risk from losing key programmers.

That's some pretty good ammunition. If that fails, get some experiential evidence. Don't take pot shots at something potentially beneficial without actually trying it.

When Not to Pair

This may be heresy within the XP community, but there are certain rare times when it makes sense not to pair. Notice that important word "rare."

When not to pair will vary by team. Our rule is that mavericking shouldn't happen often. It should never happen on tough code. But there are some instances when it makes sense not to pair. In these cases, working parallel for a short time and then coming back together is often smarter. Ken calls this "pairallelism."

There are two cases where we've found pairallelism works, although it's important to note that there may be some advantages to pairing in these cases as well:

1. When you are exploring something new
2. When you have multiple ideas about what might be causing a bug

When you're exploring, it's wise to give both members of the pair room to move in their own direction at their own pace. Some of the more extreme XPers would say that any code developed solo (e.g., during exploration) should be thrown away and rewritten with a pair. We say, "Give us a break." We're prepared to refactor or rewrite if necessary, but we aren't going to do it just because we *might* benefit from doing it. Pair until you reach something you don't understand. If you struggle with it together for a long time, split up and search alone. Keep each other aware of what you're finding as you go. When you think you know enough to move on, pair up again.

We've found there are times when a pair is following a path and gets totally surprised by behavior that has escaped the tests. Their discussion turns to brainstorming. Often they come up with two or three likely possibilities. When faced with this situation, it might be effective to split up and track down the problem separately, each looking down a different path. When either thinks they have identified the problem or have ended up at a dead end, they come back together as a pair and share what they have learned.

Trying to follow a line of thought when somebody else is clicking all over the place can be very frustrating. It can be just as frustrating for someone with a hunch about how something works, to slow down to explain the hunch before exploring it further. The pair should get past the frustration and use it as a training opportunity. But there are other times where there just isn't any payback. Try it both ways and ask both people what they think.

Pair Debugging
by Steve Hayes

Debugging sessions are rare and usually occur when the customer reports a fault. We treat the correction of the fault as a story, just like any other story, and assign a pair.

The first step for the pair is usually finding the fault, and they usually need a debugging session to find it. Following a line of thought while somebody else is clicking all over the place is frustrating, but it's also a great opportunity to learn about the component that's being debugged and about different approaches to debugging. We make the person who knows the most about the component the driver and encourage them to give a running monologue about their activity, including the hypotheses they are testing at each point, even if this slows them down somewhat. Hearing someone say, "I'm going to check the contents of X because at this point I expect that the object looks like this . . ." is fantastic. It's such a concrete statement. It either lets you learn by saying, "Why do you expect that?" or it gives you the opportunity to improve the debugging by saying, "I don't agree with that—I think. . . ."

My experience is that many junior developers are very weak on debugging because they have worked with only small-scale systems they wrote when they were in school. They often don't have a systematic approach to debugging. Working with a senior developer on a debugging exercise can make a huge difference.

Both exploration and debugging illustrate a fluid pairing environment. Not only will you be switching pairs, but you'll be moving in and out of your current pair when it makes sense.

Some people suggest that getting a second set of eyes on your code after you have done some solo development is just as good as pairing. If you're serious about it, it can work well. It's better than mavericking with nobody to keep you honest. The main problem we see is that when we don't pair program, we're prone to assuming we don't need the second set of eyes. There is also something lost in the transfer of knowledge. The second pair of eyes learns what has been done but didn't influence or learn from the path to get there.

When in doubt, pair and see if it works. Odds are it will. Most importantly, don't simply avoid pairing because you don't feel like it. Sometimes feelings aren't trustworthy—they might be leading you to avoid something that's good for you, just because it might be temporarily uncomfortable.

The Balance Between Pairing and Working Alone
by Steve Hayes

Everyone experienced in XP development will happily tell you that we should be pair programming all the time. And we should. Other people have explained the benefits, and I've observed them myself. But there is something else left unsaid, an evil twin to pair programming, locked out of sight in a darkened XP tower. Every one of us feels the urge to program alone, to spurn our potential partners and lock ourselves in that tower. If pair programming is the Jedi Force, then this is the Dark Side. You can't overcome the Dark Side by ignoring it. There will always be a part of you saying, "I'd rather be doing this by myself." So I'm going to spend some time shining a light on my own dark side and show you how you can embrace it.

Sometimes I want to work alone because I want to be a hero. I want to sit back and write some code that accomplishes something wonderful, that demonstrates that I am the genius that I think I am. There are a couple of problems with this. The first is that I'm not really the genius that I think I am. I'll probably deliver something that does the job I thought it should, but my work will be subject to all the failings that pair programming is intended to overcome. I may not have had the right job in mind, so I may have included features that aren't really necessary, and I may have left out features that are essential. I will have gone down some dark alleys and spent more time in them than if I'd had a partner to help ground me. My code probably won't be as clean as it would have been if I'd been working with someone all the time. But worst of all, I won't actually be a hero. If anything, I'm doing my teammates a disservice by creating code that only one person understands. If I'm really a genius, and I want to be a hero, then I'll find ways to help other people see what's needed and help them develop it, making the work into a learning experience for everyone. So I shouldn't work alone because I want to be a hero.

Sometimes I want to work alone because I'm afraid of exposing my deficiencies. I've always been proud of the quality of my finished software. It's tempting to present my development as a linear progression from initial spark to finished product. Of course that's not accurate. In reality I make lots of missteps, back up a lot, and sometimes simply just throw it away and start again. But I don't want to display all these warts to the world, which is what I have to do when I work with a partner! Part of establishing a successful XP environment is learning to check part of your ego at the door, to be fearless at the personal level. When communication includes all those small, daily failures as well as the grand success at the end, everyone benefits. Less experienced people see that everyone goes up and down the same slippery slopes that they do. The more experienced get the pleasure of seeing people improve their skills much faster when the process is completely open. No one learns effectively when half the story is hidden from them. So I shouldn't work alone because I'm afraid, either.

Sometimes I want to work alone because what I'm doing is pure speculation and I don't want to waste my partner's time. There are times when I think that I have some idea that will make the work a lot easier, but I can't quite explain what I'm trying to achieve. I don't like these situations, because they tell me that either I don't understand what I'm doing as well as I should or I'm doing a lousy job of explaining, but they still crop up. Worse yet, there are times when my half-baked explanation leaves my partner convinced this is a bad idea that we shouldn't waste any time on, but I'm still convinced it's the right way to go. What should I do? Maybe I have become attached to a bad idea. Well, XP encourages us to make things concrete, so I should come up with the smallest example I can to test my idea. My partner shouldn't feel obliged to hang around while I demonstrate my own confusion, so I might do this alone. The key is to keep the investigation time as short as possible, and then to get back together and talk about the conclusions. Don't use a disagreement with your partner as an excuse to work alone indefinitely. If you are taking small steps then this shouldn't be hard.

Sometimes I want to work alone because I'm in a bad mood. I've had a bad trip on the subway, I spilled my breakfast down my shirt, there were production problems when I got to the office, and my headache just won't go away. This doesn't sound like a good time to pair program. In fact, it doesn't sound like a good time to program at all. It's time to focus on my nonprogramming problems and get them under control, to get myself to the point where I can work with other people. If you're like me, sometimes you write code because it lets you ignore your other problems for a while. This isn't really healthy. So take some deep breaths, sit in a quiet place, and relax for a while. Remind yourself that your teammates didn't arrange your subway trip, clean up your shirt, do whatever you need to do to make sure the production problems don't recur, and take something for the headache. Then get back to working with the team again. Maybe you shouldn't drive. But don't work alone because you're in a bad mood.

Sometimes I want to work alone because I enjoy the meditative sense I achieve when I'm in the flow. Over the years I've become accustomed to spending a lot of time working alone, wrapped in my own thoughts. I've come to enjoy it. Pair programming strips this away. Instead of spending time with my thoughts I spend time with other developers. It's not a better or worse experience, but it is a different one and it takes a while to become accustomed to. Some days I still need a bit more alone time than others, but it doesn't have to come at the workplace. It can come while I read the morning paper over breakfast, while I run the treadmill at the gym, or while I work on my other hobbies. Since an XP team works a 40-hour week I have more time to be meditative outside of the office. It's a difficult transition, but a worthwhile one.

The key thing to remember is that everyone around you feels these impulses to the Dark Side. There needs to be give and take between the individual and the team. Individual programmers need to admit to themselves when they are trying to be a hero or they are feeling afraid, acknowledge to themselves that it's okay to have these feelings, and move on. Your team-mates have these feelings and desires as well, so they won't be surprised if you admit yours to them. The team needs to understand that there will be times when someone needs to program alone for a short while, or when someone isn't fit to program at all. Of course there are limits—you can't have a team member who never wants to pair program at all—but the team can be remarkably flexible. XP recognizes that we are people with feelings and emotions, not just plug-compatible units, and it turns this into a strength. Just like the Jedi Knights.

Unusual Pairs

We've seen lots of times where working in pairs makes sense, whether temporary or permanent. Writing books, for example, often can be done in pairs. We've alluded to some others:

- Programmer and customer or QA person working together to write acceptance tests
- Programmer and customer working together to identify tasks
- Programmer and customer debugging something very specific to a domain

Pairing allows two people to produce something greater than either one could produce alone. It is worth the extra effort, even when pairing isn't the obvious choice. Finding a way to do it can pay you back many times over.

Pairing to Build Bridges
by Steve Freeman

I was technical lead and principal XPer on a project to build a financial pricing library. The group was essentially the maintenance team for the previous product, which management felt had reached the end of its useful life. We started a rewrite to allow us to support server-based calculations that we thought were impossible with the old version.

One of the main issues that we were concerned about was how to integrate our programmers and mathematicians. Traditionally, good mathematicians do not write well-structured software because their training and mind set are just too different from software developers. Conversely, our programmers did not understand the math well enough to make judgments about algorithms and results. XP provided an excellent, pragmatic solution for writing good mathematical software by pairing across disciplines. We didn't switch pairs as often as other XP projects because the intellectual costs of understanding each algorithm were high, but we did eventually manage to achieve reasonable coverage within the group.

At the time, we were worried about how to structure the group to avoid intellectual black holes. We considered setting up pools of mathematicians and programmers to force the combinations, but in the end the answer, as always, was to keep things simple and let people sort it out themselves. Interestingly, another mathematician outside our group picked up our development style, particularly the test suites and refactoring. He later joined an investment bank and, the last time I spoke to him, his colleagues could not understand how he could deliver software that ran so reliably and quickly.

We also put a lot of effort into writing test spreadsheets to automate acceptance testing of the library. At times the overhead seemed tremendous compared to how we traditionally tested our code. The benefit was that we could always show how much we'd achieved, we understood our target platform really well, and we caught a number of bugs that might otherwise have shipped—including one in the underlying floating point library.

In the end, we didn't convert the entire team, but I was really pleased when two of our best programmers said, independently, that they didn't see how we could have achieved so much without XP.

Personal Space

One of the arguments we've heard against pair programming is that people need their personal space. Someone on an XP mailing list once said that depriving people of a place to call their own dehumanizes them.

We don't know of any XP proponents who want to deny people their personal space. But cubes are a lousy team working environment. You might be surprised to find out that XP teams often choose to give up personal space voluntarily, but if your team needs personal space, find a way to give them some. Just don't substitute it for a team working environment—it is secondary space. Give everybody a drawer, a locker, or a cubby.

There is a big difference between valuing individuals and promoting individualism. XP values individuals so much that it chooses not to isolate them. If isolation is "humanizing" then we should all find employers who prefer that their people telecommute, stay or become single, order everything over the Internet, and don't participate in team sports. And never, ever leave their homes. We have found that people warm to the idea of team space. They start valuing the team environment more than their personal space and might even give up that personal space. If someone spends lots of time in his personal space to avoid the team, you need to fix that. Help such people realize that this behavior is devaluing the other members of the team, and possibly even hurting themselves.

You can actually make team space more attractive and get more people per square foot. The authors have done that in their studio. The main room is shown in Figure 14.1.

FIGURE 14.1 Team space

How to Start Pair Programming

Many people say that pairing is such an intense learning and doing activity that they can't do it for a whole day. Treat it like running. If you've been a couch potato for five years, you shouldn't try to run a marathon. Likewise, give yourself time to work up to full-day pairing sessions.

Switch pairs often, especially when you're starting, but not in the middle of a task. Let yourself get used to rhythm of switching, but stay with a pair long enough to get the full experience of melding minds with that person. The goal is to pair with lots of people, to get used to splitting pairs and initiating new ones at natural points. Pair with people of different levels and personalities. As Chet Hendrickson, Ron Jeffries, and Ann Anderson say,

> *It takes a little time to get used to pair programming, and, at first, it will feel a bit awkward. Then you'll get good at pairing with someone, and finally you'll get good at pairing with most anyone.*[11]

The point is that you shouldn't just stick with one person. If you do, you'll start believing that pairing with that person is the model for how all pairings should be.

Be introspective about this. Be open to learning where you aren't good at pairing, then work on correcting your shortcomings. Attack your own resistance to pairing before you get on somebody else too much. After you pair for a period of time, you'll find that you don't like coding any other way. We have found that after working with a partner, going back to working alone feels like part of our minds are gone. We constantly kid each other about our codependence.

Starting to Pair
by Roy Miller

When I first joined RoleModel, I was brand new to XP. I was convinced it was the correct approach, but I didn't have any experience doing it. I had tried pair programming before, as I understood it, but I hadn't done it enough to get used to it. In my first week, I felt like I wasn't being very helpful to my partners at all. I didn't even know Java very well, so I had a hard enough time following what was going on technically.

Then one day, I was talking with a much more experienced developer during a break in our pairing session. He said, "I can't believe it. I worked on that problem for four hours and came up with nothing. Then you sat down and we had it fixed in a half hour. That's cool!" Right then it hit me how powerful pairing could be.

---

11. R. Jefferies, A. Anderson, C. Hendrickson. *Extreme Program Installed.* Addison-Wesley, 2001, p. 90.

One temptation people face when they're trying to get used to XP is that they don't want to jump in the pool. As soon as they find a particularly knotty problem in the pairing dynamic, they punt and start tweaking the process. Don't. Pairing isn't easy, and it is hard to get used to. Do it by the book first, then figure out what to tweak and how. If you never do it by the book, you won't be able to be very objective about what you might be missing.

Chapter 15

Making It Right

In anything at all, perfection is finally attained, not when there is no longer anything to add, but when there is no longer anything to take away.

—Antoine de Saint-Exupéry

If you do not develop the habit and discipline of refactoring your code, it eventually will be nearly impossible to move at top speed. This will happen sooner than you think.

The mantra Ken drums into people is, "Make it run, make it right, make it fast." Refactoring is the technique of improving code without changing what it does. It is the "making it right" piece of the puzzle.

If your system is to last for any length of time, it is inevitable that your code will change. Your problem is how best to accommodate that reality.

Refactoring keeps you ready for change by keeping you comfortable with changing your code. You just remove "unsightly buildup" out of habit, no matter where or when you find it (within reason). This keeps your code clean, which will let it survive longer.

Refactoring also makes change possible. It is an investment in future speed, and the future could be tomorrow. The cleaner your code, the faster you will be able to move when it comes time to change existing features or add new ones.

Refactoring has another advantage. In XP, you should write the simplest code that could possibly work, and learn along the way. Refactoring lets you incorporate learning into your code without breaking it.

Being Ready for Change

You do not have to think about acting on a habit. You just do it. In the software world, we have been taught that change is dangerous. Change causes delay, and costs too much. It is risky to change a system close to production, or in production. So we get in the habit of avoiding change. We must break that habit in order to move forward. The only way to do that is to form a new habit that takes the fear out of change.

Refactoring gets you in the habit of changing your code. Once we have code that runs, we don't waste time debating refactoring too much, unless it's a major refactoring. When we see an opportunity to do it, we do it. The only way to get over your fear of change is to face it. Refactoring is your weapon.

Making Change Possible

It may seem counterintuitive that you should invest time now to save time later, but it is true throughout life, not just in programming.

A couple of years ago, Roy was a couch potato. As his weight began to balloon, he decided to start running. Like lots of recovering couch potatoes, he did too much too soon and hurt his knee. He expected to get in shape without working for it. After his injury, he wised up and began by walking. Pretty soon he was running. Within four months he was running five miles a day. Within a year he was running five miles in 35 minutes. It took energy to get to this point, but he now has more energy on a daily basis. He is more effective in many ways.

But what about "You Aren't Going to Need It" (YAGNI)? What about not doing big design up front? Doesn't the rest of XP say don't do today what you can defer until tomorrow? We can put off those things that *may* help us in the future, because we are doing something that *will* help us in the future.

Refactoring your code takes more time than writing code and leaving it alone. But this is true only at the time you write the code, and only for a little while.

If you refactor your code after you add a new feature, this can take a few minutes or a few days. You can avoid that cost in the short term by skipping refactoring. Soon, though, clutter will begin to overwhelm your code.

Without a constant cleaning process clutter will obscure your design, making it harder to preserve and making the XP practice of simple design impossible. Refactoring is the essential first step toward maintaining the simplest possible design. Clean code simply gives you more room to maneuver. It is more flexible. Michael Feathers puts it this way:

I used to think that systems could be made more flexible by adding things. Now I realize systems become more flexible when you take things away. The area around the code has much more potential than the code will ever have.[1]

Adding code is much easier than removing it. Refactoring keeps your code as simple as possible, so that you can focus on adding things. When you boil it down, the primary goal of refactoring is to keep your code easy to modify so that you can move at maximum speed indefinitely.

You will get immediate gratification from even simple refactoring, but you will see the real benefits of it in the long run. You have to trust that you will see these rewards. When you do, you can't go back to being afraid of change. It costs too much.

Putting Learning into Your Code

The simplest thing that could possibly work changes over time. What could have worked yesterday won't cut it today and will change again tomorrow. If you are paying attention, you are learning along the way.

Refactoring lets you build that learning in. It helps you form the habit of changing your code so that it doesn't scare you. It keeps your design as simple as possible so that you can see where new things should fit. It helps you understand your code.

Martin describes an interesting phenomenon in *Refactoring*. He talks about using refactoring to help him understand code. In fact, one of the first things he does when he meets new code is to think about refactoring it to make it more understandable to him.[2] That is building learning in. Something that perhaps was clear as crystal yesterday can end up being foggy today. Refactor it to make the intent clear.

Refactoring is the practice of refining your code as you get smarter. A nice side effect is that being temporarily dumb ("What in world was I thinking here?") won't cost you anything. Refactoring helps you keep your code so clear that the code can answer your questions when you temporarily forget how brilliant you were.

---

1. M. Feathers. *OaooBalancesYagni* at http://c2.com/cgi/wiki?OaooBalancesYagni.
2. M. Fowler. *Refactoring: Improving the Design of Existing Code.* Addison-Wesley, 1999. pp. 57–58

How to Refactor

Martin's *Refactoring* is the definitive text on refactoring, which you should buy, read, and put into practice. Here are what we see as his main "how to" points:

- Develop the habit of writing tests first and running them compulsively before you even think about refactoring.
- Write your code first, then refactor it.
- Treat adding a new function as an opportunity to refactor the code around it.
- Treat fixing a bug as a refactoring opportunity.

Refactoring is a way to improve code without breaking it. The only way you can prove you didn't break the code is by testing it every time you make changes. Refactoring will work if you have unit tests to back you up. In fact, testing is such an integral part of refactoring that we shudder at the idea of refactoring without having tests to confirm that we didn't break anything. You might have seen the carnival game that involves quickly and repeatedly hitting the heads of mechanical moles with a mallet as they pop up from their holes. As soon as you hit a mole, another one pops up randomly somewhere else. Bugs in software are like that game: You fix one and another one pops up. The same one probably pops up over and over again. You tire yourself out and probably look stupid flailing about. Running all of your tests often helps this problem.

So remember to write the tests and the code first. Then refactor both to make them progressively less wrong. This will improve your speed later in two ways:

1. **It will make changes less risky.** Refactored code is easier to change without introducing bugs that slow you down. It also will make it easier to find new bugs that crop up, because your code will be clear.
2. **It will make optimization easier.** You eventually get to "make it fast." Refactored code is easier to optimize because you can pinpoint performance bottlenecks easier, and you can make the changes to correct them in one place.

Refactor whenever you add something new. If you put on your refactoring hat when you hit code you need to modify, you will come to understand it better by making it easier to add the new feature.

The same holds true for fixing bugs not caught by unit tests. Refactor the code to improve your understanding of it while you're trying to figure out what the problem is. This alone can help you find the bug. If it doesn't, at least you'll leave the code better than you found it.

When to Refactor

Kent uses the term "code smells" to describe that uneasy feeling you get that should tell you when to refactor. When you catch a whiff of one of these smells, you should clean it up. If you think it's ripe now, let it sit for another month and you won't be able to get near it without protective clothing.

To be honest, though, some people aren't as sensitive to smells as others are. They need a little help. Fortunately, there are two regular opportunities for every programmer to be extra sensitive to smells: before implementing a feature and after implementing it. Developers try to determine whether changing existing code would make implementing the new feature easier. Developers look at the code they just wrote to see whether there is any way to simplify it. For example, if they see an opportunity for abstraction, they refactor to remove duplicate code from concrete implementations.

The point is not to procrastinate. Refactor when you see the opportunity. Do it as you go along. See something in the code that takes you a while to figure out? Refactor it so it is clear immediately upon looking at it.

When Not to Refactor

You should not refactor when the code doesn't work and needs to be rewritten.[3] That's where Martin's list of times not to refactor ends. Refactoring needs to be as much a part of writing code as writing code. In fact, the reasons most people give for not refactoring aren't good reasons at all. They are excuses for laziness or justifications for fear. But don't think that's a reason to refactor indiscriminately.

Don't refactor if you are not sure how to make it better. We've seen several times where developers saw some complicated piece of code and thought, "I should refactor this to make it simpler." Unfortunately, they didn't really have a plan on how to simplify it. They just started changing things that they didn't think looked good with no vision of where they were headed. Soon, a bunch of tests would break, and they'd start hacking things in to get the tests to pass again. Two days later, the tests are working and the code looks different, but not significantly better. In fact, the worst wart from the earlier version of the code was removed, but it was replaced by a different wart. Don't do this. If you don't have a plan to make it better, don't just start changing things.

A more important question than when you should not refactor is how much refactoring is enough.

When to Stop Refactoring

Most people who think refactoring is good believe you should never stop. We understand the sentiment, but we disagree.

As one of Roy's managers used to say, "Good is better than perfect." As admirable as it is to try to get all the junk out of your code, it's unprofessional not to ship a system because there is room for improvement. Being professional doesn't mean being perfect.

All programmers find themselves leaving code in the system that they think could be better. The key is never to insert bad code that has a known

---

3. M. Fowler. *Refactoring: Improving the Design of Existing Code.* Addison-Wesley, 1999, p. 66.

cure, and to remove the existing bad code the next time you have to add something where it lives. Never pass by bad code and say, "It stinks, but I'll get to it later." Later won't come soon enough.

Knowing When to Stop Refactoring
by Ken Auer

I find that Java's typing model causes me to encapsulate casting in order to keep users of a class from having to cast. After coding on a system for a while, I often end up with lots of small classes that exist mostly to encapsulate the generic stuff underneath and to insert some type intelligence. The code looks almost exactly the same as a couple of other classes that also add similar intelligence for a different type. I hate it, but it's not always obvious how to get rid of it without replacing it with a different monster (where everything is of type Object and users of the class have to cast to the real type).

Sometimes I learn a new trick. I usually don't immediately find all of the places in the system where I can apply that trick. The customer would be rather bothered if I took two or three days to do that and missed the iteration. However, I do communicate the trick and encourage people to apply it when they're in the code containing the particular suspect "cruft*." Eventually, the existing cruft works itself out and new flavors of cruft work their way in.

---

* No one really knows for sure where this term came from. Some have suggested it refers to Cruft Hall at Harvard University. Since WWII, the windows of this physics lab have appeared to be full of random techno junk.

Don't refactor beyond what the customer needs. You'll get diminishing marginal utility. There will be some refactoring that you won't be able to get done, just like there are some features that you won't be able to include. Ward describes unfinished refactorings as going into debt on a project. The future reductions in project speed are the interest you pay on that debt. Sometimes, a little debt is good management. You just need to manage debt well by keeping the balance low with refactoring.

How to Start Refactoring

Start by reading Martin's book *Refactoring*. Get familiar with the code smells and the appropriate refactorings to sanitize them.

Then go with what you know. Refactor before you add a new feature and after you finish adding it. That will get you used to the process. At the same time, practice looking for specific smells. Over time, your olfactory sense will get better at picking up bad code odors. If you've been around bad code all your life, you might not notice the smell. But if you force yourself to recognize garbage when you see it, it won't be long before it starts to smell bad to you.

Don't refactor too soon. Get your code to run first. Hack a path through the jungle, then figure out if there is a better way to go. Make sure you have a solid test suite (ideally, both unit and acceptance tests), then start refactoring.

The real trick is to develop the habit of refactoring. Not all of your refactorings will be profound. Some will be pretty basic. The habit is priceless.

Why People Don't Refactor

If refactoring is such a great thing, why don't all programmers do it instead of letting junk build up in their code? There are three primary reasons: impatience, cost, and fear.

You see some short-term benefits when you refactor, but you get the big payoff later when you continue to move at maximum speed indefinitely. Deferring gratification takes discipline, but it pays off.

The economics aren't clear yet, but the main driver behind the traditional cost curve is code that is dangerous to change. Refactoring is one of the tools XP uses to flatten the curve.

Fear usually comes from ignorance. Habitual action overcomes fear. The United States military trains based on this principle. Basic training is essentially a gradual conditioning to fear. Recruits learn to obey orders out of habit, even if those orders seem silly at the time. This gets drilled into them 24 hours a day, to ensure that they will act instinctively in the heat of battle, when an untrained person might run away screaming. The only way to get rid of your fear of changing code is to do it over and over again.

Chapter 16

Pulling It Together

Integrating your code more than once per day helps you avoid integration nightmares, and will help you go faster.

"Continuous integration" doesn't mean "continuous" integration. This is a slogan, not a description. In XP you do not integrate every second. But even daily integration isn't enough to avoid integration nightmares.

You should integrate new code into the existing code base multiple times every day. If you don't do this, your speed will suffer. You will spend days, or even weeks, trying to fix the backlog of bugs that surfaced during your "big bang" integrations.

Integrating this often also reduces your risk of missing dates. It spreads the risk of a single integration event around to multiple small ones. Continuous integration also makes it easier to pinpoint the source of a problem in one of your small integration events.

Maintaining Speed

Both of the authors have worked on projects that integrated in big bang fashion. Roy can remember one project where integration meetings were held to resolve conflicts, take ownership of bug fixes, and so on. These meetings lasted for hours.

Going for two weeks, or a month, before you integrate is working under one of two faulty assumptions:

1. That your code won't cause anybody else's code to blow up.
2. That nobody else's code will cause yours to blow up.

Both assumptions are wrong. No one can understand an entire system well enough to inoculate code against problems caused by somebody else. Problems will occur. Ignoring that is delaying the inevitable and storing up pain. If you do that, you'll be up against time pressure that will make maintaining discipline tough. It will hurt badly, too.

Consider how continuous integration changes the picture. You code for an hour and then you integrate. This exposes otherwise unseen problems early and lets you address them while they're still small. That lets you maintain maximum speed all the time.

You also have everyone else's latest working code at your fingertips to use as you need to. When you combine this with switching pairs you often have conversations like this: "Man, it would be nice to have a utility that does XYZ for us." "We do, I integrated that yesterday with Joe. See, it's right here."

Reducing Risk

Cecil B. DeMille created and directed some of the grandest epic films ever to come out of Hollywood. There is a scene in *The Ten Commandments* that shows the exodus of the Israelites from Egypt. The huge number of extras cost the studio a ridiculous sum. The story goes that there was only one chance to get it right. To be absolutely safe, DeMille had three cameras set up to film the scene from different angles. If one failed, there would be two backups. It was inconceivable that all three would fail.

DeMille called, "Action!" and the scene was off and running. It went just like he'd planned. Everyone performed beautifully. When it was done, he discovered the first camera had failed. No problem, he thought, that's why we have the backups. He radioed to the second camera, which had been down in the crowd of extras, and was told that somebody had kicked out its electrical connection. By then he was feeling quite thankful for having that second backup. That crew was closer to him, so he called to them on a megaphone to see how it had gone with them. They called back, "Anytime you're ready, Mr. DeMille!"[1]

---

1. We've heard this story several times. Nobody seems to know whether it's true or not. Even if it's not, it's a great story. We would probably have that kind of luck if we made a movie.

You create crazy "only one shot" situations like that for yourself when you try to integrate lots of code in one big bang. The longer you wait before you bring things together, the worse off you'll be. The antidote is continuous integration.

We integrate multiple times every day. This is like distributing a force. It's the difference between standing in the shower for three hours and standing under Niagara Falls for three seconds. If all the force is concentrated in a single infrequent integration event, it will crush you. It will take you a relatively long time to recover, to sort everything out. By that time, you probably have missed an important date. Since the fixing effort carries over into your next phase, where you'll do yet another big bang integration, you'll probably miss your next date. Continuous integration allows you to fail fast and early—and on a manageable scale.

Distributing the force of integration over multiple small integration events makes it easier to figure out what caused a problem when one crops up. Suppose you code for an hour and you get all your unit tests to pass. Then you integrate. You know that the last pair to integrate made sure all their tests passed on the integration machine. If you get a unit test failure when you integrate, it's probably your new stuff that caused the problem. Finding the problem is much easier, so you'll maintain your speed.

How to Integrate Continuously

Each pair writes code at their pairing station. They write their tests first, then they write just enough code to get those tests to pass. After they take any significant step, they make sure all of the tests for the entire system run in their own workspace. Nobody can integrate broken code. Then they move to the integration machine.

The single biggest aid to making continuous integration work is an "integration machine." This is a separate computer, within earshot of the entire team, where each pair goes physically to integrate their code. Kent talked about having a "refactoring hat" and an "adding code" hat. You also have an "integrating" hat. Having a separate integration machine makes it clear which hat you have on. The team knows they can integrate only when the integration machine is free, so they won't step on anyone else's integration effort.

When a pair moves to the integration machine, they may run the tests. The last team to integrate was supposed to leave all the tests in working order, but you always want to be sure. (If the tests take more than a minute or so to run, it may not be worth this step.) The pair next updates the integration workspace for their project, meaning they bring in any code that they changed. Then they run the tests again. If nothing breaks, they yell, "Fore!" to tell the rest of the team that they just integrated successfully. If something breaks, they work on it until all the tests run, or, if it's not trivial, they back it out and work on it at their own station. That leaves the integration workspace ready for the next pair to integrate.

When the pair gets back to their own workspace, they bring in the latest working code, which includes not only their latest work, but also that of others who have integrated successfully.

If you hear more than one or two shouts of "Fore!", you know that you need to integrate right away. Working on old code that hasn't been integrated is a recipe for a headache the next time you integrate. So keep up.

How to Start Integrating Continuously

Continuous integration is a habit, just like refactoring. You just have to start doing it. If you aren't used to doing it, it might seem crazy. The reason it seems crazy to many people is that they are conditioned to fear integration, or they haven't worked on a project where they've experienced integration at all.

If you come from an environment that doesn't integrate continuously, you probably view integration like going to the dentist. You know you should have been brushing and flossing more regularly, but you didn't. Now you have to endure the dreaded pick. You might even have a cavity. It's your own fault, but you have become conditioned to loathe visiting the dentist.

What's the solution? Simple. Brush and floss. This is one of those things that nobody particularly enjoys doing. You do it to avoid the pain that you will have to go through if you don't. Integrating continuously is the same way. Pretend that integrating this way will save you pain. Once you do it for a while, you'll have firsthand experience to prove it.

Pessimistic Locking
by Steve Hayes

When we started using XP we changed a lot of things, but rather than change everything, we kept our tool set the same. As a result, we didn't have good support for merging code changes, and we opted for "pessimistic locking."

At first, we locked at the Java package level. As packages (and the team) got larger, we locked at the class level instead (the smallest level supported by our tool set). If we were working in small steps, completing them and checking the code back in, there wasn't much contention. When we did have contention, we usually found that we needed to look at how we were working, and in particular how much work we were doing at once, rather than at our locking

Techniques to Make It Easier

We do most of our development work in Java. We use IBM VisualAge for Java as a development environment. Its repository is extremely powerful and makes integrating code much less painful. Even so, we still encounter problems when we integrate.

Using a simple naming standard for code versions in VisualAge helps. We include the date, the client project name, the integrating pair's initials, and a version number in the version name. This makes it obvious whose code we're replacing when we integrate. If there are problems that aren't obvious, we know exactly whom to talk to.

Package Early, Package Often
by Joseph Pelrine

Package early, package often—I personally think this should be one of the basic XP practices. Any professional software developer knows that there's a big difference between a program that compiles and runs on his personal machine and a shrink-wrapped application sold in a computer store. Whether it's stripping and packaging a Smalltalk image for production, making sure that the installation program sets CLASSPATH correctly, or setting up Apache and Tomcat configuration files to publish Servlets properly, there's a lot of room for error to creep in and a lot of additional risk. The sooner you start practicing your delivery and deployment strategy, the more you reduce this risk. Plus, it's impressive for your customer to receive each milestone's release all toasted and ready to run on a CD.

Chapter 17

Staying on Process

There are no shortcuts to anyplace worth going.
—Beverly Sills

Straying from your process can wreck your project. Staying on process can be hard for human beings. You must make a conscious effort to stay on process or to get back on if you fall off. This will pay off in the end.

When you get the essential practices running well on an XP project, you will start to see some amazing results. The problem is, many teams start trying to do XP but don't see those great results. What goes wrong?

The most prevalent answer is that they get off process. Most of the time, they don't intentionally deviate from the XP practices. They simply get distracted for one reason or another. Staying on process is the only way to get the full benefit of the XP practices working together. Fortunately, there are ways to get back on if you fall off.

Why Teams Lose Their Way

There are three primary reasons people deviate from the XP practices, despite their desire to adhere to them:

1. Lack of attention
2. Lack of discipline
3. Time pressure

Sometimes you can deviate from your process without even thinking about it. There may not be noticeable pressure to deviate. In fact, things might be running smoothly. You just get complacent over time, not really paying attention to following the process rigorously. Before you know it, the small deviations build up and you're so far off track that you might not be able to find your way back.

One of the first things you'll notice when you try XP is how much discipline it takes. You will quickly see that accusations of undisciplined hacking are unfounded. It is hard to adhere to that practices by accident. It requires conscious effort, particularly if one or more of the practices are new to you (such as pair programming or continuous integration). If you aren't vigilant, you'll fall back into old habits.

Even if you are diligent, time pressure often will work against you. When you're up against a deadline, the apparent inefficiency of working in pairs (for example) will seem glaring, even if it's an illusion. In times of panic, maintaining discipline becomes difficult. Perhaps it requires too much faith, especially when you're first trying XP.

Time Pressure
by Ron Jeffries

Suppose there's just one day left in the iteration, and you and I each have a task to do that we estimate will take half an elapsed day to complete. The team's best chance to complete both tasks is for us to work together, first one task, then the other. But we each think, "If we start on this task, we won't even get to mine until this afternoon. What if it's harder than I think? I might not get done! What if his is harder than he thinks? I might not even get started!" So we decide to split up.

Now we're working alone. We still feel pressure to get done, and we probably feel even more stress because there's no one helping us. We know we should take small steps and test first, but we feel that pressure. So we skimp a bit on the tests, and we take bigger bites than we should. We've actually increased the team's risk by splitting up.

If—and it's a big if—we both get done on time, we get a little positive reinforcement for doing the wrong thing, even though we have probably left the system worse off than it was. And in any case, we have weakened our good habits and strengthened bad ones.

We're in this for the long haul—the next release and the releases after that—not for getting done with just the next thing. We want to deliver a quality version every iteration, now and into the future. We have the best chance of delighting our customer over the entire project if we do the right thing every day.

It's tempting to go off process under stress, and sometimes it just happens without anyone noticing. Everyone on the team can help by observing, by speaking up with the truth, by assisting others, and by finding simple measures of how things are going. Every team has problem times, and most teams probably play some shaky games. How you get back on track shows what you really are. Be extreme!

Using the practices even when there is pressure not to increases your chances of success. Pay now or pay later. Each time you deviate from the process, you are digging a hole. At first, the hole is shallow and you can walk in and out of it. Over time, though, as you keep deviating, the hole gets deeper. Now you have to climb out of it. If you dump a practice altogether, but it still makes sense in your local context, you might have dug a hole so deep you can't get out of it without dropping everything else and having somebody throw you a rope. How can you avoid digging the hole?

The best way to stay on process is not to get off in the first place. Of course, that's easier said than done, especially since you can get off process without noticing it. Here are a few practical ways to catch yourself when you drift:

- ✧ **Pay attention.** If you aren't thinking about your process and how well you're following it, it's easier not to follow it. Keep your eyes and ears open.
- ✧ **Make drifting obvious.** Track a few key metrics and post them in public. This makes it easier to pay attention.
- ✧ **Get ahead.** Remember that time pressure can push you off process, despite your best efforts. Relieve the pressure whenever you can by getting ahead on the hard stuff or the stuff you aren't sure about. If you finish early, you can always ask for more work. That's easier than asking for more time.
- ✧ **Practice discipline.** Discipline is a habit. If you want to follow your process consistently, everybody on the team has to mind himself. When you personally feel yourself drifting, don't do it, or ask for help on what you are doing. You are less likely to break your process if somebody is holding you accountable.

This is hard. People tend to be naturally selfish, lazy, and undisciplined. They like to hide their failures and to suffer no consequences when they screw up. Sweeping all those habits under the rug will hurt you in the long run. Recognize your own bad habits, and get them out in the open so that there will be positive peer pressure on everybody to do the right thing.

How to Stay on Process
by Ron Jeffries

Here's some techniques I'd recommend to stay on process:

- **Avoid deadline stress.** Keep your estimating skills sharp. Make sure to start early on tasks you're not sure about. Keep a close eye on how everyone is doing as the iteration wears on.
- **Go "breadth first."** Work whole stories in multiple passes, adding more detail each time. This can ensure that you deliver the most visible business value by the end of the iteration. If you do fall short, it'll be on something less important.
- **Renegotiate with the customer.** It's better to go back to the customer and negotiate leaving something out in order to deliver full quality on what you get done. Working in less effective ways will slow the team down for more than just one task. Giving the customer the choice is better than missing some features at random. The reduction in stress may even increase the likelihood that the team will finish all the tasks after all.
- **Stick together.** Even if one person is signed up for a task, the whole team succeeds or fails together. Check with the team. Maybe someone else can pick up the slack.
- **Defer nonbusiness items.** Was someone going to clean up some code, or improve the build procedure? Maybe that can be deferred so that the team can deliver what it estimated it could do.
- **Work a little overtime.** Yes, I know the rule. But a little extra push once in a while, to get everything all done, will make you feel good and look good. Just don't make a habit of overtime. That will slow the team down over the longer haul.
- **Know and track the effects of your practices.** Keep a few simple metrics in Big Visible Charts. Worried about missing testing? Then track defect insertion versus how well tested the object with the defect is. Worried about pairing? Track defects versus paired or nonpaired coding. Even simple metrics can be very sensitive. If everyone stopped pairing for a

single iteration, you would feel the impact in the next. Similarly, you will be able to see the effect of not following the practices on specific patches of code just by looking. If you can make yourselves more aware of the impact of the team's practices, you can make better decisions about what to do.

How to Get Back on Process

If you're in a hole, there are basically two things you can do. You can keep going, do your best, and hope to deliver something of value. That might be the best you can do. It might even be the most responsible thing you can do. Or, if you're not in too deep yet, you can choose to stop, climb out of the hole, and fill it back in. Then you can put up a sign that says, "Beware of digging a hole here." Next time, it will be easier to avoid.

The Pig That Went off Process
by Ken Auer

A task is not done until it is successfully integrated and all the tests pass. The rule is that when you integrate, all the tests have to pass, or you back out your changes. Backing out changes is a pain. So, early on in a project, someone integrated and two tests were not working. They had just made a bunch of changes before integrating and didn't want to go through the hassle of backing it out. They were sure that they would be able to find and fix the problem quickly. Of course, they didn't. Someone else went to the integration machine, brought in their new code, and ran the tests. They were surprised to find those tests failing and couldn't imagine how their changes could have broken those particular tests. They started debugging. After getting nowhere, they asked for some help. The guilty party apologized and fessed up.

They were forgiven, but the following day, someone else did the same thing. It was starting to become a habit. Nathaniel came in the next morning with a pig nose mask and announced, "This pig nose must be worn by anyone who leaves the integration machine in a hosed state. It cannot be taken off until the integration machine is back in a working state." Sure enough, within a couple of hours, someone was wearing the pig nose.

The pig nose is still in use, but it is worn much less frequently these days.

Part III

The Rest of the Story

Once you have the XP essentials down, you should begin thinking about the rest of the practices, if you haven't already. At that point, they make a huge difference. Master them, and you go from walking to running, from contending to winning. These remaining practices are as follows:

- ✧ Simple design
- ✧ Collective code ownership
- ✧ On-site customer
- ✧ Acceptance testing
- ✧ Coding standard
- ✧ Metaphor
- ✧ Forty-hour week

You also should think seriously about two roles identified when XP began to proliferate:

- ✧ Coach
- ✧ Tracker

These things are not less important than the XP essentials, they just don't have to be concentrated on as much when you start in most environments. Some (simple design, collective code ownership, coding standard, the 40-hour week) will fall into place naturally if you develop the right mindset (Part I). Others (customer on site, acceptance testing, coach, and tracker) might just take some time until they can reasonably be put in place in some environments. Then there is the infamous metaphor, which seems to be a practice that is hard to implement as prescribed but, nonetheless, seems to address an important issue that shouldn't be ignored.

If you are doing any of these within the first three days, you haven't necessarily done anything wrong. In fact, in some environments, getting people to understand and appreciate the practice of simple design may be the biggest and most important hurdle to overcome and should possibly be tackled early. We believe that introducing this via the other practices is often the easiest way to go.

These things are important, but you can defer getting them down until you have the bare essentials (Part II) humming. There is a good chance that your implementation of these practices and roles will be unique to your environment. In a way, it's like iteration two.

Chapter 18

Designing the Simple

Out of intense complexities intense simplicities emerge.
—Winston Churchill

Change is inevitable. Keeping your design as simple as possible prepares you for change.

Detractors claim that XP neglects design. On the contrary, in XP design is simply not done all at once, up front, under the delusion that things won't change or that all changes can be anticipated.

XP isn't an excuse not to do good design. We want good design. Good design comes from good designers working in a realistic environment. Good designers will produce better designs in an XP environment, because it's more realistic. Novice designers will have a better opportunity to learn good design techniques in an XP environment for the same reason.

Big Design Up Front approaches operate under the fallacy that you can look at a static picture of the horizon, stay still, and draw a perfect picture of how to get to the point you're looking at. XP recognizes that you are better off with a simple plan that will get you moving in the right direction, and that your view of the target will improve as you move toward it. XP considers design so important that it should be a constant affair. We always try to have the simplest design that could possibly work at any point, changing it as we go to reflect emerging reality.

Defining Simplicity

What is the simplest design that could possibly work? Kent defined it as the design that

- ♦ Runs all the tests
- ♦ Contains no duplicate code
- ♦ States the programmers' intent for all code clearly
- ♦ Contains the fewest possible classes and methods

Requiring a simple design doesn't imply that all designs will be small or that they will be trivial, they just have to be as simple as possible and still work. A simple design does not include unused features.

Well, Duh Design
by Tom Kubit

When I worked with Don Wells at Ford doing XP, he came up with a saying that we used which was, "Finding the simplest thing may be the hardest thing you'll ever do." I then added "But when you find it, the design will be so obvious that anyone who looks at it will wonder why it took so long." Don't be insulted, take it as a big compliment. This rings true so many times because the simple ideas just don't come to mind first. But when you do find them you can look at it and say, "Well, duh."

Your design should be simple enough that its intent is clear to the people who will be modifying it. That doesn't mean that somebody without any domain knowledge or history with the team should be able to pick everything up in an afternoon. But the folks who have been on the team for a while should definitely understand it, and new team members shouldn't have to climb Mt. Everest to get up to speed.

Steve Hayes told us

I think that the statement "state the programmers' intent for all code clearly" (in its slightly different forms) is one of the deepest statements in the XP books to date. Initially I didn't realize how deep. If you leave this out, the "simplest" solution to a problem would be one class, with methods only where there was duplication. Everything else would be procedural. When I first started to do XP presentations this is how everyone interpreted the "simplest" constraints. Many people told me that XP discouraged design and good OO principles like encapsulation. Clearly this isn't so, but you can get this impression from the literature to date. We need to spell out that "conveying intent" means creating objects that do one thing and do it well (because this makes the intent of the software clearer); it means using design patterns; it means separating model from view from controller. It means all these things and more.[1]

Why People Don't Keep It Simple

Nobody comes out and says, "Our goal is to create the most complex design possible." Well, almost nobody. Jim Highsmith told us

Actually, I worked in a group one time where the implied rule was that if I could write code that you couldn't understand then I was, by implication, smarter than you. You can imagine the stinky code that came out of this group![2]

The more typical problem is that people miss the forest for the trees. They start with grand intentions of keeping their design clean, then they get distracted. They forget that simpler is usually better, because it's easier to understand and it makes it easier to change things later. Why does this amnesia happen?

Software developers favor complexity out of habit. In school they learn that complex problems probably require complex solutions. Or they don't have the discipline to think about the problem first and look for the simplest solution. Complexity tends to happen naturally, which is why design tends to degrade over time. Martin describes this in making his case for refactoring as a critical software development practice:

The harder it is to see the design in the code, the harder it is to preserve it, and the more rapidly it decays.[3]

---

1. S. Hayes. Private e-mail correspondence with the authors, March 2001.
2. J. Highsmith. Comment made in technical review of this book.
3. M. Fowler. *Refactoring: Improving the Design of Existing Code.* Addison-Wesley, 1999, p. 55.

Even if this weren't true, developers are bad at predicting what they'll need later. They can't guess requirements very well. If they guess right about something they'll need later, it probably will look at least a little different by the time they get there. That's why you'll hear the term "YAGNI" a lot in XP circles. XPers know that most guessing ends up being wrong and that keeping it simple is the best way to avoid wrong guessing.

But don't apply YAGNI to the cleaning up of code. If you don't refactor, you can't keep your design simple. This is because you lose the design in all the junk. If there's junk in the way, you can't see how everything relates and where new stuff should go.

Keeping a design simple requires several things:

⬧ The ability to think simply in the first place

⬧ The courage to understand code and to change it

⬧ The discipline to refactor regularly in order to keep entropy from destroying your code

Developing these skills requires practice. Often, a programmer's background, habits, biases, and peers fight against development of these skills.

Why Keep Things Simple?

Change is inevitable. Habits and skills that make responding to change easier dramatically increase a project's chances of success. Simple systems are easier to change. Keeping them simple makes change easier. Therefore, fight for simplicity as if your life depended on it. Eventually, your quality of life as a developer does. As Martin put it

> *The compiler doesn't care whether the code is ugly or clean. But when we change the system, there is a human involved, and humans do care. A poorly designed system is hard to change. Hard because it is hard to figure out where the changes are needed. If it is hard to figure out what to change, there is a strong chance that the programmer will make a mistake and introduce bugs. . . . The program may not be broken, but it does hurt. It is making your life more difficult because you find it hard to make the changes your users want. . . . Any fool can write code that a computer can understand. Good programmers write code that humans can understand.*[4]

---

4. M. Fowler. *Refactoring: Improving the Design of Existing Code.* Addison-Wesley, 1999, pp. 6–7, 15.

Martin makes the case that this is where refactoring comes in. But refactoring is simply the primary means to an end. Humans understand that simplicity, not technical elegance, is the goal.

How to Start Doing Simple Design

As we said before, simplicity is difficult to maintain. It's also hard to learn. The only way to start is to be a little ridiculous.

When you study economics in school, the examples are full of simplifying assumptions that make the examples easier to understand. As you learn, you can get rid of the simplifying assumptions and get closer to complex reality. It is the same with simple design.

Remember the rules from Chapter 8. Think simply when you start focusing on keeping your design simple. Recall Roy's first day at RoleModel. Roy spent four hours on the problem and came up with something ridiculously complex. Ken came over to help and had a great solution with about one third of the code within 30 minutes. What was the difference? Roy overheard another member of the team ask Ken how Roy had performed on his first test. Ken replied, "He just needs to learn to think more simply." Exactly.

For your first cut at a problem, write something that is so simple it makes you laugh. Assume the simple way will work until you see that it doesn't. Simplicity is no excuse for not thinking, but you'll be surprised at how close the ridiculously simple design can get you to solving the problem.

Retraining My Mind to Think Simple
by Jeff McKenna

One of the more difficult areas of XP for me has been the idea of simple design. Because I am so gray, in most projects there are situations that I have seen numerous times before. It is difficult for me to not use my experience and go directly to the "more complete" solution, the better solution.

Here is an example. We implemented a domain model that supported a single user. The release plan (meaning it would be in place within two iterations) specified multiuser support. I coded assuming multiuser by, say, using synchronized collections. A simpler design that would work would not use them (although it does not hurt!). My approach is to use the longer-term design if it takes no more time to implement. But this is a slippery slope. How do I or how does anyone else judge how large the implementation time difference will be? Am I not allowed to use my experience, which says do something in a particular way? This is a real dilemma for me.

This example is interesting. I wrote the initial description of the dilemma for the OOPSLA 2000 workshop on Extreme Programming. It turns out that later the multiuser requirement was slipped. It was slipped for six months! Thus my better design was overdesign, with associated performance degradation. To add insult to injury, when the multiuser story finally appeared, a better partitioning of the problem, an even better design, did not require synchronized collections. This story clearly illustrates the YAGNI principle.

Over the years I have found some ways of thinking that help me find simple designs.

Write the acceptance tests first. This keeps me from writing too much code; which by definition is simpler. I wish I always did this!

Keep classes to one responsibility. Simple classes cannot do more than one thing well.

Use the Law of Demeter. * Following the Law of Demeter when refactoring will result in the behavior ending up in the "right" class. If this is done and a class ends up having too much behavior (more than one responsibility) then it can be split up. If a class ends up having no behavior then you can throw it out.

Use the concept of stereotypes. Rebecca Wirfs-Brock introduced the concept of typical types of classes based on responsibilities.** She called them stereotypes. Examples are a Controller or a Data Store or an Interface or a Dispatcher. Identify the stereotypes in your design and let them just be one of those.

Use CRC cards to explore. You can understand design if you can act it out. Acting it out often makes it simpler.

---

* K. Lieberherr, I. Holland, A. Riel. "Object-Oriented Programming: An ObjectiveSense of Style." *OOPSLA '88 Conference Proceedings.* ACM Press, Volume 23, Number 11, pp. 323–334, November 1988.

** R. Wirfs-Brock. "Characterizing Your Objects." *Smalltalk Report.* Volume 2, Number 5, February 1992. And R. Wirfs-Brock, "Adding to Your Conceptual Toolkit." *Report on Object Analysis and Design.* Volume 1, Number 2. (Reprints are available at http://www.wirfs-brock.com/pages/resources.)

Why Not Start with Simple Design?

Simple design is essential to making a project successful in the long run, but you need to be focused on developing a few other habits first:

- ✧ Focusing only on the current iteration
- ✧ Writing tests first
- ✧ Writing code that makes those tests pass

- ✧ Refactoring that code with a passion
- ✧ Working with others in pairs

Focusing on these habits will naturally encourage simpler design than you may be used to. From there, it won't be a big step to the simplest design possible. As Martin says,

> *The best advice I heard on all this came from Uncle Bob (Robert Martin). His advice was not to get too hung up about what the simplest design is. After all you can, should, and will refactor it later. In the end the willingness to refactor is much more important than knowing what the simplest thing is right away.*[5]

Other natural forces present in XP will encourage simple design. We have often found that business people often encourage simple design, too, if you present the issue to them in the right way.

Ken remembers when the GoF book first came out.[6] Some people were so enamored with the patterns that they tried to use a pattern every time they tackled a problem, no matter how simple. Sometimes it made him sorry that he'd ever turned people on to the book. He'd come across the application of the State pattern that somebody used to avoid a single conditional statement. In that case, YAGNI applies. Use the conditional statement. If the same condition proliferates throughout multiple methods of the same class, consider the state pattern. This is something an experienced designer already knows, and a novice designer who wants to be a brilliant designer might miss.

On the other hand, armed with XP, the novice designer might miss things an experienced designer can see coming a mile away. The experienced designer suggests taking some time to add something like a state machine where it is not obviously needed for the task at hand. The less experienced partner says, "YAGNI." Maybe the experienced designer is wrong. They could argue about it, but the real test is whether it is a sound business decision to go with the more sophisticated design. Instead of arguing with the other developers, present the issue to the customer. Present the trade-offs—the cost and benefits of doing it the YAGNI way or the sophisticated way—and let the customer make the call.

---

5. M. Fowler. "Is Design Dead." Available at http://martinfowler.com/articles/designDead.html.
6. As we mentioned earlier, GoF stands for "gang of four," E. Gamma, R. Helm, R. Johnson, and J. Vlissides, the authors of *Design Patterns: Elements of Reusable Object-Oriented Software*. Addison-Wesley, 1995.

Simple Design Can Be a Business Decision
by Ken Auer

Our customers trust that we know more about software development than they do, and we trust they know more about business priorities than we do. Sometimes we think we know more than they, but we're usually wrong. Let's look at a scenario that really happened and then offer an alternate scenario that could have happened to illustrate the importance of trusting the roles will get us to the right place.

We were building a system with many different screens (tabs on a notebook mostly). After we did a spike to get the feel of basic functionality (in which no buttons were ever disabled) we talked about the "finish the order entry screen" story for the next iteration. It went something like this:

COACH: OK, let's break down the "finish the order entry screen" story into tasks. What does it have to do?

FRANK: We need to change the X field to a ComboBox and ...

COACH: (Interrupting) Frank, why don't we let the customer tell us what it needs to do, and we can ask questions whenever we're confused or we suspect there might be holes in what they ask?

CUSTOMER: Actually, couldn't you just make X a ComboBox, internationalize the labels, and disable the buttons appropriately?

FRANK: Well, I guess we could.

JOE: May I say something?

COACH: Go for it.

JOE: You know, I've done a lot of these systems, and there are basically two ways to disable buttons, menu items, and so on.

CUSTOMER: I don't care how you do it.

JOE: Well, I think it will impact the overall schedule.

CUSTOMER: Do the one that has the least impact.

JOE: It might mean that it takes a little longer to get the order entry screen done right, but I think it will pay off in the long run.

CUSTOMER: Are you sure?

JOE: Give me a minute and I'll explain it to you at a high level. You can write all of this really brittle code that explicitly finds each button and menu item. People do this all the time, and it's a pain to keep all the logic straight. (Several other developers nod or say "Amen" or show other signs of agreement.) Or you can create a set of conditions that are active values and enablers that hang off those conditions. For example, the "test is selected" condition could be defined once. Then you can hook all the buttons/menus affected by that condition with enablers. All the wiring of enablers to conditions happens in one place. If the conditions you want to key on change, you do it in one place and you're done. If we add security, whether or not the user has permission is just another condition. You hook it up and it works. The rest of the code doesn't have to do anything else. It will make changes so much easier as we go forward. We just need a few days to put the basic framework together. I did this in Smalltalk on several occasions in less than a day. I think it will be a little hairier in Java, but I don't think it will take too long.

CUSTOMER: How many days?

JOE: Well, we need to analyze exactly what kind of conditions we need and how we define them. The enablers are the easy part. So, depending on the kind of conditions we need, we're talking about at least two ideal days, potentially four or six if we find some unpleasant surprises. But the types of conditions can evolve. If we can identify the major types of conditions we need, I can give you a better answer.

At the point where we've got a cost for doing more than the one-time obvious but less technically satisfying solution, the conversation could go a couple of ways:

Scenario 1

CUSTOMER: That sounds technically interesting, but we only care about the order entry screen for now. Put that enabler stuff off. I don't think it will be worth that much time.

Scenario 2

CUSTOMER: I'm sure we're going to be changing stuff all of the time. How much time do you think it will really save when we get to the Navigator screen?

JOE: Well, it's hard to say. In my experience, doing the stuff by hand can burn you a lot, but sometimes you get it right the first time. I'd guess that it would save about one-half day on average anytime we define or do some major rework on a screen.

CUSTOMER: Can you do enough of it to get the remove button disabled when nothing is selected this iteration? I really want to show the order entry screen to tech services at the end of this iteration.

JOE: Sure, that's one of the easiest conditions to define, we can have that condition and the rest of the framework in place in three days max. And it will make all of the other screens easier as we go forward.

CUSTOMER: Go for it. Just make sure we get the order entry screen done this iteration.

In the enabler discussion, the customer went with Scenario 2. If the team stopped at the first screen and the screen didn't change much over time, not doing enablers (Scenario 1) might have been the right decision.

Say the customer does go with Scenario 1, and the developers go forward implementing the spaghetti of explicitly enabling and disabling buttons. Then just one more story comes along, and finally a developer says "this stuff smells, I'm going to refactor it" and essentially implements the condition or enabler mechanism at that point.

That decision then would not involve the customer. It would be a technical decision that is obviously justified based on the amount of cruft in the code.

We're not really asking the customer to approve the additional time to be spent and make a design decision. We're asking the customer to assume the risk that it won't be needed. Because if it turns out we need it, we'll spend the time anyway, without asking her.

If your system potentially calls for a state table, you should be able to justify it to the customer in economic terms. If you can't, maybe YAGNI or maybe you just need to do a better job of presenting the reasons. Assume the customer can make intelligent choices. They could be wrong (they often are), but so could you. Let them make the call. They've kept me from putting a lot of features that I was sure they were going to need in the system. When they were wrong, they eventually see it. When they were right, I haven't wasted any time arguing with them over something that will eventually work itself out.

Simple design is not an accident. But once you have the core habits of thinking simply, forging ahead without fear, and refactoring, simple design will happen, and you will get better at it over time.

The Essential Design Tool

CRC cards are fine. We like them. But the best design tool is shown in Figure 18.1.

Get away from the computer to do design. It's too constraining. When you are caught up in the details, get away from the code long enough to see the big picture.

You should have an environment that invites this. We have whiteboards on virtually every wall in our studio, and people are always writing on them. It's amazing how people elsewhere get any work done without them. Make sure they are available within every few steps of any place where people are creating something.

FIGURE 18.1 A whiteboard

Don't focus on whether XP encourages enough design. Focus instead on an environment that encourages collaborative design. If there aren't enough whiteboards, just go out and buy some mylar panels and some dry erase markers and put them to use!

Chapter 19

It's Everybody's Job

Turf battles over code stand in the way of developing a system at maximum speed. Get past this by making each programmer responsible for the whole thing. No code is off limits. Nobody likes to make a mess he'll eventually have to clean up.

Every person on the development team has both the authority and the obligation to change any part of the code to improve it.

Everybody owns all the code, meaning everybody is responsible for it. This allows people to make necessary changes to a piece of code without going through the bottleneck of an individual code owner. Making everyone responsible also avoids the chaos that erupts when nobody owns the code.

Collective code ownership isn't the norm in software development. Developers tend to resist it, usually because they don't understand what it means, so they assume it's like no code ownership at all, or they fear giving up control of "their" code.

What Collective Ownership Means

Collective code ownership is not the same as no code ownership. Kent talks about this in *Extreme Programming Explained*.[1] In the bad old days, nobody owned any of the code. Everybody changed code to suit his purpose, whether or not the change fit well with what was already there. Chaos was the natural result, especially with the dynamic nature of objects. Code grew fast but it was a mess. In self-defense, development organizations opted for individual code ownership. The only person who could change code was the owner. This created stability, but change became agonizingly slow. If the code owner left the team, change in his code stopped.

Saying that everybody owns all the code isn't the same as saying that nobody owns it. When nobody owns code, people can wreak havoc anywhere they want and bear no responsibility. Unit tests must run all the time. If you break something, it's your responsibility to fix it. This requires discipline. If you develop that discipline, collective ownership can work.

Moving From "I" to "We"

The biggest barrier to collective code ownership is a programmer who feels hurt by the practice. A developer who is used to owning code can be intimidated by not owning it anymore. It feels like losing control, like not being responsible for producing anything. That can be scary. It also can be a blow to the ego: If everybody owns all of the code, no one person can be a hero because of "his" code.

The only way to get past this is to conquer your fear and to beat your ego into submission. Neither one is easy.

Collective code ownership doesn't work without trust. You have to give up control. You have to give up the idea of exclusive ownership. You have to believe that "we" produce vastly better results than "I." If everybody owns all the code, anybody can change any of it to meet requirements better or to be more understandable. This will keep the code clean, and will increase speed. If everybody owns all the code, the team's ability to deliver isn't destroyed when the owner of a particular piece of code leaves the team. The only way to understand the value of collective ownership is to give it a good try.

---

1. K. Beck. *Extreme Programming Explained: Embrace Change*, Addison-Wesley, 2000, p. 59.

The hardest hurdle to clear is the ego problem. Nowhere is humility more important than right here. To make collective ownership work, you have to change your definition of what it means to be a hero. Heroes aren't the ones who have the best code with the most clever tricks; heroes are the ones who make the team better—the best pairs, the best refactorers, the best encouragers of other people. If people don't change their thinking, it will be tough for them to change their behavior, no matter how compelling the argument is about results. As someone once said, "It's easier to act your way into a new way of thinking than to think your way into a new way of acting."[2] So act.

Why Have Collective Code Ownership?

Consider the alternatives to collective code ownership. If nobody owns the code, nobody can be held responsible for messing it up. When there is a problem with integration or a production bug, things will degenerate into finger-pointing sessions.

When individuals own parts of the code, code gets further and further away from the team's understanding of what the customer wants. You essentially have mavericks, even if they're pairing. They are always thinking about "their" code, worrying about how others are messing it up. Some might even cheat and clean it up when the pair partner isn't around. Even worse, change ends up being practically impossible. It isn't worth the pain of going through submitting a change request that the developer will get to when it's convenient. Either alternative guarantees that a development project will move slower than optimal speed.

Collective ownership of all the code binds the team together. Everybody has a sense of ownership and empowerment. Turf battles go away, and the team can concentrate of the real goal: making a system that users want and developers can be proud of.

Communication and collaboration are at the heart of the XP values. Collective code ownership is one of those seemingly simple rules, with powerful consequences. It can rapidly show who really believes in collaboration and who doesn't. XP isn't designed for those whose personalities tend toward doing their own thing their own way for their own reasons. Collective ownership is a good way to flush out real collaboration issues early in the team's history.

---

2. Nobody seems to know who said this. Some sources suggest Millard Fuller, Founder and President of Habitat for Humanity.

How to Start Having Collective Code Ownership

There are three things you can do to start implementing collective code ownership:

1. Check your ego at the door. Just give it up for a while as an experiment.
2. Look past the short-term discomfort of giving up control of code to the long-term benefits it can produce.
3. Use tools that make mistakes easy to recover from and that provide robust version control.

Then act like you own all of the other code. Focus on the results the team can create if everybody acts that way. When somebody doesn't act that way, don't let him continue. The grand experiment will fail if even one person doesn't play by the rules. This is the positive incentive. The negative one is, in reality, that the troublemaker will stand out like a sore thumb and be asking for attention he doesn't want.

It's easier to experiment if the risk is low, and the lower the risk, the faster you can go. Good tools can be your safety net. We use an Envy-backed tool for all of our Java development (IBM VisualAge for Java). An Envy repository is a wonderful thing. We have version history for every single change we make. We can always go back to a version that worked. The team can stay in sync all the time. If somebody hammers something beyond all recognition, we can revert to a clean state. A tool like this makes collective code ownership easier.

Why Not Start with Collective Code Ownership?

When you have unit tests, you no longer have a reason to have individual code ownership. As soon as you start breaking work down into stories and tasks, working on them in pairs, integrating continuously, and keeping all the tests working, you will realize that you mostly have collective code ownership already. If you don't, figure out why not. It's probably because you are implementing one of those other practices incorrectly. Talk about it at your stand-up meeting. This is why having stand-up meetings in place is more important than collective code ownership at the start of a project.

Chapter 20

Where's the Customer?

If the client won't give you full-time, top-flight members, beg
off the project. The client isn't serious.

—Tom Peters, *Reinventing Work*

Customers decide which system features get built first. When a question
arises about a requirement, they have to be available to answer it. The best
way to ensure they are available is to make them be part of the development
team.

Over half of all software projects fail. Many of these failures are due to poor
communication between the customer and the development team. The development team makes assumptions about what the customer wants or needs, and
builds the wrong system. Having real users around to answer questions, to set
priorities, and to nip misunderstandings in the bud avoids this problem.

Why Have an On-Site Customer?

To function optimally, an XP team needs to have a customer available on-site to
clarify stories and to make critical business decisions. Developers aren't allowed
to do that alone. Having a customer available also eliminates bottlenecks that
can arise when developers have to wait for decisions.

A story card (or a requirements document) is not all the direction a developer needs to deliver the necessary code. Each story is a commitment to a later conversation between the customer and the developer to flesh out the details. Communicating face to face minimizes the chances of misunderstanding, unlike writing all the requirements down in a static document.

Again, the process of defining requirements is a dialogue, not a document. Having the customer around to clear up ambiguities and to provide direction keeps things on track.

The most common objection to having an on-site customer as a member of the team is that it costs too much, that real users are too valuable to give up their time. That is usually short-sighted thinking. Having real users around to answer questions for the development team ensures that the software will be useful sooner. If that's not worth the time of a user or two, the system isn't worth the expense.[1]

There are a few possible exceptions to this rule:

- When a manager or developer is a domain expert
- When doing exploration work, because the customer admits he doesn't know what he wants
- When the customer and developer have already established good communication, and the few questions that do come up can usually be answered via phone or e-mail

Manager as Customer
by Steve Hayes

My boss actually came up with an objection to the on-site customer that I couldn't really overcome without changing a large Wall Street Bank en masse. The bank culture assumes that technology staff will know enough about the business so that they can make both business and technical decisions. I've actually seen my boss correct business people about how their business worked. This is expected, and without it you won't get promoted. So if you let technical people make technical decisions and business people make business decisions the technical people may not have a career path.

---

1. K. Beck. *Extreme Programming Explained: Embrace Change*, Addison-Wesley, 2000, p. 61.

These situations are not ideal from a development perspective, but it's not usually enough of a reason to quit your job or to abandon XP.

On-Site Versus Available When Needed

The customer needs to be available at a moment's notice to answer questions that will let the project move at maximum speed. If you have to wait a week to get direction, you're sunk. That said, it is important to be practical.

Sometimes, the customer cannot be located physically with the project team. We have found that a remote customer who is available at any time is often good enough. We developed a framework for a wireless application company based across the country from our office. The customer was always a phone call away. If he was too busy to respond right away, he usually got back to us the same day. When he did, it usually worked fine, but we'd still rather have him on site.

Similarly, sometimes a customer cannot devote every hour of every day to the project. The important thing is that the customer be available when needed, within reason. You simply don't have to talk to your customer every minute. If your customer can't be close by, figure out how to work with him.

Developer On-Site
by Uros Grajfoner and Matevz Rostaher

Our company specializes in insurance information systems. At this point, eight insurance companies in seven different countries in Central and Eastern Europe use our insurance information system. So how do we practice "customer on-site" with eight customers?

Kent Beck once said, "The customer speaks with one voice." In our case, a person who has over 25 years of experience in the insurance business and information technology mostly represents the customer. With that much experience in the domain, it is as if the customer was always on-site. Of course, there are details on every project that have to be discussed with the real customer. In these cases, we strive to get the customer on-site or get the customer to be always available.

The idea for "developer on-site" came during educational seminars done by developers for end users. Developers started to program, with the end users by their side, letting them see the prototypes and the development speed, and letting them comprehend the scope of a certain change or of adding some new functionality.

The practical result was that communication and resulting feedback added to its value from both sides. The customer got a better idea of what priority a certain change might be. That way, the developer could indirectly include end users in the Planning Game, even if they didn't seem to be prepared for it. The developers understood the customer's working environment better and saw the customer's problems. End users could talk to developers and show them everyday problems from their point of view. Some of the problems were annoying for the customer but easy for the developer to solve (these "little things" usually get lost in long lists of top-priority projects that have to be done first). Developers could create a short patch to show the customer a short and easy solution.

The satisfaction was mutual: The end users felt their contributions to the system were useful. The use of the system was simpler. Confidence in the system and in the developers increased, not to mention that the "little problems" were fixed. The developers on the other hand had the satisfaction of helping. They received new feedback, which can always prove useful. All they had to do next was take the patches home and integrate them in the base system.

On the other hand, users wanted the developers to solve everything at once. With developers there in person, users thought: "Now is my chance, it can take months to get the developer back here." The result was a large list of top-priority stories that couldn't be solved at once. A small Planning Game can help in this situation.

This practice breaks the rule of continuous integration. It's often not possible to pair with another developer because only one developer is visiting the customer. It can take days for the developer to get back and integrate the changes. The cost for additional communication of the remote developer with the rest of the team is high, but on the other hand, the benefit of feedback from the end users prevails in many situations. Problems in information systems are often in details; this practice helps solve them.

If you can't have an on-site customer, make sure you can have one that is available whenever needed. We wouldn't turn down work where our customer couldn't be physically present with our team. We *would* turn down work where our customer didn't care enough about the project to give the team whatever it needed to produce a useful product.

How to Get an On-Site Customer

The best way to get an on-site customer for your team is to ask for one. If the person authorizing and paying for the project objects, confront that person with the choice of getting better software sooner or increasing project risk.

If you can't get an on-site customer, do your best with an "always available" customer. That might work well enough. If it doesn't, document the snags and make the problem very obvious. Be a squeaky wheel. Don't accept failure as natural. Continue to press for an on-site customer if the alternative doesn't work.

If you can't get either an on-site customer or an always-available one, you can go ahead with the project and accept the reduced odds of success, or you can call it quits. Regardless of which option you choose, you should go in with your eyes open.

Why Not Start with an On-Site Customer?

If you can, start from day one with an on-site customer. You can start doing XP without one. Beg, borrow, and steal time from your customer to get going. Just recognize that you'll go a little slower and there will be a little more friction between developer and customer. Once you're used to the practices, adding an on-site customer will help you make the quantum leap to the next level.

Chapter 21

Knowing When You're Done

Acceptance tests are the proof that your system does what your customer requires it to do. Have customers write acceptance tests before you write the code to implement them. You, as a developer, probably will have to help. As with unit testing, writing acceptance tests will feel odd, but you'll get better with time.

Acceptance testing is actually more important than unit testing in many ways.

The way you do acceptance testing isn't as important as doing it. Acceptance tests are the only things that prove to your customer that the system works. Without these, you're just asking your customer to trust you. Proof removes all doubt. It is the customer's equivalent of the JUnit green bar. Nothing gives a programmer a shot in the arm quite like seeing that wonderful green bar. Give your customer the same confidence.

Acceptance tests also give the customer a real idea of how close the developers are to being done. This lets your customer make informed decisions about whether a system is ready for release.

Customer Confidence

As we said in the Chapter 13, unit testing is about confidence. As a developer, if you have an immediate indication that something has gone wrong, you can fix it immediately. Conversely, if the tests confirm that everything works, you can celebrate. Both outcomes allow you to proceed with confidence.

Acceptance tests can give your customer the same confidence boost. A comprehensive suite of acceptance tests that the customer can run anytime allows him to get immediate feedback on how "done" the stories are. If some of the tests fail, the customer can make an informed decision about what needs to be addressed before the system is ready for release.

Lack of customer confidence can slow a project down just like lack of developer confidence can. Acceptance tests help you guard against that.

How Did All These Bugs Get in Here?
by Ken Auer

Although we had suggested working on automating acceptance tests in the early iterations, our client didn't seem to feel it was very urgent. Our unit tests were growing. We had several hundred unit tests running all the time, and the product demoed very well, with rarely a bug. At the end of every iteration, the project manager would demonstrate the functionality to our customer and other managers and business people, and there were few glitches in preparing the demo. Other people from tech services or other parts of the company would hear about the project and occasionally drop into the lab to see a demo at a moment's notice. We'd just show whatever was on the integration machine and rarely had a problem.

The customer was excited about the product and decided to take it to a big trade show. She was excited about how new functionality was being added so quickly and the stability the system seemed to have. So, instead of locking down a version of the system and having QA pound on it before a trade show like they would normally do, the project manager and the customer figured they would just package up what we had a week or two before the trade show and build a demo script. What could possibly go wrong?

Well, we soon found out.

The first day we packaged it up for her, there was some unexpected behavior. No problem, we'd tackle those problems and give her a new version the next day. We did, and she found a lot of other problems—problems no one had suspected existed. Whenever we had given a demo in the past, the developers had given it following a simple script they had in their heads. It was a very different script than our customer wanted to follow when demoing to end users.

After a pretty stressful week that brought the iteration to a halt to tackle all of the problems the customer was finding, we had something for the trade show. It showed well, but some additional problems were discovered.

In the next iteration, getting acceptance tests on all of the primary functionality rose to the top of the stack of potential stories.

It can take a while to get a suite of acceptance tests built and running. If you've been running without them for a while, they can shake your confidence in what you are doing when you run the first set and they don't work. This is another taste of reality. The earlier you get that taste, the better off you are. Your confidence will build over time as the acceptance tests start passing.

Acceptance Tests as Documentation

If a developer wants to know what the code does, often the best way to begin is to look at the unit tests for that code. This is some of the best code documentation we've ever seen.

The same holds true for acceptance tests, but at a different level. Acceptance tests are documentation for the customer, for users, and for nontechnical people who need to know what the system does and how. These tests can be useful for developers as well, if they need an overview of what the system needs to do.

In XP, user stories are "letters of intent" for developers and customers to work on a problem together. They are commitments to a future conversation that yields detailed understanding of the story, estimates of the amount of effort each task will take, intermediate candidate solutions, and ultimately acceptance tests.

Acceptance tests are a contract between the developers and the customer. Preserving those tests, running them frequently, and amending them as requirements change prove that there has been no breach of contract.

Acceptance tests can save you from having to loop back and write documentation later. These tests are more detailed than descriptions on paper. They are basically step-by-step user documentation that is directly verifiable. Want to know what the system does? Look at the acceptance test for the part you're curious about. What more could you ask for? In fact, the technical writer on our largest ongoing XP project is investigating ways to use the input files for the project's acceptance tests to generate at least part of the end user documentation.

As with unit tests, acceptance tests should be absolutely up to date all the time, unless you're cheating.

How to Write Acceptance Tests

There is no acceptance testing equivalent of JUnit. You can't just download some free software and start testing on day one. Even if you could, you still would need customers to help define the tests.

Customers often have as much trouble writing acceptance tests as developers have writing unit tests. Give them time to practice. Developers may have to help them in the beginning.

Customers and developers often have naive perspectives on how to write testing scripts and what to test. It's wonderful when you have experienced software testers available. They already know a lot about testing and may have experience with various automated testing tools available on the market. Whenever possible, bring in experienced people to help customers and developers get the tests together.

On the other hand, we've found that many software testers are experienced in an environment where the only interactions with developers were one-way conversations: "What you gave me was not ready to be tested" or "Here's a list of bugs. When you think you have them fixed, give me a new version to test." Only use software testers who are interested in having a dialogue.

On most larger projects we worked on before using XP, a separate group did acceptance testing. This group was often made up of people who had very little understanding of software. This is good and bad. The end users of software also tend to be pretty naive, so the testers represent the end users well. On the other hand, there are more efficient ways to test your software. For example, it is probably more cost effective to give an early release of your software and a developer to a small set of end users, and to have the developer take notes on what doesn't work. The feedback will be direct and the cost will be much less.

Roy remembers a large project with over 20 testers on the team doing various kinds of testing. This army of people interacted with the system almost constantly to determine whether or not it was working. This attitude and group setup is nuts.

In his article "Testing Fun? Really?" Jeff Canna talks about how developers should do acceptance (or functional) testing:

> *Functional testing should be approached much like unit testing. Write [the tests] before writing code, as soon as there is code to be written that produces something a user will interact with (such as a dialogue). The developer should work with a user to write functional tests that capture the user requirements currently being worked on. Whenever a developer starts a new task, he should describe the task in the functional testing framework. Development then moves forward, unit testing as new code is added. When all of the unit tests pass, the original functional test is revisited to see if it is passing or if it needs modification.*

Ideally, the concept of a functional testing group should disappear. Developers should be writing functional tests with users. Once there is a suite of functional tests for the system, the member of the development team responsible for functional testing should bombard the system with variations of the initial tests.[1]

Before working on the story for a particular feature, a developer should have a conversation with the customer to understand acceptance requirements for that story. Ideally, the customer will write the acceptance test. In our experience, developers have to help customers to create acceptance tests, much as they had to help customers write story cards in the Planning Game.

Jeff's article brings up an interesting point, though: Exactly when should you write acceptance tests? There probably are several strategies that will work, but on our largest XP project to date

- ✧ Developers write a rough initial test, after one or more conversations with the customer
- ✧ QA fleshes out the test suite
- ✧ Developers make sure they have one or more valid test before they write code for most stories

When to Write Acceptance Tests
by Duff O'Melia

Like many in the XP community, we have experienced the joy of writing unit tests before writing code to implement a feature. We have found a similar joy in writing acceptance tests before writing the code to complete a story. We have even tried writing acceptance tests before estimating a story; however, this approach hasn't worked well because the customer often needs an estimate as soon as possible to determine if the story should even be part of the upcoming iteration.

We have had success in writing the acceptance tests just prior to coding a story. These tests increase our knowledge of the story and force us to speak in depth with the customer about any questions that arise. This helps us give the customer exactly what he wants. The process of writing acceptance tests may or may not affect our estimates. Identifying potential issues early on in the iteration helps to give the customer plenty of time to adjust priorities.

---

1. J. Canna. "Testing Fun? Really?" *IBM developerWorks Java Technology Zone*, March 2001.

Automating Acceptance Tests

Automate acceptance testing whenever you can. This makes it a normal part of life. Run the tests daily. This will give your customers the confidence they need to remain enthusiastically involved with the project.

Producing charts to show the results over time is a great idea. They show you how much progress you are actually making. Don't kill yourself producing charts, however. We've found that the simplest thing that can possibly work is finding a spot on a whiteboard and simply listing the last few weeks' worth of acceptance test data. It looks something like Figure 21.1.

	1/3	1/4	1/5	1/8	1/9	1/10	1/11	1/12	1/15	1/16
Run	92	95	95	95	96	96	96	95	97	97
Pass	42	48	62	63	64	43	58	76	80	83

FIGURE 21.1 Acceptance test tracking

More acceptance tests get added over time and should eventually level out. The number passed should get closer and closer to the number run. If the number passed takes an unexpected drop, it is probably because something in the system changed that broke the test scripts. It might mean the scripts need to be revisited or it might mean that you've introduced an unexpected side effect that had ripple effects throughout the system. Either way, it means that you've taken a step backward and need to figure out how to recover. Charts like this show that you are focused on making progress.

Remember not to turn your brain off when it comes to automation, though. The general rule should be to automate when it gives you good value for your time and money. In some cases, automated testing can cost significantly more than a nonautomated testing effort, so be sure you understand the short- and long-term trade-offs.

Automated Acceptance Testing
by Roy Miller

Acceptance tests capture user requirements in a directly verifiable way, and they measure how well the system meets them. They also expose problems that unit tests miss. Perhaps most importantly, they provide a ready-made definition of how "done" the system is. I would hate to work without them (and I have).

Unfortunately, writing a suite of maintainable, automated acceptance tests without a testing framework is virtually impossible. The problem is, automating your acceptance testing can be expensive. On the upside, if the automation framework is reusable, the up-front investment can save lots of money in the long run.

That's why some of the developers at my company (in cooperation with our client) created the first cut of an automated acceptance testing framework during their first big XP project. Developers and analysts worked with the customer to enter tests into Microsoft Word tables. Tests consisted of actions that could be performed on the system being tested, such as manipulating widgets in a user interface, interacting with a serial port, and so on. A set of Java classes read the test files each night (we actually generated HTML files from Word, which helper classes then parsed) and ran the tests automatically. Results were written to an HTML output file.

We have since enhanced the framework to be entirely XML-based. We anticipate using it on future projects in order to help our customers reduce their testing costs. The client for which the original framework was created is subject to regulatory approval by the FDA for all software systems. We anticipate that having automated acceptance testing in place will reduce the time for FDA validation at this client from five months to several weeks.

What to Test

The customer controls what features need to be covered by acceptance tests. A good rule is that every story has to have at least one acceptance test that shows whether the story works in the way the customer wants it to work. Many stories will require many more tests than this, but it's a start.

As with unit tests, err on the side of having too many acceptance tests. When in doubt, write one. Again, there aren't hard and fast rules here. Write the tests needed to instill confidence that the system will work as expected. If the customer isn't confident, ask yourself whether you have enough acceptance tests, and whether each test covers enough.

It doesn't hurt to read a lot of the classic literature about testing. Certainly, those sources tend to emphasize the formality of things and the scientific proofs that every possible situation has been covered (which is very important if you are building something that deals with people's lives). Existing literature offers a lot of insight into the kinds of things that are important to test and that might not be intuitively obvious. Being thorough in your testing gets you to the point where the customer is confident in the product.

As mentioned in Chapter 13, you should test user interfaces with acceptance tests. That's true, but that's not the end of the story. Unit tests validate the guts of the code—the way various components interact. Acceptance tests validate business transactions—what the system does. Sometimes these results show up on a user interface, but sometimes they don't. For example, a component of a system Ken was in charge of building for a client involved communication with an external physical device through a serial port. No user interface there, but there was an interface to the system that needed to be tested.

Often, significant parts of a system provide a service to various end-user applications. The user interface is not the driving factor in whether the system is functional. In these cases, figure out how to automate testing of whatever drives the system.

Grammar School
by Rob Mee

One of the things people find hardest about writing tests is creating test instances of objects in code. Often, a developer spends more time creating these instances, known as fixtures, than writing the test itself. What if you had a simple, succinct language that clearly expressed your application domain, so that writing test instances was really easy?

In the container shipping business, for example, you might want to describe something like Service from Oakland to Tokyo via Shanghai carrying toys: 20ft $500; 40ft $750.

How do you get from a statement in a domain-specific language like this to an instance of a domain object in a language like Java? Essentially, you have to write a compiler for it. Sounds hard, right? It's not—you just have to use the right tool.

The first thing to do is to get your hands on a parser generator. This type of tool has been around for decades and is available in just about any language you can think of. For Smalltalk, there's T-gen, downloadable free from the University of Illinois. If you're using Java, you can go right to the source. Get JavaCC from Sun Microsystems—it's free too.

Now write a grammar that describes the rule—the syntax—of your little language. For those of you who had a compiler class way back when, or maybe just read the "Dragon Book*" for fun, you're pretty much home free. If you've never been exposed to compiler technology before, don't worry, it's not all that hard. The tool will use your grammar to generate a parser for you. You tell the parser how to generate domain objects. Once all this is done, you can use

---

* A. V. Aho, J. D. Ullman. *Principles of Compiler Design*. Addison-Wesley, 1977.

your little language to create test instances, even quite complex ones, using as little as a single line of code.

Not only can a language like this dramatically reduce the time you spend creating fixtures, but it can also provide a means for business users to express acceptance tests. Put a few statements from your language together and you've got a powerful script, enabling anyone in the organization to express a range of scenarios and acceptance conditions. At Evant, where I currently work, we've developed a language called ESP (EVant Script Programming) that we use for acceptance tests, data loads, presales demo configurations, and so on. Domain-specific languages can also be used to augment XML capabilities you may already be building into your system—in fact, ESP uses XML as an intermediate language. The advantage of a domain-specific language is that it can be much more concise and readable than XML. It's certainly easier to convince product managers to use it.

Sometimes it can be tough to determine what should be covered by a unit test and what should be covered by an acceptance test. Jeff Canna discusses this in "Testing Fun? Really?" He describes how the line between unit testing and acceptance testing isn't always clear:

> Often it isn't clear where to draw the line between unit and functional testing. To be honest it isn't always clear to me where this line is either. While writing unit tests I have been using the following guidelines to determine if the unit test being written is actually a functional test:
>
> - If a unit test crosses class boundaries, it might be functional.
> - If a unit test is becoming very complicated, it might be functional.
> - If a unit test is becoming fragile (i.e., it is a valid test, but small parts of it have to change continuously to handle different user permutations), it might be functional.
> - If a unit test is harder to write than the code it is testing, it might be functional.
>
> Notice the phrase "it might be functional." There are no hard and fast rules here. There is a line between unit tests and functional tests, but you have to make your own decisions about where the line is. The more comfortable you get with unit tests, the more clear it will be when a particular test is crossing the line from unit to functional.[2]

---

2. J. Canna. "Testing Fun? Really?" *IBM developerWorks Java Technology Zone*, March 2001.

How to Start Writing Acceptance Tests

You should be convinced that you need to write acceptance tests before you implement system features. If unit testing before writing code was new to you, acceptance testing might terrify you. Join the club. Since acceptance testing usually is done by people who are not developers, a good number of developers aren't skilled acceptance testers.

There are three keys to writing acceptance tests:

1. Regular conversations among developers and the customer to discuss the acceptance requirements for each story
2. Clear responsibility for making sure the tests are written and executed
3. A pre-determined format for the tests to facilitate automation

Communication is the single biggest factor. Developers probably aren't used to talking to their customer about acceptance tests. Customers probably aren't used to that either. If this discussion is happening, you can figure out how to get the tests written. If it isn't, you can't write valid tests at all.

Regardless of who actually writes the tests, somebody has to be held responsible for them. Just as pair programming can help developers be diligent about writing unit tests first, there needs to be some mechanism for ensuring that acceptance tests are done diligently. We think the best way to do this is to make acceptance test writing part of fleshing out the details of a story. Unless one or more acceptance tests for the story exist, the developer can't implement the story. You may miss a few in the beginning, but the more you hold yourself to this rule, the better off you'll be in the long run.

The first acceptance test you write should always include a script of the simplest path through the system. If you can't create a test to handle the simplest path, rest assured you will not be able to create one for the more complicated ones. Only after you've got a script through the simple path should you focus on all of the variations to the path.

Unless you already have an automated testing tool in house with which you are very happy, you probably won't begin with an automated acceptance testing framework. That's not a problem. You can still do acceptance testing. This might be a great place to use people, such as QA staff, who typically don't show up on the XP radar screen. Have them work with the customer to write some generic scripts until you can figure out how to automate the tests. As soon as you get more tests than a single person can run in a short time (for example, in less than an hour) on a regular (perhaps daily) basis, you should begin to see the value in getting the tests automated. Once you have a few generic scripts that you find helpful, you can evaluate how to automate the scripts.

The quality of the tests is more important than the quantity. You must make sure that you are testing things that prove or disprove your product's usefulness. Don't worry about the details of what happens when somebody types a thousand random characters into a field, if doing so won't cause anything worse to happen than three random characters. Don't worry about stress tests if your system won't be under stress. Don't ignore performance tests just because your automated test tool allows you to record and play back user events easily but doesn't provide performance feedback.

There are many automated testing tools on the market. We cannot recommend one more strongly than another. We have polled many XP groups about the tools they are using to automate their tests. What works for one does not seem to work for another. Some ignore the value of simplicity with a plethora of bells and whistles. Others seem to twist the XP slogan and provide "the simplest thing that *can't* possibly work," because of something unique to the project environment. The appropriateness of one tool or another to your project depends on many variables. We think it is worth investigation, however, because just about every XP team we know that has found or developed a tool for automated acceptance testing is glad it has it.

Even if you don't have an automated framework in the beginning, making one doesn't have to be a huge undertaking. Remember to do the simplest thing that could possibly work. We have heard of people entering test scenarios into Microsoft Excel spreadsheets, parsing them, and running tests with a few simple helper classes in Java. When Ken's team wanted to automate acceptance testing to facilitate regulatory approval for RoleModel's first big XP project, it started by entering tests in Microsoft Word, generating HTML, and parsing that. The fancier automated framework that exists today grew from those simple beginnings.

Why Not Start with Acceptance Testing?

You can start an XP project without a strategy for acceptance testing, but it's risky. You have no way to prove directly that you have met customer requirements, other than having your customer eyeball the user interfaces, output files, and so on. But you can do that. That's what a lot of people do at the beginning of projects anyway, so don't sweat it.

In the beginning of the project, it is more important to get your development team programming in pairs, writing unit tests consistently, integrating regularly, and refactoring code along the way than it is to have it help customers write acceptance tests. It is more important to get your customer involved in planning, answering questions for the development team, and communicating in a new way with the developers than it is to have him write acceptance tests. Once the developers and the customer are doing these essential things, writing acceptance tests can make things even better.

On the other hand, don't talk about acceptance testing as an afterthought. Plant the seed of customers producing acceptance tests up front. Talk about the confidence it will give customers when the tests are running. Within your first few iterations, you should begin getting scripts in place and determining how to automate them. If you are in a culture where testing is typically held off until the end, it might be difficult for people to understand how you can write acceptance tests before the coding is done. But when they start seeing the results of the first few iterations, they'll begin to realize that there are things to test.

A caveat to putting automated acceptance testing off too long is that you'll often be lulled into a false sense of security by the unit tests. You've been warned.

Chapter 22

Don't Get Distracted by the Code

The nice thing about standards is that there are so many to choose from.
—Author unknown

Coding standards keep the team from getting distracted by useless trifles.

Coding standards used to be a big deal. Some people claim it's impossible to develop maintainable code without them. We certainly have seen plenty of cowboy code, with formatting that could be described as random at best.

In XP having a coding standard is important. The particular one you pick really doesn't matter that much. Keep your standard simple and practical. Complicated standards get ignored most of the time.

Why Have Coding Standards?

Having a coding standard does two things:

1. It keeps the team from being distracted by arguments about things that don't matter as much as going at maximum speed.
2. It supports the other practices.

As Kent put it, with XP you spend so much time looking at code created by somebody else that consistent formatting is quite important:

The conventions for naming and method size are more important than where you put returns and tabs, but knowing exactly where the white space will be when you look at a method reduces friction considerably.[1]

Without coding standards, it is harder to refactor code, harder to switch pairs as often as you should, and harder to go fast. The goal should be that no one on the team can recognize who wrote which piece of code. Agree on a standard as a team, then stick to it. The goal isn't to have an exhaustive list of rules, but to provide guidelines that will make sure your code communicates clearly. As Martin says in *Refactoring*, the compiler doesn't care whether code is ugly or clean, but humans are the ones who change the system and they do care.[2] The more hoops you make people jump through to change the system, the more they will avoid change.

How to Start Having Coding Standards

If you have a current standard, use it. If you don't, code for a while until consensus emerges, then implement a standard. Don't spend too much time up front trying to decide all of the coding rules. That will just slow you down.

An easy way to set standards is to use a tool that automatically formats code and encourage everyone to use it. But, as stated above, code formatting is only part of the issue.

If the lack of standard approaches is causing concern to some of the team members, simply arrange to have a team meeting to discuss it. Don't allow the meeting to turn into the formation of an ANSI standards committee.

---

1. K. Beck. "Coding Conventions" at http://www.c2.com/cgi/wiki?CodingConventions.
2. M. Fowler. *Refactoring: Improving the Design of Existing Code.* Addison-Wesley, 1999, p. 6. Martin was referring to design being ugly, but the argument holds for formatting. Formatting isn't as important as design, but bad formatting can slow you down, just like bad design can.

Why Not Start with a Coding Standard?

If you already have a coding standard, use it. For coding standards to matter, you have to be coding first. It is far more important to make progress in the beginning than it is to be sure everybody puts their curly braces ({[<or whatever>]}) in the same place.

Once you start coding, minimize distractions from that activity by killing petty disagreements (arguments over tab width count as petty, in case you were wondering). This will improve communication (everybody's code will look similar), make it easier to refactor (same reason), and minimize integration headaches due to having people reformat code simply so they can understand it.

The Simplest Coding Standard That Can Possibly Work
by Ken Auer

We have a special XP Wiki we use as the document repository of choice. However, other than using it to keep track of stories, we find that we almost never use it.

On our largest current project (still going in May 2001), we have a "Coding-Conventions" page that was last updated 27 Sept 99 and that consists of the following:

```
"* NamingConventions"
```

The "NamingConventions" page consists of the following:

```
"* NameClassesBasedOnWhatTheyDo"
```

This page actually has several paragraphs about why we should name classes based on what they do instead of how they are used. This one "convention" is mostly followed on the project.

During the second week of the project, we spent an hour or two talking about what conventions we should follow. To the best of my recollection, we agreed to the following.

- All methods should be short (less than 10 lines in general, with most being much less than that).
- When you do something unconventional with reason, you should (only after determining there isn't a better way to do it) document why in a comment.
- Don't abbrev when naming vars.
- It is acceptable and sometimes preferable to return from more than one place in a method if the method is short.

We discussed but never reached consensus on other things like where brackets go, when to use lazy initialization, and so on. Some of the discussions were pretty good and planted some seeds.

We then just continued to program. At first, some people became uptight about where the brackets went and changed every method that didn't conform to their idea, but this wore out pretty quickly (quicker for some than others).

Over time, the coding style converged. The best stuff became the de facto standard, because little discussions popped up, someone convinced someone else, and the pair-vine eventually worked to make stuff converge.

There are still times we can guess who wrote a particular method, but sometimes we're wrong. I kind of like it when people blame some ugly code I wrote on someone else; sometimes I even let them in on the secret that I actually wrote the ugly code. Either way we fix it!

There is still some ugly code in the system. Every once in a while we add some more. However, the overall quality of the code is getting higher every day.

Personally I think the only coding standard that matters is that everyone agrees to write code of the highest standard . . . that highest standard is always a moving target, and always getting higher.

Your mileage may vary.

A de facto coding standard will often emerge if you implement the other practices well and communicate.

Chapter 23

Overtime Is Not the Answer

Every now and then go away, have a little relaxation, for when you come back to your work your judgment will be surer. Go some distance away because then the work appears smaller and more of it can be taken in at a glance and a lack of harmony and proportion is more readily seen.

—Leonardo da Vinci

If you burn the candle at both ends for too long, pretty soon you run out of wax.

There is a practice of XP that has been named "40-hour week." The exact number of hours each member of the team works during any week isn't important. It has been suggested that this practice be renamed "sustainable pace." Forty hours is an arbitrary number used to represent a "normal" week where there is a healthy balance between work and nonwork. That balance has been forsaken for lots of reasons, very few of them any good.

Many people in the IT world have a problem with working too much. With the explosion of e-commerce and the intoxication people seem to have with doing things at Internet speed, the problem has gotten much worse in recent years.

Working too much is a recipe for failure and disillusionment. It also doesn't produce the desired results.

Working too much usually keeps you from accomplishing the short-term goals you were shooting for in the first place.

Working too much will burn you out in the long run, even if you love your job. This will keep you from accomplishing your goals in the future.

Why People Work Too Much

People work too much when

- They are hiding from something else in their lives that they can't or don't want to deal with.
- Overtime is a status symbol.
- It will help them get ahead, or they think it will.
- They have no choice (if they want to keep their job), usually because somebody in power requires them to work too much to meet a deadline.

The point is that, when people work too much, there usually is a deeper problem that hasn't been addressed.

What's Wrong with Burning the Midnight Oil?

If you are working too much, or you are forcing others to do so, stop it. Attack the underlying problem and fix it. Not doing that just delays pain.

If there is a problem in some other area of your life that you're running from, take the time to fix it. If you don't, you will regret it. Most people regret not focusing on the nonwork things that have lasting significance once their working lives are done.

If you are in charge of an organization where working too much is a badge of honor, fix that problem. Roy used to think he could work anyone under the table. In the end, he was the one on the floor. Now he thinks that working too much is a sign of insanity, not honor. There is nothing wrong with working hard. There is a problem with killing yourself.

If you are in charge of an organization where working too much lets people get ahead, change the incentive structure. The irony of this "work to get ahead" mentality is that it usually makes you fall behind. Attrition rates are high at organizations that burn people out. Amazingly enough this leads to higher recruiting and training costs and disrupts client service. High pay can compensate for no life only so long. Working too much will cause other areas of your life to suffer, which will reduce your effectiveness when you are at work. Even if you love your job, too much of a good thing is unhealthy. Think of a job you love like dessert. It's all right to eat it, but you need to eat other things in order to stay healthy.

"Balance" should be more than a platitude HR groups use to convince prospective employees that they won't die young. It is the only thing that can keep you producing over time. Stephen R. Covey, in *The 7 Habits of Highly Effective People*, describes the balance between "production" (P) and "production capacity" (PC). Nonwork time is when you can focus on the PC side of the equation.[1]

If you burn the oil long enough, sooner or later you run out of oil. Burnout can happen when a person is forced to work more hours than he wants to for an extended period of time, or works more hours than he should for an extended period of time.

Recognize that an organization does not control your life—you do, by the choices you make. If you work for, or are in charge of an organization that requires you to work yourself to the bone, consider whether that is the best choice for you to make. If you are trying to be a change agent, but your organization refuses to change, maybe you should actively seek other opportunities. Change your organization, or change your organization.

Working more hours is almost never the solution to a productivity problem. It can be a solution to a short-term schedule problem, but it rarely works. Tired, overworked people tend to make mistakes and are usually unhappy. Their productivity goes down, not up.

Negative Code
by Steve Freeman

In a previous job, the boss used to stay late and code. We would come in in the morning and find things broken with no idea what had happened. (The boss was too clever to write tests.) It could easily take several of us a morning to fix the result of an extra few hours of code. One of my colleagues called these late night bursts "Negative Code."

The C3 project defined overtime as time spent at work when you didn't want to be there. That's as good a definition as we've ever heard from people who aren't running from something. The reality of it will be different for each

---

1. S. R. Covey. *The 7 Habits of Highly Effective People.* Simon and Schuster, 1989, p. 54.

person, but everyone has limits. Also, people who have a life outside of work may be spending more hours at the office taking care of things that they would normally take care of at home anyway, so you probably aren't getting as many hours as you think.

Sometimes you just have to work more than you want to. Usually that's because you or somebody else mess up. You underestimated a task, you promised too much, or your boss promised too much or doesn't have the guts to say no. Think of working overtime like using a credit card. It's more convenient than cash, and it lets you defer payment in the short term, but the interest is a killer. If you build up too much debt, you'll go bankrupt. Overtime is the same way. You can do it sometimes to help smooth things out. If you do it too much, you'll be spending money you don't have.

How to Start Working Normal Hours

If your current work culture isn't used to working normal hours, this can be a tough thing to adjust to. This is especially true if some people on the team refuse to cut back.

First, define what is normal for you and your team. This depends on your own physiology, as well as on your outside commitments. Not everyone will hit stride at the same number of hours per week. For some, 40 hours is too little; for others, it's too much. It's important for everyone to be on roughly the same work schedule. You can't pair if your partner doesn't show up until you've been at work for several hours.

Second, cut back gradually to that normal schedule. Working too much is a bad habit and it's hard to break a bad habit cold turkey. If you can, do it. Try cutting back first. Once you've identified your normal week, try to split the difference between that and what you're working now.

Third, practice not compromising on the hours unless you mess up. If you mess up, admit the mistake and correct it, then work on preventing the mess-up next time. Practice being honest during planning. That will support a sane work schedule.

Fourth, have some courage. It takes guts to work a reasonable schedule. When someone demands that you work too much, reflect on the situation to determine whether you made a mistake. If you didn't, have the courage to say no.

Increasingly, true balance is something you have to fight for. Sometimes it requires making tough choices, but it is worth the effort.

Why Not Start with a 40-Hour Week?

You can do XP without working normal weeks. It's just harder. If you do this for too long, any approach to software development, XP or otherwise, will fail.

At first glance, a normal work week might seem to be the oddball XP practice. To understand how it fits in, remember what happens when people on the team consistently work huge amounts of overtime. Overworked people are prone to make mistakes. The likelihood of such people being effective pairs, of seeing opportunities to refactor, or of communicating very well is extremely low.

Mess with people's lives, pay the price.

Chapter 24

Painting a
Thousand Words

A system metaphor represents a common understanding of the system for everybody involved. It makes design easier and keeps everyone focused on the goal.

A Chinese proverb says, "A picture is worth ten thousand words." Images, even mental ones, often communicate more than words alone.

When a programmer writes code, he should choose his words wisely—they convey rich meaning. Code should communicate the programmer's intent clearly. Ward talks about the Thesaurus pattern—having a thesaurus on your desk to help you find the right nuance for the names you use in your code. The point is facilitating communication. The goal is to have a system of names such that every programmer on the team who reads the code understands what it says and why.

Where the Concept of Metaphor Came From

One of the biggest challenges of developing software is having customers and developers talk to one another in a language they both can understand.

In XP customers decide the features of the system based on business value, which is their language. Programmers then decide how those features get built, in their language. When a customer and programmer need to talk, a metaphor can ease the translation. Rodney Ryan put it well:

> *Isn't the intent of the system metaphor to improve communication among the entire team (customers and nonprogrammers included) by creating a common way for all to view the system, rather than just expressing an architecture to the programmers?*
>
> *"The system is a bakery" jibes better than "The system interprets text as commands and executes them against builders that produce resultant objects and attach assorted decorators, sorting them via pipes and filters to the correct bins; the user can than browse and eat them as needed."*[1]

Programmers might understand the latter description, but communication with the customer will break down if it's all you've got. It focuses too much on implementation details. A metaphor lets the team focus on "what" rather than "how" in the beginning. If you can find a good metaphor, it can be a powerful tool.

How to Start Creating Metaphors

The real point of a metaphor was always to have a common understanding and a shared vocabulary. You can't always find a killer metaphor. Sometimes you can come up with a shared vocabulary based on a description of what's in your domain, such as a contract management system with contracts and customers. There is nothing wrong with this if there is common understanding.

A few rules might be helpful here:

1. **Pick a vocabulary that's consistent with your domain.** This was what the Chrysler C3 project did. Chrysler makes cars, so the project team used a "production line" metaphor with "parts" and "bins." A metaphor about "cakes" and "ovens" wouldn't have made as much sense.

2. **Don't waste time finding the perfect metaphor.** Find a useful vocabulary and go with it. The beauty of a metaphor is not critical; having everybody understand how the system fits together is.

3. **Remember the limits of a metaphor.** Don't let it hold up your progress. If something doesn't quite fit into a metaphor you chose, that's fine. Stop using a metaphor that isn't working.

---

1. R. Ryan. *System Metaphor* at http://c2.com/cgi/wiki?SystemMetaphor.

Why Not Start with a Metaphor?

You need to develop the shared understanding and common vocabulary embodied in a system of names eventually. These things evolve, so you typically can't have them when you start. If you have a sudden flash of insight that reveals the perfect metaphor, go with it. Metaphors can be powerful tools, providing everyone with a mental image to facilitate communication and helping keep design simple.

A metaphor is an instance of a common vocabulary that reflects a shared understanding of the system. It's a convenient picture that makes those things "gel."

A lot of people doing XP say they haven't really found a good metaphor or that they use metaphors only for certain parts of the system. All of the people we've talked to who don't use a metaphor haven't seen it as a significant problem. If you have one, great! If you don't, communicate anyway, and wait for the insight that reveals the shared understanding and common vocabulary you're after.

Chapter 25

Looking for Guidance

Better than a thousand days of diligent study is one day with a great teacher.
—Japanese proverb

A good coach makes following a new process, and staying on process, a lot easier.

We've never heard a convincing argument that says you need to have an experienced coach in order to do XP. The developers on the first XP project didn't have an experienced coach. They had an experienced developer/leader who had direct access to Kent, who was still formulating XP. They didn't have all the resources we now have at our disposal to learn all about XP. In fact, there have been many projects since then who have not had an experienced XP coach.

At the time we're writing this, you can probably count on two hands the number of people with over one year of experience coaching XP projects. So it would be foolish to say that you can't do XP without an experienced coach. But a team could certainly benefit from one.

Missing It
by Ron Jeffries

As I visit clients and give talks on XP, I keep running into teams who are doing two-thirds XP, and to teams who have picked up XP on their own who are really in the "but at least we don't write documentation" form of XP.

I started out thinking that XP teams needed experienced coaching almost unconditionally. More recently I was thinking "This isn't so hard, people can just pick it up." But my experience is suggesting to me that teams really don't get XP from the books, lectures, and Web sites. I'm coming back to thinking that most teams need coaching from someone with experience.

Why You Do Need a Coach

When we ask ourselves what we can do better without a good coach, nothing comes to mind. If you can get a good coach, hire him. We believe there is value in having a big open office space, doing all our work in pairs, having a customer on site, and making requirements a dialogue instead of a document. This is all highly interactive, multisensory engagement stuff. We'd be hypocrites to tell you that all you need to do is to read this book and everything will come out rosy.

Why Do Basketball Teams Have Coaches?
by Don Roberts

Basketball teams have coaches because players are too involved in the game to make optimal decisions. Many other influences affect their judgment. Emotions get in the way. If you've ever played organized basketball versus pick-up basketball, you'll immediately recognize the difference.

I've watched good coaches pull players out of games after making an amazing hot-dog play (that was successful). Not because they failed, but because continued play in that manner cannot be successful in the long run. I see coachless XP as allowing hot-dog behavior to occur unchecked.

"Yeah, we're supposed to refactor relentlessly, but we're behind schedule." "Yeah, we should have written the tests first, but I already knew how to implement it, and I did write the tests later." "Yeah, I know I shouldn't program alone, but everyone else slows me down," and so on, and so on, blah, blah, blah.

XP is pretty simple. Basketball is pretty simple. Simply knowing how to do something well doesn't mean that you will execute it well.

A distant second best to having an experienced coach is having an inexperienced coach who gets advice from the writings of pioneers. The context of the pioneers' experience is multisensory and much bigger than can be reduced to the written word. The newbie is left to read between the lines, then figure out how it all applies to his situation without the benefit of being able to ask the pioneer. It is hard enough trying to figure out what we are saying to each other when we're in the same room, even if we have whiteboards.

A distant third is coaching by committee. If people are all committed to doing XP, they can hold each other accountable to some extent. It's difficult to coach when you are playing the game. If you find yourself in this situation, force yourself to be more reflective. Have stand-up meetings more often. Schedule time to have reflection meetings where you talk about how well you are doing on the process, perhaps once a week.

What If We Don't Have a Coach?

Ken has found that when he's away from a project for a while it is not uncommon to hear about problems coming up. The conversation might go something like this:

KEN: So, Ralph, how's it going?

RALPH: Well, it was really bad for a couple of days. Joe was actually encouraging several of us to work by ourselves. It wasn't too bad for the first few hours. I was just exploring for the first hour. But then we tried to integrate. It was a nightmare. My stuff had some problems, but you should have seen what Sue did when she was working by herself! I was afraid that was going to happen, but I didn't want to say anything because Joe's the project manager. We finally got the integration problems worked out at five-thirty that night. The next day Joe told us to work alone again! Finally, after a while, I couldn't take it anymore. I just said I needed a pair. It got a little heated. But this morning we met and worked it all out.

At times (usually in an earlier part of the project), Ken comes back to find bigger problems that haven't been resolved. It sometimes takes a couple of days to find out about some problems. The integration machine has some failed tests, and no one seems to be concerned. An expedient developer decided that there was an easier way to handle security and replaced a bunch of stuff with uglier code. How did it happen? Mostly he worked by himself. When he called someone over, it was to get the bugs out. They hacked it together to get it to work. His pair wasn't aware of how drastically he changed the design for the worse. That's why you need a coach.

We've started several small projects without a coach. Inevitably, someone comes up with a reason not to follow a practice. They tried what they thought was the right way to do something but, in this case, things didn't seem to work. So, since the two pairs of people were working on different things, it didn't seem to be important to do continuous integration. Now work has to stop for a day to get the two things integrated. Maybe both people solved the same problem in two different, incompatible ways and both have built several sets of assumptions based on the mutually incompatible approaches to the base problem.

Maybe the team appears to have all of the practices down. But, there are two stories. One story is a challenge and the two most experienced people on the team both feel that they can tackle it with the other's help. The two junior guys are left on their own to tackle the "easier" story. Neither of the experienced developers has ever used JSPs so it isn't important that they be on that story. Three days pass. The two experienced developers finish the first story and start a second. They're just pairing away. At the stand-up meeting, the junior folks declare what they were working on and that they are making progress, though not as much as they'd like. They've been driving in a ditch for three days, creating some complex code without knowing it could have been done any simpler. It seems okay to their inexperienced partner. That's why you need a coach.

Rookie Coaches

Not everyone can hire an experienced coach. Even if everyone were convinced they needed one, there are not enough to go around.

If the best you can do is come up with a good leader who believes this stuff will work and has enough experience in software to have some credibility, let him lead. In all but the rarest occasions it will be difficult to coach by committee. Of course, coaching by committee can be better than coaching by ignorant despot.

What do you look for in an inexperienced XP coach? Ken has met some successful coaches who had to figure it out without an XP guru at their sides. They tended to have the following characteristics:

⋄ They are generally positive in their outlook. They look at problems as opportunities to learn and are confident that they can figure out whatever they don't know.

- ✧ They look at software as a craft rather than as a manufacturing process.
- ✧ They are good listeners and good teachers.
- ✧ They have been involved in a variety of software projects in the past and can tell you what worked well, what didn't, and why.
- ✧ They prefer to work with particularly talented people but value every individual as a potential contributor to the success of the project.
- ✧ They prefer to find out the facts rather than the spin about any problem. They don't shy away from the truth and they have little tolerance for people who are more interested in looking good than dealing with the problem they are supposed to be solving.
- ✧ They are very energetic and do not tire easily when problems land on them one after another.

How to Coach

The job of the coach is to make sure the team is playing to win. Just like in basketball or other sports, it's not about having everybody show off how great he is. Sure, you want to give everyone his moment in the spotlight and let him know how proud you are of him. But you need to focus on team performance.

First, the coach has to make sure everyone is executing the fundamentals (Part II). If they are not, the team may continue to keep the game competitive for a while with some stellar individual efforts, but will lose eventually.

But it's not enough to have the fundamentals right. You need to produce. All of the things in Part III are necessary to make serious progress. Make sure those things are happening, too.

You need to cheer the team on when it is doing well. You need to pull people aside when they are actively resisting or not contributing. You need to compensate for weak links without drawing too much attention to the weakness. You need to nurture people who aren't doing well. You need to coach!

Minimal Coaching

When Mike Krzyzewski, coach of the NCAA Basketball Champion Duke Blue Devils, saw his team down by 22 in a crucial game, he told his team, "Forget the plays, just go out there and play your game." For the next 15 minutes or so, he just watched as his team steadily closed the gap. He couldn't have motivated a less talented team that way. Sometimes you are very active when you are coaching. Other times you can just point people in the right direction and do very little else. And some teams need less coaching than others.

A team that is executing the XP process well could probably get by with minimal coaching. In that case, an experienced coach who knows the team could come by every so often, ask a few questions, observe a few things, make some recommendations, and disappear for a while. Here are some guidelines for this approach:

◇ This typically works best when the coach was there in the beginning and knows the project, the unique implementations of the practices, and the people on the team.

◇ Make sure the times the coach visits are not too far apart. Sometimes even the biggest problems go unseen by people stuck in the middle of them.

◇ Problems or potential problems can come up at any time, so the coach should be available to ask questions while problems are still small.

How About a Player/Coach?

Coaching can be a tough job. On most teams of any size, it's a full-time job. That's why it has been argued that you should not have a player/coach. It is hard to do both and do them well. The reality is that it's harder for some than for others. It's also harder in some situations than in others.

Sometimes you need a star player more than you need a coach. It's more important for the technical work to be done competently than it is to make sure the process is running at maximum efficiency. If you're facing a difficult challenge, adding Michael Jordan to your team might be more important than having a great coach. Having both would be best. If your most qualified coach also happens to be one of your most talented or experienced developers, you have to make a tough choice. That person may have to wear both hats, but realistically he can wear only one effectively at a time. He has to get good at switching them.

If you find yourself in this position, hand off one hat as soon as possible. Ken seems to be able to switch hats pretty well. He does what makes sense, most of the time. Sometimes it's more important for him to tackle stories. Other times it makes more sense for him to make sure the process is working and people are okay. Is he always in the perfect role at any moment of the day, day of the week, or week of the month? Of course not. It's a tough balance and it changes from minute to minute.

Player/Coach
by Ken Auer

About two years ago, when RoleModel Software was just becoming more than a one-person company, I was leading a team of about eight that was very "junior heavy" on a significant system, which was being written in Java. Greater than half of the team was made up of our client's employees and the rest were employees of RoleModel Software. I was only on the project slightly over half time. My "second in command" (Duff) was very bright and had some good Java experience, but was still relatively green. Among the client developers were some very sharp people with little programming experience, and some experienced developers with little OO experience. One of RoleModel's developers was a 19-year old apprentice (Nathaniel) who was also very bright and has an amazing amount of experience for his age, but who lacked experience on projects of any size. Another, more senior developer (Jeff) joined the project midstream and was just beginning to understand the system. So, on any given story/task, we had a pretty high risk that those driving the task had many weaknesses that outweighed their strengths in bringing the task to completion with a high level of efficiency and quality.

The project manager (from the client) wanted progress on the project, but wanted their people to be mentored and to take responsibility for tasks. XP, at the surface, seems to be the ideal approach to address these simultaneous goals. Early on, I'd spend a lot of time mentoring. I would get someone started on a story, and then, once it was well under control, I would switch pairs, sometimes being the odd person out, exploring some of the more complicated technical challenges while keeping one eye out for anyone who was having problems.

A few months into the project it was clear that we needed to hook a recently selected object-oriented database into the system, and that there were some very hairy issues that were going to need my attention. We were behind where we wanted to be. Some business issues held up the decision about who the database vendor was going to be, but it was now set. I had, by far, the most experience with persisting objects. There were some characteristics of the objects we needed to store and retrieve that made this a significant challenge. We had to do some creative, unnatural acts with the database. I needed to roll up both sleeves.

Though I could and did certainly work with a partner on these tasks, it was clear I was going to have to drive and that this would need a lot more of my attention for a few weeks than I'd have liked.

While I gave those things my attention, there was little to no time for coaching. More often than previously, more junior people were working together. I recognized the following problems (often after they had reached an alarm stage):

- Developers were commonly ending up "in the ditch" on tasks that they seemed to be "driving steadily down the middle of the road" only an hour earlier.
- Estimates were often significantly off as tasks were confidently oversimplified. (They didn't think they needed to verify the approach with someone more senior because it was "so obvious.")
- Pairs were thrashing but thought they were doing fine.
- A story was under control until a new partner came in and put a twist on a task that made the task owner panic.

If I were focused more on my coaching role, I would have caught many of these things before they became serious issues. Instead, I ended up putting out a lot of "brush fires," due to manifestations of these issues. I wasn't the only one noticing the problems. Since I couldn't sit down with everyone for very long, we tried to identify a few rules to prevent some of the problems (e.g., whenever possible, pair up a RoleModel person with each client employee), but there were always exceptions to those rules. They had some positive effect but not as much as we'd like. It was a rough couple of iterations.

Eventually we got back on track. By the way, we succeeded with our unnatural acts on the database. Nobody else on the team thought they would have been able to pull off the story without me.

Did I focus my time well? I'm not sure. I'm positive the persistence work wouldn't have gotten done, but I'm not sure how much better off the rest of the project would have been if I had spent more time coaching. I probably wouldn't do it too much differently if I had to do it over again and had no control over the makeup of the team. The team did very well considering the challenges they faced versus the experience they had.

Why Start Without a Coach?

If you don't have a coach available, that shouldn't keep you from starting.

If you can get an experienced coach, get one. If you can't, find someone with potential and grow one. You've already showed enough leadership to buy this book, maybe you are the one who can grow to be the coach.

Chapter 26

Keeping Score

There are many forms of feedback. Capturing and tracking a few key pieces of data can be extremely valuable.

We've mentioned the value of feedback. As a group, you need to have it, and in all but the most exceptional cases, you want to have some real numbers to tell you how you're doing.

If you have someone who is naturally good at gathering metrics without being a pest, you've been extremely blessed. Otherwise, come up with a system that allows people to collect data on themselves and that doesn't emphasize individual track records. The goal isn't to give awards for the best estimators, or punish people for missing their estimates. The goals of tracking are

- ✧ To encourage everyone to get better at estimating
- ✧ To identify as soon as possible when the project is ahead, behind, or on the expected schedule
- ✧ To identify problem areas

What to Track

What you should track is going to vary widely from project to project. What seems to make the most sense on every project is to

♦ Track estimates and actuals
♦ Track acceptance tests created and passed

There are plenty of other things to consider measuring, but these are the basics. If you are doing well on the basics, there might not be any point of measuring anything else. If you are not, find things to measure that you suspect might be causing problems. But don't go crazy measuring everything. The goal for winning projects is to get the product out the door, not to collect data.

How to Track

The role of the *tracker* was defined early in the life of XP:

> *"The Tracker goes around a time or two a week, asks each programmer how she's doing, listens to the answer, takes action if things seem to be going off track. Actions include suggesting a CRC session, setting up a meeting with customer, asking Coach or another Programmer to help."*[1]

In *Extreme Programming Explained*, Kent warns us a tracker needs the ability to collect information "without disturbing the whole process more than necessary." And, "you can't be such a pain in the neck that people avoid answering you."[2]

We've found that the job of the tracker is typically not one that many programmers want to do. In fact, the kind of person attracted to this job is often exactly the person you don't want: the controlling type who finds fault with anyone who misses a detail and can't see the forest for the trees. When Ken first started doing XP, his initial reaction was that he'd rather not have a tracker than have the wrong person as a tracker.

On the other hand, not having a tracker is not really an option. You can't get better at estimating if you don't have feedback on how well you've done on your estimates to date. You can't rely on people to admit they are having a

---

1. From http://c2.com/cgi/wiki?ExtremeRoles.
2. K. Beck. *Extreme Programming Explained: Embrace Change.* Addison-Wesley, 2000, p. 145.

problem with their tasks because of their natural inclination to hide bad news. Progress is shown by marking off tasks and stories as completed. Without a chart, how do you know you are or are not making progress?

We've found that the best way to avoid disturbing the process is to automate tracking as much as possible. There are a lot of things you might want to know that are simple to track without being invasive. For example, if you run acceptance tests every night, just write a routine to count how many passed and how many failed. If you are ambitious enough, you can even store that data someplace where another program can read it and chart it. If not, just ask someone to check the results in the morning and write up the numbers on the whiteboard.

Story cards and task cards are a great way to plan and operate an XP project. However, they leave a lot to be desired when it comes to tracking. For most projects, the cost of a full-time manual tracker seems high considering the return. Some sort of automatic tracking, even as simple as a group-accessible spreadsheet, might be the simplest thing that could possibly work, and have a lot of good side benefits.

AutoTracker
by Ken Auer

When we began using XP, we'd write our estimates on cards and move them from the "not done" to the "done" board. We could see some form of progress of the iteration, but if no one asked "how well did you do on your estimates?" as the cards were moved, we were not learning to make better estimates and had no idea how well we were really tracking. Of course, we'd often forget to ask this question. When we did ask the question, we didn't do anything with the data except file it in our heads.

We recognized that there were certain data we felt we had to enter manually. The most obvious were

1. The person who took responsibility for a task.
2. His estimate.
3. The actual time it took to complete.

As we examined both the people we had and the kind of company we wanted to become (a custom software development company), we recognized that we and our clients would need tools. We would want the data and statistics to be up to date in pseudo-real-time and accessible from multiple sites. We basically wanted something even more flexible than cards that can only be at one place at a time. We also recognized that something like a spreadsheet could roll up the estimates vs. the actual and help us examine the trends. If we could find or build some set of tools that would have these attributes, then the coach, as well as the developers and customers, could simply look at the results and make appropriate adjustments.

The answer seemed to indicate a Web-based set of tools where data could be entered from multiple sites and viewed from multiple sites with a reasonable level of security. This data would have to be very simple to update and easily associate with stories/tasks. We also didn't want to sacrifice the "token" quality of the cards, which identified task ownership.

We thought that something like a Wiki* would give us a good way to enter and save stories, break them into tasks, and add data to the tasks as we had it. However, the Wiki was text-based, and we feared there was no room for analysis of data. We discussed the possibility of a Wiki-based project management tool with Ward Cunningham. Ward agreed to experiment with some way to tally up the results of special fields and add security to create a private Wiki. In short order the first pass at RoleModel's Online Extreme Project Tracking was born. After several months, another iteration was done and we have been using this version as it stands for over two years, giving each project we take on its own Wiki.

We created a couple of templates for stories and tasks and a special Perl script rolls up all the data from numeric fields. The script looks for any field with numbers in it. "Field" is defined as a leading space followed by text, followed by a colon. This allows us to define new fields as we desire. The reality is that we've pretty much stuck to three fields of interest. Since the script does not discriminate, it will also roll up our "as of: 991229" date fields. We found the simplest thing to do was to ignore this side effect.

We use our Wiki for all sorts of things about the project. We follow the rule that we create no unnecessary documentation. Most of the necessary documentation is on the Wiki or at least pointed to by it. We can add stories and tasks as necessary, and then we organize them by creating a page for each iteration.

For a given iteration, we have a page describing each of the stories/tasks we're tackling. (An example is shown in Figure 26.1.)

We can break each story or task into subtasks (or not). If we do, it looks like any other node in the tree. (See Figure 26.2.)

---

* W. Cunningham. *The Wiki Way: Quick Collaboration on the Web.* Addison-Wesley, 2001.

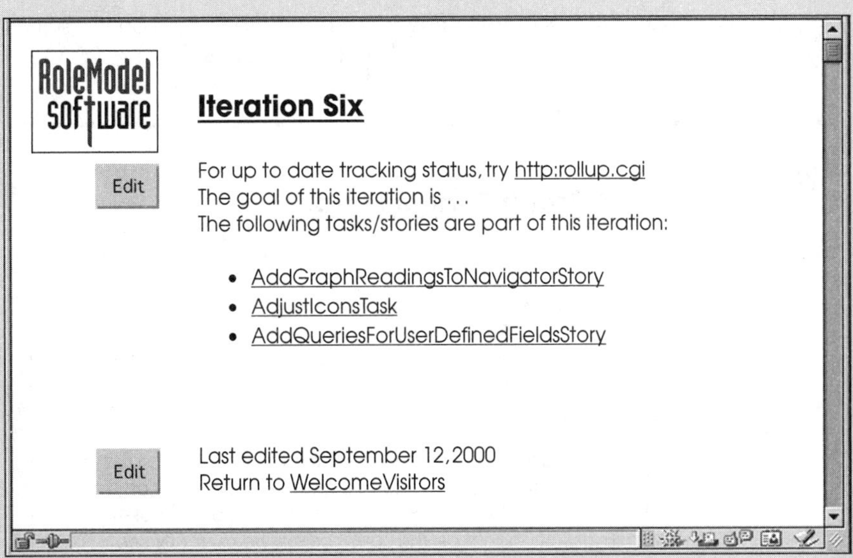

FIGURE 26.1 Iteration page

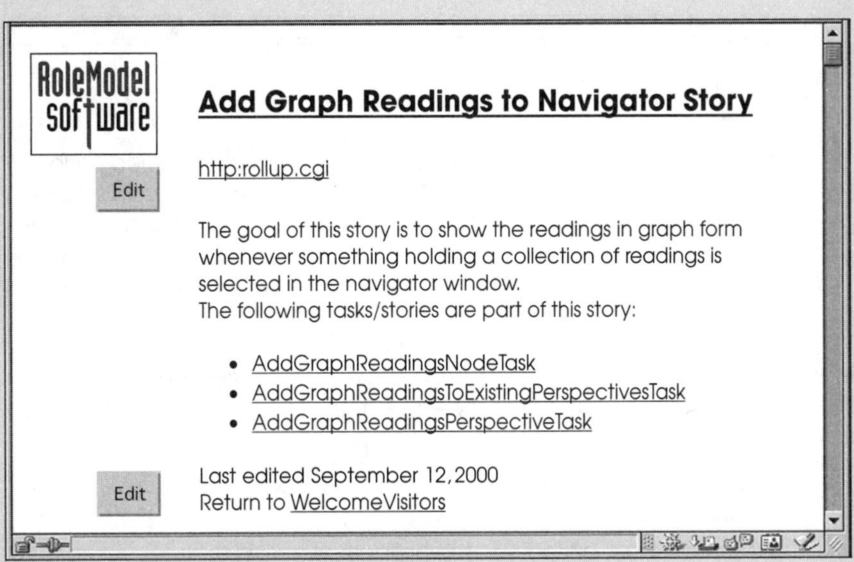

FIGURE 26.2 Story page

Eventually, we get to the leaves. They use a template (keyed on the suffix 'Task' in this case) when created, and we fill in the details. (See Figure 26.3.)

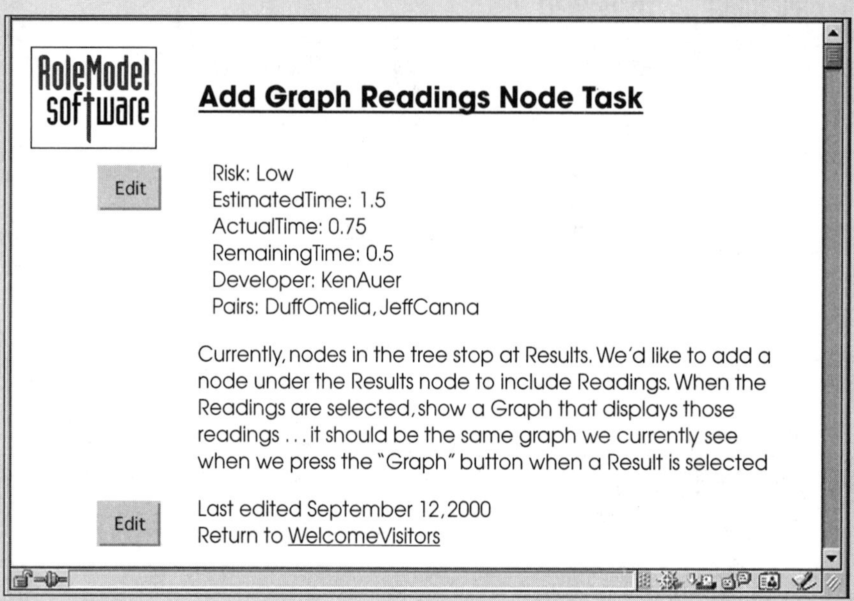

Add Graph Readings Node Task

Edit

Risk: Low
EstimatedTime: 1.5
ActualTime: 0.75
RemainingTime: 0.5
Developer: KenAuer
Pairs: DuffOmelia, JeffCanna

Currently, nodes in the tree stop at Results. We'd like to add a node under the Results node to include Readings. When the Readings are selected, show a Graph that displays those readings . . . it should be the same graph we currently see when we press the "Graph" button when a Result is selected

Edit

Last edited September 12, 2000
Return to WelcomeVisitors

FIGURE 26.3 Task page

At the beginning of each iteration, developers who have signed up for tasks enter the EstimatedTime and the RemainingTime (which should start out the same). During the iteration, at the end of each day (or more often), developers update the ActualTime and RemainingTime fields for all of the tasks they worked on. Note that ActualTime plus RemainingTime will not necessarily equal EstimatedTime.

At any point, someone who wants to see how a story or an iteration is going (with respect to estimates), can just go to the corresponding *http:rollup.cgi* to see a table that shows the items and the totals (see Figure 26.4.). So, I can see at a glance things like:

- How much more time is needed to finish the assigned tasks of the iteration
- Whether we are currently in the ballpark of our estimates
- Which particular story/task(s) are threatening the completion of the iteration
- Whether there's more time than work remaining (or vice versa)

RoleModel software

Rollup of IterationSix

	Actual Time	Estimated Time	Remaining Time
. . Add Graph Readings Node Task	0.75	1.5	0.5
. . Add Graph Readings To Existing Perspectives Task	0.75	1.5	0.5
. . Add Graph Readings Perspective Task	0	1	1
. Add Graph Readings To Navigator Story **total**	1.5	4	2
. Adjust Icons Task	0.5	0.25	0
. . Add Queries For User Defined Date Fields Task	2	1.5	0
. . Add Queries For User Defined String Fields Task	1	1	0
. . Add Queries For User Defined Number Fields Task	0	1.5	1.5
. Add Queries For User Defined Fields Story **total**	3	4	1.5
Iteration Six total	5	8.25	3.5

10 pages examined starting with IterationSix.
Return to WelcomeVisitors

FIGURE 26.4 Rollup page

This ever-present feedback helps me (as the coach) or anyone else on the team (e.g., the official tracker) ask some good questions at the next stand-up, such as

- Has everyone been updating the Wiki at the end of the day? (Hopefully the answer is no when the data that prompted me to ask showed we were behind schedule.)
- It looks like the XYZ story has been giving us some problems. Is it under control? Is the customer aware of the issues?
- It looks like Joe has more tasks than he can finish in the remaining five days of the iteration. Joe, how can we help you out? Mary, it looks like your tasks are done, can you help?

This allows us to make the role of the tracker a lot less time consuming. It is also much less obtrusive.

During development, the unobtrusiveness of the Wiki is excellent. During the day, as we understand what we have to do, we can simply push the edit button and add a note or two for ourselves (or the next person who visits the page). At the end of a task or at the end of the day, we simply edit two numbers, Actual-Time and RemainingTime. We don't need to get grilled by anybody. Before the end of the next day's stand-up meeting, several people usually roll up the iteration and might drill down a bit if something seems to be out of whack. The stand-up meeting is usually where concerns are communicated.

We also like the idea that the customer and others interested in the project can look at how things are progressing from wherever they are sitting. Because of the security features (simple log in name and password), we can limit exposure as much or as little as we want. The message to everyone around is that we have nothing to hide. We want open communication. Most others don't spend too much time looking at it but like the idea that they can.

Backups are done every night, so we don't have to worry about where the cards are.

Customers can edit the stories. (In reality we have a problem getting them to do it, but we don't think Wiki is the issue here.) If we need some sample data and customers are not on-site, we can call them up and they can update it.

The Wiki is also a great place for storing other stuff about the project. When new people come on board, they know that they can go to the Wiki to find things they don't feel they can ask or just to study something deeper. For example, we have our integration process described there. Even though we walk them through it, some people just feel more secure knowing they can read about it to reinforce what they just saw.

Moving the stories around on the Wiki is not as easy as moving the cards around. With a card, a story on the back burner is just on the other side of the table and easy to find. You don't even have to remember its name. On the Wiki, there have been several times during a discussion when someone has said "Don't we have a story for that?" Finding it on the Wiki is not easy, especially if you don't remember what you called it. This could theoretically be faster if we organized it better. Psychologically, we've found sorting through cards at the Planning Game easier than sorting through Wiki after the Planning Game.

We use cards at the Planning Game, and then someone enters them into Wiki afterward. This gives us a higher "shuffling ability" during the Planning Game and lets us track more easily during other times. However, Wiki tends to be the database of record and the cards don't show up at the Iteration Planning meetings. We've tried printing out the data on the Wiki, but sheets of paper are a poor substitute for smaller index cards. So we tend to do our Iteration Planning meetings just by writing candidates for the iteration (based on past planning and performance) on the whiteboard and sorting them there. It just doesn't feel right when you are trying to make trade-offs this way because you can't sort as efficiently when you have to erase and rewrite, but it hasn't been a big enough bother to make people re-create the cards.

We currently don't have a good way to throw out anomalies (other than removing them from the record) or to create pretty charts. On the other hand, we have thought of a lot of things we can do with the data we have collected; it doesn't seem productive to extend the capabilities yet.

For example, we could also organize pages by developer (which tasks are assigned to whom), or any other means. We could roll up the entire project, or any part of the project simply by creating a new Wiki page with bullet items that point to the pages that contain stories/tasks. It doesn't seem to us that any of these organizations are really that valuable and worth the effort (even if the Wiki were easier to use than it currently is). For example, if we rolled up individuals' estimates, the concern would be that there would be incentive to record only numbers that would show themselves to be good estimators. By not doing it, we instead focus on the tasks that were difficult to estimate, not on the person as a poor estimator. We discuss what threw off the estimates and, as a team, look out for that next time we estimate. Instead of picking on the poor chap it happened to, we all learn from the mistakes.

This kind of tracking also helps keep the focus on how well the team is doing toward completing an iteration. Although you can drill down on a problem task and find out who has taken responsibility for it, this is typically used to find out who needs help, not to point fingers. There is still the occasional ribbing, but I think the finger would unnecesssarily be pointed at the individual far too often if we tracked that more explicitly. It's obvious that a person needs to make adjustments when he's off on his estimates by a significant amount three times in a row. How well (or poorly) they estimated three months earlier just isn't very relevant.

Theoretically, we can get a lot of historical metrics also. So far, we have found that rolling up the current iteration tends to give us all the feedback we need to make forward-thinking decisions.

What other things might you want to produce besides the actual, estimated, and remaining time and their rolled up totals? There are a lot of candidates, but we've never found many others that important. If we are doing pretty well with our estimates, and the number of acceptance tests passed is going up steadily, you may not need more. If not, you might want to measure the things you think might be contributing to the disappointing numbers.

Why Not Start with a Tracker?

When you are first starting XP, you are just beginning to look at stories and then begin exploring. Eventually, you'll start having things to track, but the chances are good that what you track during the first few weeks will not be extremely useful. However, from the start, everyone should make estimates and track how accurate those estimates are.

It's important to track data to meet your goals. How big a deal you make out of the tracker role is up to you. It is easy to distribute the role as long as there is some central place where everyone can get at the data.

The group should be the one doing the analysis of the data you gather. Stand-up meetings and retrospectives[3] are the times to talk about it. A coach can easily play the role of the tracker if the data is gathered unobtrusively and presented at a glance. Of course, once you really get the first practices going, and until you have it all automated, you may wish to identify a part-time tracker or just assume the manager will play that role.

---

3. N. Kerth. *Project Retrospectives: A Handbook for Team Review.* Dorset House, 2001.

Part IV

Uncharted Territory

XP is an evolving reality. As it becomes better known and more popular, companies not known for being pure innovators are seeing how it can help them leapfrog their competition. That means more people accustomed to formal approaches are beginning to talk about agile ones.

When folks new to XP start talking about it, especially those with a business focus, they ask questions that often make XP converts uneasy. These are the hard questions. They expose the parts of the discipline that haven't been explored fully yet. They force people to think about XP at the boundaries.

Up to this point, everything we've talked about is based on the confidence produced by visible results. We've not only gone into the wilderness as pioneers, but we've built settlements. Sure, there are times of uneasiness, but most days people are quietly and confidently going about their business.

The following few chapters are a bit different. These are stories from pioneers who have explored some new territory, but haven't yet gotten the desired results. The good news is, the wilderness hasn't eaten them alive.

Chapter 27

Selling XP

If you're trying to persuade people to do something, or buy something, it seems to me you should use their language, the language in which they think.

—David Ogilvy

Don't sell XP. Sell the results of XP. Prove that it can do what you said it could, without unacceptable risk to your customer.

We believe that more agile approaches are the future of software development. XP is the most intuitive and practical agile approach we've ever seen. Programmers who try XP love it. Anecdotal evidence suggests that it helps teams produce great software quickly, and that the software is valuable to customers. The more we've applied XP, the more we're convinced.

RoleModel Software's ideal client is the one who calls us and says, "You know, we've got this idea for a new product. We've identified a representative customer who will define the product for us and be dedicated to working with us wherever and whenever they need to. We just need a crack software development team to come in and work with them to turn the concept into reality. The management team has decided that we need to use an agile development process. We've got a lot of money in the bank and a sales and marketing team that has their own agile process in place waiting for the customer to define the evolving product and ready to adjust the message as they learn. All of the support organizations are ready to do the same. I've heard you guys are the experts in this situation. Is there any amount of money that would convince you to come work with us?" We're still waiting for that call, but we're not holding our breath.

The reality is that many have heard about XP and are intrigued by it but their world isn't lined up to work that way. They want to buy a quick solution to today's problem. Changing their approach is something they'd rather not do.

Let's face it. At the time of this writing, XP is in its relative infancy. No one has an overwhelming portfolio of years of successful XP projects.

As a development team, RoleModel Software has been at this as long as anyone. We were able to start without any resistance. We've only hired people who want to do XP. This is good and bad. As a company, we can truly say that we have always believed in XP and our developers came here because they believed in it. It's not just lip service. On the other hand, because we are a young company, we can't point to decades of satisfied customers.

In two and a half years of focusing exclusively on XP, we've successfully sold XP on occasion, but we've also failed on many attempts to sell our services. There are a lot of other things that have to happen to make XP work wonderfully.

When we've attempted to sell services into existing software houses, there are several sales that have to happen. First we sell to the decision makers. Then we have to sell to the development team and to the customer. If the "customer" isn't defined well, we have to try to sell management again on how to identify the customer better. Then there are all of the support organizations that have to adjust to the new way of doing things. For many, it is not a major adjustment, and once they understand it, they like it. We must expect that until and unless XP becomes mainstream, the selling will never stop.

The following are our current views on selling XP, based on what we've learned to date.

Erasing Objections

The primary reason customers don't buy projects that use XP is that they are afraid of it. They may give other reasons, but fear (or "risk aversion") underlies them all.

The name "Extreme Programming" conjures up images of snowboarders slinging code with reckless abandon. Customers don't understand the discipline that XP requires. People trying to sell XP suffer because of this assumption, but the name is just an excuse. The root of the problem is that customers are afraid to try something new and different.

Anything that challenges conventional thought within a discipline will seem radical and XP is no exception. The XP practices (especially pair programming and collective code ownership) are uncommon in the industry. Even programmers resist them sometimes. Given that, customers have another convenient excuse not to try XP: If they try it, they'll run off their best people.

Traditional approaches have been tried for over 30 years. Teams have used each of them to produce great software. But the overwhelming evidence suggests that teams using heavier approaches don't produce results reliably, they bust the budget, or they require a much bigger budget than seems reasonable. Often they deliver late, if they deliver at all. Those approaches simply put too much in the way of a project to be successful. Potential customers who claim that other approaches are proven are ignoring these facts. As we said in the introduction to this book, these old ways are comfortable because they are acceptable.

How to Sell XP

The primary reason customers are afraid of XP is that the proponents of XP (including us, until recently) haven't focused on selling what customers really care about: results in terms of positive impact to their business. That is what we need to be selling.

The only way to sell XP is to overcome customers' fear of giving it a try. The only way to overcome that fear is to

- Focus on the results of XP (the value that it adds to the customer)
- Convince customers to let you prove it
- Take their risk away while you prove it
- Develop a track record of delivery you can show to other potential customers

The Results

Customers don't speak the language of XP and they shouldn't have to. XP should speak the language of business. This means that you shouldn't sell XP at all. You should sell the *results* of XP.

Your odds of failure are astronomically high if you try to sell XP itself. No software development organization that we have heard of advertises that their process stinks, or that they deliver low-quality software, or that they're slow. If you try to sell XP as a better mousetrap, you will be one more voice in an already crowded field.

Instead, identify your market's needs for value. Sometimes you can quantify that value in terms of dollars, sometimes you can't, but you had better know what it is. Once you've identified it, determine how XP can help you partner with customers to deliver that value. Translate XP into a means of delivering that value. That's what you sell.

What kind of results do potential buyers care about?

- Improved profits
- Improved process
- Repeatable ability to deliver
- Competitive advantage

Of these, competitive advantage is most important. Sustainable competitive advantage is the lifeblood of business. XP can help you give it to your customers. XP supports radical innovation in their products and services by being fast, flexible, and focused on value. Customers can be faster to market with better products and services. They can respond to customer needs more quickly. They can expand their markets faster and easier. They can reduce the cost of maintaining their software assets over time. That is a compelling financial picture.

If XP can't live up to its promises, you won't be able to sell it no matter how good a story you tell. If your story is good, though, and you reduce the customer's perceived risk, you'll get the opportunity to prove XP can deliver spectacular results that will make a difference to your customers' businesses.

Proving It

The only way customers will let you prove yourself to them is if you do three things:

1. Provide something of obvious value to get you in the door
2. Minimize their risk while you are proving it
3. Once you prove yourself, renegotiate based on that proof

Getting Our Clients Started
by Roy Miller

We charge our customers for an Initial Planning Game, which we call "The Planning Workshop." XP says that you shouldn't try to set scope in stone before the project starts, since requirements evolve throughout the project as the team learns. However, customers typically want an approximate cost and delivery date for the project so they can determine if they want to sign up for it. That requires a broad understanding of scope.

Our workshop is basically an Initial Planning Game. We run a Planning Game at a coarse resolution to help our customer answer the question, "Should we invest more?" We simplify the exercise by assuming stories are independent of each other, and that we will develop necessary infrastructure along with each one. We move fast, guess about some estimates, and leave plenty of padding.

The deliverable for the workshop is "the big plan." Customers get a set of story cards for the next release, the prioritization of those stories by business value and technical risk, and a first cut at a project plan. The plan contains a ballpark estimate of effort, time, and the number of developers necessary to get the job done. An actionable plan like this, even though it's at a coarse resolution, is very valuable to customers.

If the customer wants to start a project, we can sign a contract immediately. Sometimes, though, a customer is skeptical. In those cases, we sell our customers an "exploration period." This is the first one or two iterations of the project at the rates we would charge the customer if they had already signed a long-term contract with us. This lets us show the customer that it's worthwhile to have a long-term relationship with us. Once the exploration period is over, we deliver the software and tests we produced, and ask if the customer wants to continue.

We accomplish the goal of removing risk by structuring our contracts to focus delivering value from the project and minimizing risk for the customer. Our contracts do this in five ways:

1. We apply half of the customer's cost for "The Planning Workshop" toward their first iteration after the exploration period.
2. We keep the contract period short (two iterations).
3. We allow the project to change direction as the team members (including the customer representative) learn things.
4. We give the customer the option to cancel every time the contract is up, with adequate notice.
5. We bill by the iteration, so that customers can be sure they are getting production-ready value for their money.

Our contracts look something like the ones Kent Beck and Dave Cleal described in their paper "Optional Scope Contracts."* Each one contains a clause like this:

The customer will pay the team of N developers $N/iteration for the next two iterations. We will bill the customer by the iteration. The customer may terminate the project at any time by giving us notice equal to two

---

* K. Beck, D. Cleal. "Optional Scope Contracts" at http://www.xprogramming.com/xpublications.htm.

iterations or 30 days, whichever is shorter. This contract will renew automatically upon termination, unless explicitly cancelled by the customer. Whatever software is delivered will meet the quality standards defined in Appendix A. The stories, business/technical prioritization of those stories, and an initial project plan are included in Appendix B. All of Appendix B is subject to change during the project as the team learns, and is expected to change.

This is the simplest contract that could possibly work. It aligns the customer's interests with ours. Everybody involved with the project wants to deliver value as soon as possible, and everybody wants the project to continue.

Our customers have a reasonable idea of what they may be getting when the project starts, based on the output of "The Planning Workshop." But what they want, and therefore what they should get, always ends up being different from what they imagined at the beginning. Our contracts force customers to give up the illusion of control over scope at the beginning of our projects in exchange for getting the software they want at the end of a project. And every bit of software they get will be 100% done, as confirmed by automated tests they contribute, of course.

Once you are in the door, it's just a simple matter of Extreme Programming, assuming you've learned from the previous 26 chapters. XP done well will add value. We had a customer say, "We've been doing software around here for years, but I've never seen it produced at the pace you guys are doing it. It's really quite amazing."

Along the way, recognize that there will be some disappointments. You can build a product faster and better, but there are a lot of reasons it might not sell. Identify what went well and what went poorly. Learn from the successes and failures. Then get back in the game and play to win.

Developing a Track Record

Develop a track record of proof. Then sell that track record as applied to each new customer's particular situation.

Scrap and claw to get your first customers that will let you do XP projects and build a track record. Track the value that you add. The more you can quantify the value that you add, the better you'll be able to attach a price to it that will preserve your margins. Quantify it in terms of three things:[1]

- ✧ How much value will you add?
- ✧ How soon will you add it?
- ✧ How sure can the customer be that you will add it?

If you can't quantify the value that you add in terms of dollars, at least get testimonials describing the value that you added and how happy your customer was with your service.

Once you have a track record, sell from it. Talk to your customer. Get to know his industry, how his critical success businesses and functions contribute to his revenues and costs. Know how you can improve each of those. Find out how far he is from the new levels you can give him, which represent a quantifiable competitive advantage. Then sell him your ability to do that, setting your price at a level that represents an attractive return for him and for you.

If you position yourself as a value-adding partner, you can protect yourself against your competition. If you position yourself as an adder of cost, you will trade away your margins in order to undercut your competitors' price. You have to choose which strategy is better.

Relationships Sell

All this talk about selling value is great, but it is not that simple. A smooth marketing message and a compelling business case help, but they aren't enough. This is because businesses are run by people. People aren't predictable and they don't always do the smart thing. There are going to be times when buying the services you are selling isn't the smart thing.

The only way you will be successful at selling XP is to develop relationships with your customers. Treat them as your partners. They will see you that way in return, as long as you deliver superior value to them. If you are viewed as

---

1. The way to quantify value, and the process of selling from "norms" are not original with us. Mack Hanan talks about both in his book *Consultative Selling: The Hanan Formula for High-Margin Sales at High Levels*. AMACOM, 1999.

a partner, it will be difficult for competitors to unseat you based on price, and nigh on impossible for them to hijack your relationship.

The bottom line is simple. If you partner with your customers to give them the competitive advantage they want and need, they will give *you* the competitive advantage *you* want and need.

Chapter 28

XP and Startups

Selling XP is a challenge because it is difficult to find potential customers that are willing and able to try it. Startups can be both. XP is agile enough to give startups sustainable competitive advantage.

The natural question in selling XP is what type of customer to sell it to. This is not as simple as finding a prospective customer that needs software.

The Target

Good potential customers for XP

- ◇ Are open to XP
- ◇ Are willing to try XP within their organization
- ◇ Have approval and funding for a project on which to try XP
- ◇ Have an urgency to get started on that project

Startups tend to match this profile rather well. Every startup is unique, but all of them tend to have the following characteristics:

- ◇ Openness to new ways of doing things, including software development
- ◇ An acute sense of a good deal and the freedom to act on that

- ◇ Incomplete in-house software development capability
- ◇ A need for speed, to beat competitors to market

We are not claiming that all startups are good targets. Some are so strapped for cash that they cannot pay for your services at all, and we do not advocate working for free. Some have half-baked ideas that probably will fail, and we do not advocate working for lost causes. Others don't need custom software.

The point is not that all startups are good targets. Rather, startups tend to provide the kind of environment that favors XP. Uncertainty is the norm—requirements often are vague and volatile. It is clearer who the Gold Owner and the Gold Donor are (quite possibly the same person). Decisions tend to be made quicker. There is a need for a small initial investment, with the option to invest more later as growth, and more funding, become available. XP can thrive in an environment like that. The question is how to *sell* into an environment like that.

The Pitch

In the last chapter we discussed tracking the value that you add in terms of quantity (how much value you'll add), speed (how fast you will add it), and certainty (how sure your customer can be that you'll add that value). If a startup can spend a little now to get a lot of return soon, and can be sure they'll get that return, that is ideal for them. The rub is the uncertainty. Fortunately, XP addresses that by allowing you to give your customers

- ◇ Accurate and frequent feedback about progress
- ◇ Many opportunities to change requirements dramatically
- ◇ The ability to make a small initial investment
- ◇ The opportunity to go faster with quality

In an uncertain world, a strategy that does all that can give a startup significant competitive advantages. They crave it. Sell it to them. As one of the entrepreneurs we know says, "Any startup that makes software and doesn't use XP is stupid."

As we said before, it isn't always possible to assign dollars to the value that you add, and we certainly do not recommend making promises you aren't sure you can keep. In that case, testimonials from other startup customers can help out.

When you sell to startups, remember that often two parties are involved: the entrepreneur(s) who are starting the company, and the venture capitalists who fund them. You have to be aware of both and might have to make your case to both. At a minimum, you need to give entrepreneurs the material necessary to make the case to their source of funding.

Entrepreneurs

Entrepreneurs face tremendous pressure every day. Competitors are threatening to get a product out first. If an entrepreneur moves too slowly, somebody's going to eat his lunch.

Entrepreneurs need a way to develop software that lets them beat the competition to market. XP can be that way, if you make a good case.

Risk is the norm for startups. No process for developing software can eliminate all risk. The beauty of XP is that it lets an entrepreneur be as quick to market as possible with products that delight his customers in a predictable way, over and over again, with minimal risk. If a startup company can do this better than its competitors, it has a significant advantage. If it sustains that advantage, it wins. That is the case you need to make.

Venture Capitalists

Venture capitalists (VCs) care about two things above all others:

1. Getting a good return on their investment for each of the companies in their portfolios
2. Helping create companies that will yield great returns quickly (within one to three years, in most cases)

Typically, VCs try to ensure these results by assembling top-notch management teams for each company. They look for people with vision, with operational expertise, and with hard-nosed cash management skills. A great idea for a product and a big market for it can help ensure success, but most VCs believe that the management team makes the difference between a big win and a big loss.

This is true, but making a business successful is about more than just the management team. If the business plans to develop software products, or to develop software to enable their business, it had better have a technology plan. That plan must feature a way to develop that software that creates competitive advantage.

XP complements a business strategy that depends on being fast and nimble. XP embraces change, assumes it will happen, and thrives on it. No other software process we've ever used does that quite as well.

Starting a viable company is all about being fast. If the market isn't crowded now, it will be soon. Companies are at constant risk of being leapfrogged by competitors. If they move too slowly, they're dead. A team of software developers skilled in using XP can create exactly the kind of agility startups need to stay ahead. It can help them move as fast as possible while minimizing risk.

VCs are always looking for approaches that will increase the probability that companies in their portfolio will pay off. XP is just such an approach. That is the case you need to make.

Selling to Startups

In order to sell to startups and to "intrapreneurs" in established companies, you should have three things:

1. Partnerships within the startup community (e.g., with VCs and angel investors)
2. A track record of adding value in a startup context
3. A willingness to share risk

Timing is critically important to getting the opportunities you want with startups. Partners can bring you together with startups who need work done, when they need it done, before another service provider can steal the deal. These partnerships also save you the trouble of doing as much due diligence as you would have to if you were evaluating the companies alone.

Once you have a qualified opportunity, you have to present a compelling case that you are the service provider of choice for the startup. There are two components to this: a track record and a willingness to share risk.

You cannot sell effectively without a track record. Back up your track record with hard numbers whenever possible. In any case, always have testimonials to support your ability to help startups. Your track record proves your ability to deliver.

But a track record isn't enough. Startups need to manage cash flow closely. They may have money to spend, but they don't want to hemorrhage cash. The greater the degree to which you are willing to share financial risk, the more attractive you will look to startups. This involves reducing the up-front cash the company has to pay for your services. We are currently working with a local startup this way, allowing them to pay us a small amount on a monthly basis, with the balance due as a note. An alternative might be to take some payment as equity.

Be discerning. Remember, it's called risk sharing for a reason. Recognize that even if you build what the customer wants, it still might not pan out. You could end up with worthless stock certificates.

When you share risk, try to retain at least joint ownership of the software until the work is paid for in full. Sometimes startups will go for this, sometimes they won't. The key is to be willing to structure risk-sharing deals with startup companies. There are many more options than those described here. Keep an open mind and be creative. Startups will appreciate that.

Strategic Initiatives: Startups in Disguise

New strategic initiatives within established companies are "internal startups." Typically, these initiatives have some sort of special status outside at least some of the normal chain of command. They are less free-wheeling than pure startup companies, but they are less restricted than incremental changes within established lines of business.

Our specific targets within established companies are "intrapreneurs," people who have new ideas that require software. In his book *Intrapreneuring*, Gifford Pinchot III said, "Corporate risk takers are very much like entrepreneurs. They take personal risks to make new ideas happen."[1] We look for people like that.

When we can find people that fit that profile, we sell to them much the same way we sell to pure startups. You have to be aware of the increased bureaucracy within an established company, of course, but if you can identify

---

1. G. Pinchot III. *Intrapreneuring*. Harper & Row, 1985.

good targets, the sales strategies you use with intrapreneurs are similar to those you use with pure startups.

Joining Them

You may not have the development portion of an XP team. Maybe you are just trying to figure out how to find someone willing to offer you a job in which you can do XP. Startups are a good place to look. Generally, they value the kind of people who are attracted to XP, whether or not they have ever heard of it.

If you think looking for a job at a startup could be your best shot, don't sell XP during your interview, sell the values and results of XP. Try to find out whether the startup has those same values. If not, keep looking.

If you think you might want to create your own startup, consider how XP can help you hit your goals. Hire people who have already done and/or want to do XP. If you can't find them, share the XP values with them and expose the basic practices. We have told people who are looking for jobs with us to read *Extreme Programming Explained* if they haven't already. If they are not excited about it, we don't hire them.

If you are not comfortable with the more obvious risk involved with a startup, there are other options. More and more established companies are using XP or partial XP. You will probably have bigger barriers to overcome at a more established company, but it can be done.

Either way, play to win.

Chapter 29

Scaling XP

People in glass houses shouldn't throw stones.[1]
—Geoffrey Chaucer

Don't say XP will not scale until you've tried it. Some larger teams have had success with XP, and there are creative ways of scaling XP that have not been tried yet.

"XP doesn't scale." We've heard that many times. Invariably, the person saying it hasn't tried to do it. Sometimes that person hasn't even tried XP on a small scale. At best, that person is saying, "I don't think XP will scale." If somebody hasn't tried to scale XP, his criticism is theoretical. Until he gets empirical evidence that XP won't scale, he shouldn't act like he knows something he doesn't.

Even XP proponents have fallen prey to this idea that if you say something enough times, it must be true. The standard answer with respect to XP and scale that we've heard from many "XPerts" is, "XP works for teams of about a dozen or less." We think that this is a cop-out. We may not have all the answers, but we can do better.

Does Anything Really Scale?

Most processes that scale really do one thing well: They manage and satisfy the details of a contract that specifies a formal process. When people talk about large-

---

1. G. Chaucer. *Troilus and Criseyde*, 1385.

scale software projects, typically Department of Defense (DoD) projects come into the discussion. These projects are notorious for what they track, not for what they produce. The authors haven't been on DoD contracts for any length of time. We've known many who have. If you think DoD contracts and processes should be the model of the way to do large-scale software projects, may God bless you and keep you . . . far away from us.

Does Rational Unified Process (RUP) scale? We know of a sizeable RUP project that ran for over 18 months and produced a lot of diagrams but absolutely no working code. This is not conclusive proof that RUP doesn't scale. It is however, conclusive proof that poor interpretation and execution of a process that is supposed to scale will most likely cost a lot of money to produce nothing of real value. We're certain the same can be done with poor execution of XP.

Next time someone asks you whether a process will scale, ask him to define for you what his measures of success are. If the measures don't include delivering a quality product that the customer is thrilled to have paid for, he is not playing to win the same game we're playing. If his measures include these criteria, ask him whether he knows a process that can deliver that, and ask for evidence. Then ask him if there's something fundamental in that process that allows it to produce the product as reliably and as efficiently as possible. He'll probably say that you are evading the question of whether a process will scale. We say that the question is irrelevant because its answer is impossible to prove.

This skeptic may say that a process could be proven scalable if there were at least one known case of it scaling. (Interestingly, no process started out as proven based on this criteria.) We say that a known example is simply proof that someone has claimed to have done it. The example does not prove that anyone else can produce the same results applied to a different problem.

Should You Need to Scale?

If you have a project with more than 10 or 12 developers, don't jump to the conclusion that XP isn't workable for that project. First ask yourself why you have so many developers. Do you really need them, or are you throwing bodies at the problem? Would 10 great developers be enough? What if you had 10 good developers, and you got out of their way?

On many projects, more people isn't the answer. In fact, Frederick Brooks' work shows that adding people to a project actually can jeopardize its success.[2]

---

2. F. Brooks. *The Mythical Man Month.* Addison-Wesley, 1995, p. 25. Brooks' law states, "Adding manpower to a late software project makes it later."

Why Can't XP Scale?

We've heard the following reasons why XP can't scale:

◇ It would be hard to communicate at an XP level with a larger team.

◇ XP doesn't support tracking key success factors that you have to track for large projects.

◇ Large systems are inherently complex—XP requires things to be simple.

Perhaps communication with a larger team would be harder, but communication is still vital to project success. XP values communication. A larger project simply requires a different form of communication than a project-wide stand-up meeting. That doesn't mean there isn't a way to scale XP projects.

Perhaps tracking success factors becomes even more important for larger projects. XP supports tracking success factors—in fact, there's a role for it, the tracker. Maybe people who claim XP can't scale don't think the XP community has talked enough about the metrics teams should track. We think tracking acceptance tests sounds like a good idea, as does tracking estimates. Maybe someone thinks we need to measure other things. We can do that, as long as the measurement helps us achieve our goals. Measurement doesn't keep you from scaling XP projects.

Perhaps large systems are inherently complex, but XP can help you manage complexity. XP doesn't require systems to be too simple, only as simple as possible. A large system doesn't have to be unnecessarily complex—it needs to be only as complex as necessary. This doesn't mean you can't use XP to build it. XP manages complexity by breaking it down into simple steps. How else would you do it?

These arguments assume scaling XP is impossible. We disagree. The "Extreme" in "Extreme Programming" comes from the metaphor of turning the knobs of industry best practices up to 10. Thus, scaling XP is a matter of taking some of the best practices for managing large projects and figuring out what it means to turn their knobs up to 10 in a way that's compatible with the rest of XP. Every practice in XP can and probably should be used on a large project. Some of the practices probably would need to be modified a bit. You probably would need to add a few things. But there is no reason to assume it's impossible.

When to Scale

We can certainly imagine, and have seen cases where you would need more than 10 or 12 developers. Sometimes, you *can* get more done sooner if you have more people working on it. The most obvious case is when you are already going at a good pace, there is good communication, and there is more work to do based on customer requests that aren't being satisfied in a timely fashion. Another case is when there are clear system boundaries. Small teams of 12 or fewer can work on each part of the system. Then they can coordinate their efforts.

How to Scale

XP as prescribed does seem to fit better with small teams. It's hard to imagine a stand-up meeting with 50 people. However, we do know of XP projects that involve 40 or more people.

If you determine that more people are necessary to accomplish your project's goals, don't be afraid to ramp up. Keep your methodology as agile as possible, but proceed with courage. Follow some XP advice in determining how to do this. What is the simplest thing that could possibly work for a large team?

One of the ideas we've discussed with many in the community seems to have some real promise is a coaching team. We have both participated in and heard of similar set ups in non-XP projects, and have seen them have much better success rates than their alternatives.

If you need 50 people on a project, organize it into 10-person teams. Call these XP teams. Each team will function using XP, and each will have its own customer, who talks to the team directly to "drive" that team's efforts (e.g., participate in that team's Iteration Planning). Things will get a little different when one XP team needs to talk to another.

Create a coaching team,[3] whose role is to

♦ Make sure cross-team communication is happening whenever it needs to
♦ Serve as the point of contact for the customers for each XP team
♦ Do Release Planning

Members of the coaching team need to see their team as a service team, and it needs to be clear that all teams on the project fail if all do not succeed. Coaching team members must participate and take their roles seriously, or

---

3. A paper by Ron Crocker contains similar concepts (R. Crocker. *The 5 Reasons XP Can't Scale and What to Do About Them*). Preceedings of Second International Conference on Extreme Programming and Flexible Processes in Software Engineering, XP2001, pp. 62–65

things will get out of control. The coaching team should *not* be a roadblock, bottleneck, or controlling force. If this team tries to control too much, they will be the "enemy." We have seen "coordination teams" fall into this trap many times in non-XP environments.

The coaching team would have several full-time members and several part-time ones. The customer from each XP team is automatically a part-time member of the coaching team. Each XP team should have its coach and a programmer representative on the coaching team as well. Each XP team may wish to rotate several members through the representative role so that everyone gets familiar with it and nobody gets bored. Each XP team's coach is probably best suited to determine who should represent the team based on skill and on the activities happening at the coaching team level.

The coaching team does all Release Planning for the project as a whole. The customers in the room have to resolve conflicting customer priorities among themselves, perhaps by playing some version of the Senate Game (see Chapter 10). No developer can decide how to resolve conflicts between customer priorities. That is a business decision only customers can make. Depending on the type of project, the coaching team may wish only to decide on which stories are included on a broader level, such as in the next quarter.

Once the scope of a release has been decided, each XP team is responsible for planning for its own work during the next iteration. The team plans with its own customer, based on what was stated in Release Planning.

Dependencies become more important here, so each team may have to break into temporary subteams to manage the interface between two systems. The most obvious way to do this is to create stories and/or tasks tackled by pairs using a programmer from each team. Pair programming is an excellent way to build these interfaces.

Reserving Judgment

Unless someone can offer us conclusive proof that 50 non-XP developers using a favorite "method that scales" would do a better job at getting a quality product delivered than 50 XP developers, arguments about scaling are theoretical. Until someone really tries to scale XP, the question still remains, "Can XP Scale?" Don't believe anyone who tells you it can't without more evidence than the opinions of any number of people who haven't tried it.

Chapter 30

The Next Best
Thing to Being There

*My innate wit and charm don't
come across in e-mails.*

—Ron Jeffries

*There are a lot of business pressures that encourage distributed teams. Can
such teams use XP?*

When you can't get everybody on the team in the same room or even the same
town, can you still do XP?

Some people who have never done XP claim that you can and make rather
strong arguments about it. Others say that if XP can't be done in a distributed
fashion it is doomed to fail because telecommuting is the wave of the future.
They argue technology is available today that allows you to use every practice
without everything being in the same place.

Distributed teams can't do XP as effectively as co-located teams, but that
doesn't mean they can't use the XP values and practices to their advantage.

The Limits of Technology

Many geeks seem to think that using technology to address a problem will
always provide a better solution. Indeed, technology can automate tasks that
are error-prone when done manually and enhance human interaction. But let's
not ignore the obvious facts.

A VNC session (or PCAnywhere or similar session) is a much better way to help someone who isn't next to you work through a problem on-screen than trying to describe it over the phone. But two people next to each other at a computer with a whiteboard behind them can communicate more effectively than two people on VNC sessions any day of the week. End of discussion.

There are plenty of challenges to communication when everyone is in the same room. Those challenges are greater when people are far apart. Proximity facilitates communication.

Recently a director at a multinational company asked us how he could use XP on projects with teams of six to twelve people located physically in four to six countries. We suggested this was a hard problem that we don't think any methodology could address. He nodded and said

> *It has been quite frustrating. We would spend an incredible amount of money getting extremely talented engineers together at the beginning of the projects to build a team and gain a mutual understanding of what had to be done. After that we'd have regular conference calls and a ton of e-mail and instant messaging. Then, several weeks later, they would get together again and it was scary how completely different their understandings were of what they were supposed to be doing. Often the directions they had each gone in those few weeks took them as far apart as night and day."*

Can a Team Telecommute?

We think it's great when people have jobs they can do from home. In fact, it's pretty dumb to commute an hour or even ten minutes so you can work by yourself if you can work just as effectively by yourself where you are. Such a situation was a contributing factor to Ken's decision to start RoleModel Software as a one-person company out of his house. If you are not part of a team, don't bother with the façade.

But if you need a team to build something, the team members will benefit greatly from constant communication and collaboration. If you really want to contribute the maximum value to a team, you need to be part of it and be there. If it's more important for you to telecommute than to be part of a team that runs at maximum efficiency, then telecommute. Just don't act like you can have your cake and eat it, too. You can't. Don't lie to yourself or to anyone else.

You can telecommute and use a process that has a lot of the same values and practices as XP. You should probably include other practices to compensate for what you can't do as well. It will never be as effective as being there.

When to Try Distributed XP

Let's assume that you find yourself on a team that someone decided must be distributed. Let's also assume that, for the time being, there is no practical way to change that. Can you do XP?

Well, the answer is no, not in all of its glory. But you can do a lot of the practices and get a lot of the benefit. There are many companies that claim they do distributed development very effectively. A few actually do.

Talk Isn't Cheap
by Susan Johnson

I worked on a project where the five-person team was distributed across four U.S. cities and three time zones. The project was successful in large part because we didn't substitute written communication for what would otherwise be verbal communication. This personal communication was very expensive—travel, teleconferences, and lengthy phone calls. The Extreme Programming practices helped us focus our expensive time and made it more productive.

We benefited most from being together at the beginning of an iteration. Story writing and design discussions work best face-to-face. We also made sure we got a good start on pair programming the major items. Occasionally, we were forced to travel to integrate parts of the system or resolve difficult technical problems.

Pair programming is the epitome of intensive communication. We used two telephone lines, one for talking and one for software that lets both persons view the same screen. It is a low-tech solution that works fairly well, but there are two pitfalls you have to watch for. The first pitfall is that there is a delay in receiving keystrokes from your partner, so everything moves more slowly. The second is that pairing over the phone is more difficult than pairing in person. It is easier for one person to dominate. It is more likely that there will be misunderstandings. Patience is required to help with both pitfalls.

Test suites were an important contributor to good communication. Since we did not change pairs, we used the tests to communicate the interfaces between the layers in the system. The discipline of creating tests for each layer was enforced by a consumer higher up the food chain demanding a working example of the needed functionality. If the tests for a layer were well commented, the consumer of the layer could read the test as an example of how to use the layer's services correctly.

We practiced continuous integration of code through an FTP site. Everyone submitted their changes to the site at the end of their own working day.

One team member integrated them together, and a new build was available every morning, with a synopsis of the changes.

We used a daily teleconference as a substitute for stand-up meetings. The expense and tedium of conference calls usually encouraged them to be short. We found out early that less frequent calls bred bad assumptions about what was being done, which slowed us down. We also discovered early that cell phones were necessary to keep things moving. Team members needed to be reachable for quick questions and decisions, especially since our cumulative "lunch hour" was three hours long!

A distributed XP team can succeed, but it requires a highly motivated group. You must always consider what is the most effective communication medium, not the easiest or cheapest.

Those who have gone to great lengths to make distributed teams work are very proud of what they have accomplished.

If you are not ready to do what's necessary to make distributed XP work, you probably won't be doing anything very close to XP. You certainly won't enjoy all of the benefits of XP. You may even find that you were better off taking a different approach that has more of a divide-and-conquer strategy. Then you won't be very agile, but you may accomplish some other goals.

There is a lot of interest in doing distributed XP. We think motivated people will have some success. There's more to learn about how to make distributed XP work better. But it will never work as well as XP with a physically co-located team.

Chapter 31

Measuring XP

The business case for XP to this point is primarily anecdotal. There needs to be a stronger empirical case for XP as an instance of an "agile" method.

Many of the claims about XP are theoretical. They make intuitive sense, but they are based on anecdotal evidence. That isn't a bad thing, but it's not enough for industry acceptance. We need to get some numbers for XP.

What to Measure

Deciding what to measure is not as easy as one might think. XP is a new way of doing things, as are other agile methods. As overused as the phrase is, these new agile approaches represent a paradigm shift in software development. Part of that shift involves a different way of measuring.

Gary Hamel, in *Leading the Revolution*, claims that radical innovation is the only thing that will save many businesses. Agile methods like XP are enablers for this kind of radical innovation. If we measure XP the same way we measure traditional approaches, we'll fall into a trap. Traditional measurements do not capture a process' ability to enable agility.

Measuring Agile Methodologies
by Jim Highsmith

One of the issues with all agile methodologies is that they imply a different standard for success and therefore measurements are different. For example, we measure the number of features delivered rather than conformance to initial requirements, because we understand that requirements and features will change over the life of a project. A traditional measurement that focuses on conformance to requirements will show XP projects performing poorly.

Also, if we "embrace change," then one measurement we need to come up with is an "agility" measurement. If it really is more important to conform to a customer's constantly changing demands, then how do we measure that? For example, at the end of each iteration, ASD (Adaptive Software Development) advocates a customer focus group that logs change requests. I then track the status of those requests over time so that by the end of the project I can say, "We delivered 124 features, plus we responded to 89 percent of the 147 change requests the customers made." Not only did we deliver, but we responded to the customer.

We need to measure some traditional things, but we also need to measure agility. Jim Highsmith has made a point of pushing people within the agile development community to consider other measures that take into account the qualitatively new ways of doing things that agile approaches are exploring. If we try to measure these new approaches like XP with old yardsticks only, these new approaches may very well come up short. But these approaches are enabling radically different solutions to traditional software development process problems, and we need proof that XP can deliver on those radical innovations.[1]

XP should allow teams to deliver better software faster and cheaper than other approaches, and in a way that enables radical change often. At this point,

---

1. At XP2001, Jim Highsmith mentioned work done by Alan McCormack of MIT and Rob Austin and Richard Nolan of Harvard that confirms the superior ability of "evolutionary approaches" to deliver higher-quality software faster on projects of various sizes. (A. McCormack. "Product Development Practices that Work: How Internet Companies Build Software." *MIT Sloan Management Review.* Volume 42, Number 2, pp. 75–84, 2001; R. Austin, R. Nolan. "Manage ERP Initiatives as New Ventures, Not IT Projects." 1998. Not yet published.)

however, most of the data is anecdotal or limited to students in a university setting. Making the case for XP will require numbers from projects conducted in a business setting by professional software developers using XP.

Specifically, practitioners doing XP need to answer questions like these:

- ✧ Does XP increase code quality? Along what dimensions? By how much?
- ✧ Does it reduce the cost of delivery? By how much? Under what conditions?
- ✧ Does XP decrease delivery time? By how much? Under what conditions?
- ✧ Does XP reduce staff turnover? By how much? Under what conditions?
- ✧ Is XP more responsive to customer needs? How much more? Under what conditions?
- ✧ Is XP more supportive of innovation within an organization?
- ✧ Does XP really make change easier and cheaper?

XP begs these questions. Other methods, especially "heavy" ones, do as well. The reality, though, is that there are very few controlled experiments proving that any method is useful at all. In our industry, methods often get adopted because of salesmanship and popularity.

Where's the Data?
by Ken Auer

At a conference a couple of years ago, I had about 15 minutes to present what we were doing with XP and the benefits we had found. I asked if there were any questions.

ATTENDEE: You make a lot of claims about XP. Do you have proof that it works?

KEN: What kind of proof are you looking for?

ATTENDEE: Is there a company that has produced a product using XP that is still going strong after five years in production?

KEN: XP was only formulated a couple of years ago. That would be impossible. The Chrysler payroll project is printing people's checks and has been for quite a while.

ATTENDEE: If you don't have data, how do you expect anyone to use it? In my company, they have just standardized on RUP, which is a proven methodology.

XP values feedback and metrics throughout the project. We should value them in the realm of process comparison, too. So how do we get them?

There are a couple of approaches that might work well. One is measuring XP against another method. The other is measuring the impact of introducing XP within a single organization.

The XP Challenge

One of the ideas some of the people at RoleModel have had is something we call the "XP challenge." It is a real-world experiment in parallel development. The environment should be as controlled as practically possible. It should involve two teams of developers going head-to-head, one using XP and the other using another methodology, preferably a heavyweight one like many CMM-4 companies use.[2] The challenge should be sponsored by industry (multiple companies) and by academia, and the project should involve a real business problem. The two groups cannot interact, and they should have equal access to the "customer" for the purposes of gathering requirements and getting direction as the project proceeds.

The goal of the challenge is to provide a somewhat controlled environment for measuring each approach. Once completed, the data should be clear: Either XP lives up to its billing, or it doesn't. If it doesn't, more research will be

---

2. Software Engineering Institute's Capability Maturity Model (CMM) is a five-level model for identifying the capabilities of an organization to build software.

necessary to determine why. We are currently working with Laurie Williams at North Carolina State University to further define and execute this experiment.

The Before-and-After Study

Another approach involves longitudinal study of a single team, before and after XP. Laurie Williams of North Carolina State University and Giancarlo Succi of University of Alberta, Canada, have developed a proposal for a study like this at a large high-tech company. Here is an excerpt of the proposal:

> *We propose a case study with related surveys be performed at Company X to provide quantifiable, empirical results. Surveys will be used to poll a set of data from the software engineers involved in the study. The surveys will assess their reactions to the transition. Additionally, surveys will be used to measure customer satisfaction with software releases.*
>
> *In a case study, key factors that affect outcome (such as the transition to XP) are identified. Then, specific, predetermined outcome measurements are tracked and analyzed. Case studies are generally performed in a "typical project," and they can be thought of as "research in the typical." Often, a more preferred research technique is to run a formal experiment. Formal experiments can be referred to as "research in the large," and their results have greater external validity or applicability to many settings. However, experiments generally require a control group (a group that uses Company X's existing development methodology) and an experimental group (a group that uses XP) often replicating the same or very similar projects. It is very difficult to affordably run formal experiments in industry.[3]*
>
> *Our plans with the case study are to measure "this group before they did XP" to "this same group after they started doing XP."*

The methodology for the experiment is similar to the XP Challenge. The difference is that the results would provide an opportunity to examine the impact of introducing XP into an organization, rather than simply comparing the raw results of two different approaches to software development.

---

3. N.E. Fenton, and S.L. Pfleeger. *Software Metrics: A Rigorous and Practical Approach.* Brooks/Cole Publishing Company, 1998.

What Having the Numbers Will Mean

Regardless of the approach used, measuring XP is a must, although having "hard numbers" to support XP may make not selling XP easy. In the end, those numbers will do only two things:

1. Reinforce, or refute decisively, the intuitive notion that XP is a superior way to develop software.
2. Give people who believe XP is the way to go some ammunition against opposition to XP.

People who think XP is good or superior based on their own experience will continue to believe that. People who think XP is a bad idea, too risky, or just too unproven, probably will continue to believe that. But there are some people out there who will be swayed by convincing experiential arguments backed up by empirical evidence. The numbers will be useful in convincing those people.

Until then, we'll just have to play to win without the conclusive scientific evidence that we will, just like everyone else in the software industry. In the end, numbers don't matter as much as shipping quality software cost-effectively.

Chapter 32

Where to Next?

The story goes that when Alexander the Great reached the easternmost end of his conquest, he wept because there were no worlds left to conquer. We are not in that position. The XP adventure is just beginning.

We have been on the trail a while. We've discovered some things that work and others that don't. We've blazed a few new trails and are expecting the journey will continue to be fruitful. We have embraced change. We've applied XP to software development and have experienced life on a flatter curve. It's a winning strategy.

We hope you can profit from our experiences as we have related them in this book. The question now is, where to next?

Resistance to XP is growing. It is a "disruptive idea," very similar to Clayton Christensen's "disruptive technology."[1] Existing companies, some of them well run, are clinging to tried and true methods of developing software. They have applied more rules, guidelines, process improvements, and formality in the hope of increasing their chances of success. We believe those attempts will collapse under the weight of their own complexity.

The future is agile. In a software world where change is both normal and constant, approaches that handle change the best will be the most successful.

---

1. C. Christensen. *The Innovator's Dilemma*. Harvard Business School Press, 1997.

Christensen has told us the fate of those well-managed companies that respond too late to disruptive technologies. It is the same with disruptive ideas. If agile methods are the future, as we believe they are, there are two alternatives:

1. Deny this, stick with traditional methods, and watch as your competitors leapfrog you.
2. Get in the game, explore the boundaries, and shape the future.

Shape the future, or have it dictated to you. It has always been so. Doing nothing is the same as choosing to let others lead. Risk avoidance is no excuse for not acting. You cannot have change without risk. The future is coming. Lead, follow, or get out of the way.

All of this stuff is about people. People are your customers. People are your developers. People use technology as a tool. You can automate things we've figured out how to do, but you'll still need people to leverage that automation to focus on the next challenge in making lives better for people. In the long run, you will be surrounded by people who value people as much as you do. Think about it.

The business case for XP has not been made as completely as it needs to be. That is what should be done next. The only way to do that is to experiment at the boundaries of the discipline and to determine what "agile" means in a context broader than the software portion of projects having a single team of fewer than 10 or 12 software developers.

Those companies that participate in helping make the business case for agile methods will lead the way to the future of software development and business in general. We are playing to win. Are you?

Index

The XP Series

Kent Beck, Series Advisor

Extreme Programming Explained
By Kent Beck
0201616416
Paperback
© 2000

The XP Manifesto

Planning Extreme Programming
By Kent Beck and Martin Fowler
0201710919
Paperback
© 2001

Planning Projects with XP

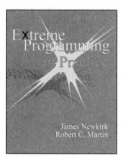

Extreme Programming Installed
By Ron Jeffries, Ann Anderson, and Chet Hendrickson
0201708426
Paperback
© 2001

Get XP Up and Running in Your Organization

Extreme Programming Examined
By Giancarlo Succi and Michele Marchesi
0201710404
Paperback
© 2001

Best XP Practices as Presented and Analyzed at the recent Extreme Programming Conference

Extreme Programming in Practice
By James Newkirk and Robert C. Martin
0201709376
Paperback
© 2001

Learn from the Chronicle of an XP Project

Extreme Programming Explored
By William C. Wake
0201733978
Paperback
© 2002

Best XP Practices for Developers

Extreme Programming Applied
By Ken Auer and Roy Miller
0201616408
Paperback
© 2002

Delves Deeper into XP Theory

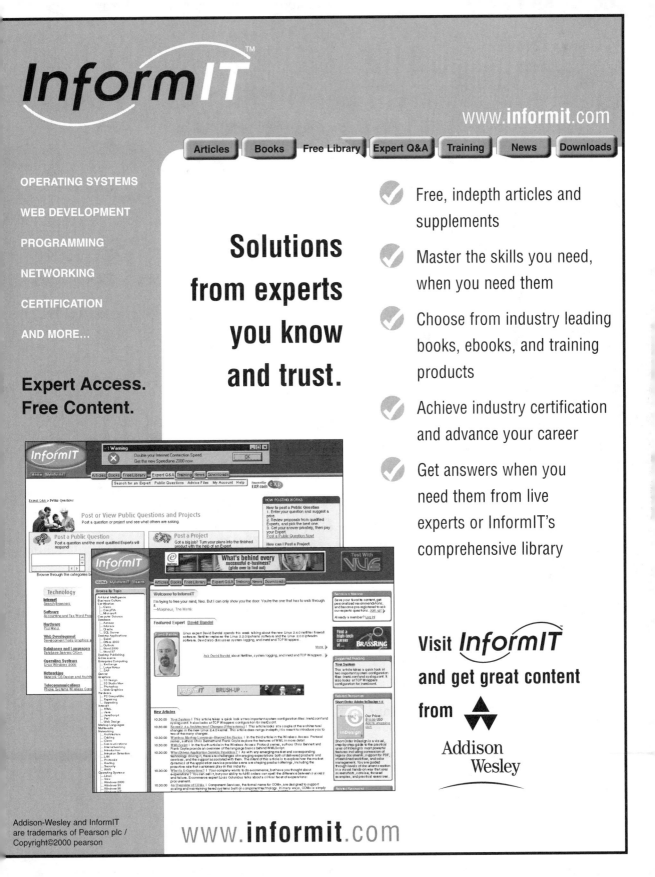

Register
Your Book

at www.aw.com/cseng/register

You may be eligible to receive:
- Advance notice of forthcoming editions of the book
- Related book recommendations
- Chapter excerpts and supplements of forthcoming titles
- Information about special contests and promotions throughout the year
- Notices and reminders about author appearances, tradeshows, and online chats with special guests

Contact us

If you are interested in writing a book or reviewing manuscripts prior to publication, please write to us at:

Editorial Department
Addison-Wesley Professional
75 Arlington Street, Suite 300
Boston, MA 02116 USA
Email: AWPro@aw.com

Addison-Wesley

Visit us on the Web: http://www.aw.com/cseng